I0458401

VIETNAM:
ON THE OUTSIDE
LOOKING IN

VIETNAM:

ON THE OUTSIDE
LOOKING IN

War Came For Our Soldiers
Returning Home With Hidden Wounds
Their Experience Changed Their Lives

RANDALL BAXTER

Vietnam: On the Outside Looking in

Copyright © 2025 by Randall Baxter. All rights reserved.

No part of this publication may be reproduced, distributed, or transmitted in any form or by any means, including photocopying, recording, or other electronic or mechanical methods, without the prior written permission of the author, except in the case of brief quotations embodied in critical reviews and certain other noncommercial uses permitted by copyright law.

Printed in the United States of America
ISBN 978-1-967279-60-9 (sc)
ISBN 978-1-967279-61-6 (e)

2025.09.22

This book is printed on acid-free paper.

The contents of this work, including, but not limited to, the accuracy of events, people, and places depicted; opinions expressed; permission to use previously published materials included; and any advice given or actions advocated are solely the responsibility of the author, who assumes all liability for said work and indemnifies the publisher against any claims stemming from publication of the work.

Blue Ink Media Solutions
1111B S Governors Ave
STE 7582 Dover,
DE 19904

www.blueinkmediasolutions.com

SALUTE!

DEDICATION

This book is dedicated to all Vietnam veterans and their families and friends.

Especially to Vietnam Veterans Freddie Owens and Ed Junod who allowed me the privilege of being a part of their efforts to help their fellow veterans.

As a non-veteran it was an honor to be included.

I also want to dedicate this book to Taylor, Henry, and Spencer McRae, my grandchildren, and Nora Marohn, in hopes that one day they will become aware of the sacrifices our soldiers have put forward to protect their freedoms.

Children, you are too young now to understand, but one day standing with your hand over your heart, I hope you will appreciate the soldiers who stepped up to represent their country in times of trouble. Some of them were my personal friends. One of these soldiers was a student of your great grandmother: Juanita Belle Kinzalow Baxter Haun. One day Henry

Cason fixed my bicycle, the next he was a fighting medic in a place called Vietnam. He came home wounded, and with an unusual medal for a soldier. Called the Soldier's Medal. 109 of these were issued. One to country boy Henry Carson, another to General Colin Powell, who later was considered for President of the United States. More on this later.

Very special thanks to Linda Marohn, my life partner, and best friend, who has helped me over the past decade in writing this book, and editing and encouraging me to complete this book.

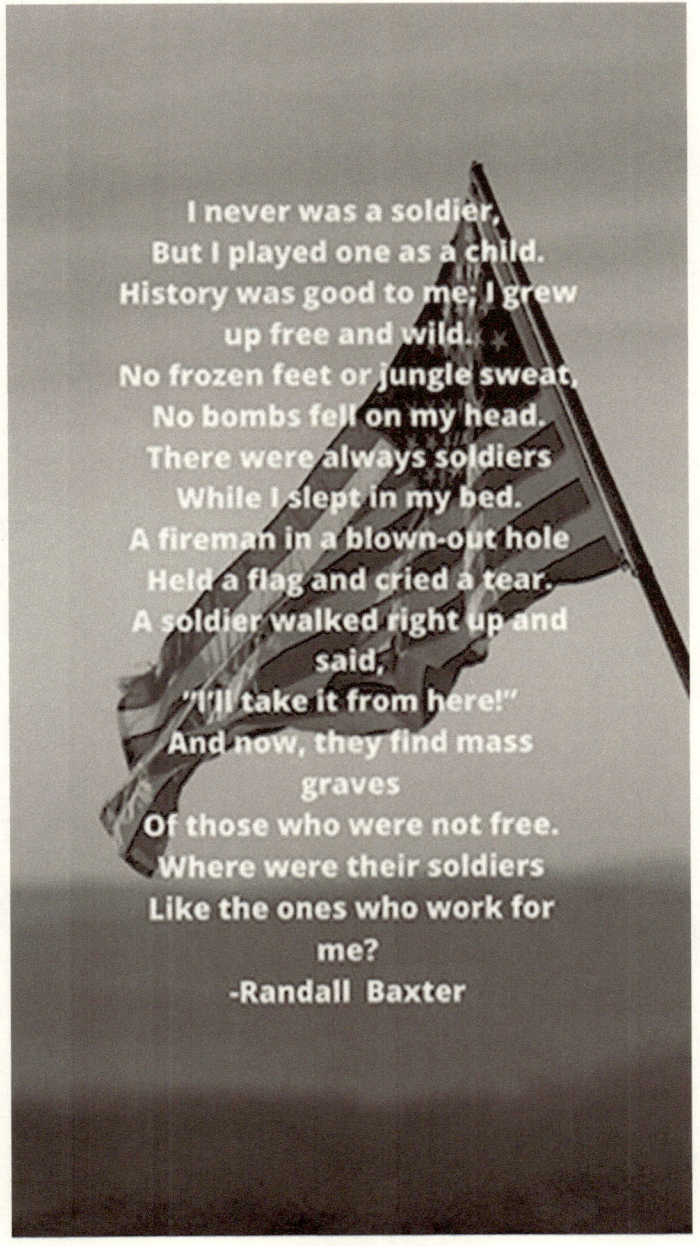

I never was a soldier,
But I played one as a child.
History was good to me; I grew
up free and wild.
No frozen feet or jungle sweat,
No bombs fell on my head.
There were always soldiers
While I slept in my bed.
A fireman in a blown-out hole
Held a flag and cried a tear.
A soldier walked right up and
said,
"I'll take it from here!"
And now, they find mass
graves
Of those who were not free.
Where were their soldiers
Like the ones who work for
me?
-Randall Baxter

Katrina Carter
13 years old and her father is a
Commander of a portion of the 101st Airborne
She mounted my poem onto the picture of the flag

PROLOGUE

I was on a business trip to Baltimore one day a few years back and realized I was a short train ride to Washington DC. Walking through our nation's capital with all its history was always a bucket list item for me, so I seized the opportunity and took the train ride.

I wanted to walk the whole city in one day if I could, I wanted to go by myself, so I could see and do whatever I wanted. I arrived at the train station, grabbed a map of the city, and off on a long walk for the day.

I was surprised that my first sight was so many homeless people in the park. Sleeping on the park benches and on the marble benches around the fountains. Using newspapers for blankets.

But I could also see the Capitol buildings and the Washington Monument. I could see on my map that I could go to the Lincoln Memorial, and along the way I could see the lake where FORREST GUMP spoke to the anti-war crowd, and in one day I could walk by Congress, the White House, the Supreme Court, the US Treasury, Ford's Theater. I also began to realize how Manassas and Gettysburg were only a short drive away.

There were a few Monuments that I will always remember. The World War II Memorials, state by state. The Korean Memorial, with the soldiers marching in rain gear and heavy coats, the Vietnam Memorial known as the WALL, and one that really sticks in my mind and is the topic of this book. The Statue of three Vietnam era soldiers returning from battle and the look on their faces. Survivors of the Vietnam War, carrying wounds no one could see, that would not manifest except over time. You can see a picture of this statue on the front cover of this book in the binocular lens.

I am not a veteran, or an expert in POST TRAUMATIC STRESS. We have all felt stress, that is easy to announce, traumatic stress is a deeper wound on people, and the fact that it develops over time is where the term POST comes in.

This book seeks to tell the History of the Vietnam War from an OUTSIDERS view point. I am a student of history, and I want to tell you the stories of veterans I have had the honor of meeting, who have shared their stories with me as guests on my radio show, THE VETERAN NEXT DOOR.

One of my favorite soldiers was Freddie Owens who died at age 76, peacefully at the University of Tennessee Medical Center in Knoxville, TN.

This is an excerpt from his obituary: He died on Friday, March 30, 2018 at 1:22 pm after an eight year battle with prostate cancer due to service related Agent Orange exposure. Survived by wife, Diana; siblings, Bettye Owens, Vivian Hayward, Sylvia Owens, Miriam Mitchell (Joseph), Sandra Brown, Reginald Lowe (Otella), Isaiah Johnson (Pam); children, Scott Owens (Hope), Michael Owens (Paula), Michelle Owens, Mark Owens, Freddie Owens, Jr (JoCherie), Helen Turner (Charles), Patrick Owens (Tamika); and grandchildren, Tristyn, Scott Jr, Sa'Taya, Lisa, Jessica and Ashley Brannon and other numerous grandchildren, great grandchildren, nieces, nephews, cousins and other loved ones.

Freddie was born on April 27, 1941 in Edison, GA.

He graduated from Middleton High School in June of 1960. Immediately following graduation, Freddie joined the US Army, where he achieved the rank of SSG and served with distinction for over 15 years. He earned the National Defense Service Medal, Vietnam Service Medal with three Bronze Stars, Republic of Vietnam Campaign Medal with 60 devise, 2 Overseas Service Bars, Expert (M-140, Expert M-16), 5 Service Stripes, Purple Heart, Air Medal, Combat Infantryman Badge, Presidential Unit Citation, Army Commendation Medal, Good Conduct Medal (4th award), Vietnam Cross of Gallantry with palm.

As president of Vet2Vet, he worked tirelessly advocating for veterans care and benefits.

He served as Co-Chairman of the Knoxville Regional Veterans Mental Health Council, Founder of Soldiers Heart Ministry, Peer Facilitator for Legacy Peer Support Group, Chairman of the Faith Based Community Committee and as a Veterans Court Mentor. He was baptized at an early age at New Bethel M.B. Church in Tampa, FL and has been a long time member of Redemption Church International where he served as a greeter, photographer, children's camp volunteer and on the security team. Freddie officiated children's sports all the way up to collegiate, from the age of 19 until this year.

I met Freddie Owens and Ed Junod both Vietnam Veterans who worked tirelessly helping fellow veterans with POST TRAUMATIC STRESS issues, and the two of them gave me the opportunity to help as a Non-veteran, by doing whatever I could to help their efforts.

There are many veterans who work in the areas of helping their fellow veterans with the unseen, unpredictable injuries of the Vietnam War and all wars that have followed.

I salute them all! With all my heart! It is impossible to name them all in this book, but not impossible to acknowledge their love and their efforts to help one another.

This book is one of the outcomes of my experience.

Having never been a veteran, I can only comment on the Outside Looking In!

ON THE OUTSIDE LOOKING IN

Prologue:

Hello,

My name is Randall Baxter. My first book was THE VETERAN NEXT DOOR 1939-1946, and over the past several years I have had the opportunity to get to know, and to renew some old friendships of men and women who had one thing in common that I could never claim. They are all veterans of The Vietnam War.

A war I came to know, through the eyes and stories of these veterans who have shared their stories and lives with me. When I add to that, the Historic records, and the 20-20 hindsight, and my own life experiences. Then you will see how my viewpoints on the war and its outcomes have developed different insights that have changed overtime. How my childhood perspective evolved into an awareness of the far reaching and long lasting life altering lifestyles these Viet Nam War veterans have experienced. How these people have influenced me, many decades after first hearing about, the unrest and violence occurring in what we now called Vietnam. As you may have noticed in this paragraph, there are two spellings of the word Viet Nam. Americanized the country is called Vietnam, As you talk with many south east Asians you will find the spelling to be Viet Nam. There are many references to the spelling in this book to both.

John Kennedy was elected President when I was 9 years old. He was killed on a day I had stayed home from school with a sore throat and I was watching a movie, and playing with my army men when the movie was interrupted announcing the President had been shot and had died from his wounds.

I have a photo of myself when I was about 4 years old, with a cowboy hat and matching cap guns in cowhide holsters strapped to my waist, and oh yeah, cowboy boots.

I was heavily influenced by Gene Autry, Roy Rogers, Steve McQueen, Audie Murphy and John Wayne.

I knew I had been born after World War II, and I was surrounded in Sunday school with WWII Veterans as my teachers. A General from that war was President, and a World War II hero was taking his place.

I could quote almost verbatim President Kennedy's statement about not asking "what my country could do for me, but what I could do for my country." That he had challenged Americans to go to the moon".

And, a statement that may have laid the groundwork, for what was to follow in Viet Nam. He told everyone involved or concerned that America would pay "any price, bear any burden, meet any hardship in the defense of freedom."

I was too young to know about a region of the world that used to be called French Indo-China. Or why it's name was changed or, why it split into two parts. I was more interested that someone had killed our young hero President and his successor was the Vice President and he had three letters for a name, LBJ. As I said earlier, I was nine years old at the time. Playing with my army men, watching war movies at the theater, starring my old cowboy heroes.

I had never heard of a man named Ho Chi Minh, or of General Giap.

Where was Diem Bien Phu? Who were the Viet Cong? The North Vietnamese Regulars? Why did they need to engage American Soldiers so they could update their battle tactics. They seemed to know that if we were going to pay that price, bear any burden, that it could well be in reference to Communist North Viet Nam wanting to unify all of Vietnam, but first it must eliminate the French supported power structures, South Vietnam forces, and the French may have America's help.

Besides, what does a 9 year old boy know, other than what he hears at home, sees on the nightly news? I do not remember a current events class in the 5th grade. We did have a news magazine called the Weekly Reader. I'm guessing, most of the soldiers who fought in Viet Nam did not have a current events class either.

By the 7th grade, I was into comic books like "Sgt. Fury" and "Sgt. Rock." Fifty years later I still have some of those comics in my personal library. I was beginning to purchase comic books about the Viet Nam War. One morning in the 7th grade there was a history quiz, and the extra credit question was what do Americans call the opposing forces in South Viet Nam? My answer was "CHARLIE", and my teacher marked it wrong. The answer was Viet Cong. I was really disturbed, the next day I brought in one of my comic books to show the teacher, my heroes in the comic books were calling the Viet Cong, "Charlie. This was 1967, and the Viet Nam war was served up for dinner every night, and even the music was changing. We were between, IA Drang and the TET OFFENSIVE. The number of soldiers going off to fight the war was way more than those coming home from the war. There were no parades for those coming home, and eventually the returning veterans were forgotten, or accused of war crimes. They were held responsible for the American Government policies in the war!

My life was becoming involved with Vietnam Veterans, and I did not realize how deep it would grow. Young men were leaving and going to war. Henry Carson, and one of my oldest brother Phil's schoolmates. Both came home wounded, one with a medal he shared with Colin Powell, one without his legs. Occasionally a Knoxville boy would be killed in the war, or one would come back wounded. It was sad, but I was generally not affected. I would read about it as I was delivering newspapers and playing my harmonica.

By the time I was in my senior year of high school, in 1972, the POW's were being released and the war was winding down as Americans knew it. We as a nation were ashamed of My Lai, and we had failed as a country to recognize or know the difference between an unpopular war, and the soldiers we sent to fight it.

My thoughts of being a soldier were behind me.

It was time to go to college, The University of Tennessee.

Should I be a news reporter?

A radio disc jockey? A lawyer, or a teacher?

Could I just do them all?

I became a teacher like my Mom.

One of my first teaching gigs, was as an instructor at Knoxville Business College. A school for people who wanted to develop business employee skills. Mostly for young and/or divorced women or women seeking bookkeeping, typing and office management skills. Average class size was about ten or twelve students per class. I taught Economics, Sociology, Psychology, History of Business, and Math. One fall, expecting the same size classes, my rosters had 30-40 students to each class, and to my surprise, the majority of the students were not the young females, but Viet Nam veterans going to school on the GI Bill. I will tell you this, it was a very interesting mix of students.

This was my first interactive introduction to Vietnam veterans. As students in my classes, with the great majority of them older than me by five years. Sometimes I wondered, who was teaching who? Many became my friends.

When I left my teaching career, and went to work with the NEW YORK LIFE INSURANCE COMPANY, many of these same students became my clients. I was allowed to share their growing families, careers and eventually began to see them retire.

My second opportunity in my life to engage with Viet Nam veterans was in my participation as a paintball Industry vendor and field operator in the 1980's and 1990's. At this time, most of the Vietnam Veterans were in their early forties.

Many of my paintball buddies were Viet Nam veterans. One day I was playing in the woods with a friend who had become an integral part of my paintball team the Tree Dancers. We were going to Nashville, to play in the International Masters. During practice, (it was raining) and at the end of the game, we were cleaning our equipment and I looked up and saw Ron crying. I asked him what was wrong, he said I would not understand, but sometimes he could not control his emotions when his feet got wet. He told me how, in the last days of his tour in Viet Nam, there was a lot of killing in the rice paddies, it was not long after that, he was a civilian sitting in a bar in San Francisco, drinking a beer. He had had no counseling or debriefing for dealing with the ordeals of battle stress, he had lost contact with his buddies, and the wet feet would make him flash back to those days, even 15 years later. My friend stopped playing paintball right after that. I missed him, but I understood.

In 2010, I was given a chance to fulfill my ambition to be a radio personality. I had to become a time broker to do it, so I had to pay for my time on the radio, so I sponsored it with products and service I sell as an insurance and securities representative in my own company called Asset Positioning Services. Some Vietnam Veterans also sponsored my show.

The radio program is called THE VETERAN NEXT DOOR, and I am the host of the show, NOT THE VETERAN! I tell stories, sometimes with guests who lived through historic military events. We did the show weekly from August of 2010 to 2016, and have covered all wars since America's beginnings, and interviewed many veterans including many World War II veterans. Korea, Viet Nam and the recent Middle Eastern wars in Iraq and Afghanistan.

While doing so, I became involved with United States Senior VETS. A 501C non-profit providing information to veterans and their families concerning their Non-service related disability benefits. I had also become active in many Veteran Advocacy panels and organizations as a volunteer.

Now you know the evolutionary progression of my involvement with Veterans. I need to point out that not one time during this Prologue did I say I was a veteran, as I am not. I just want you the reader to know that I function as a Non-veteran volunteer advocate, and that I do Estate Planning with the co-operation of local attorneys, for many of these same veterans.

Recently, my friend and occasional co-host, Tom Mercer, who just happens to be one of the soldiers in this book, invited me to attend a reunion of the Big Red One, "Swamp Rats".

It was in Nashville, Tennessee. I stayed all day Saturday, and for the Dinner, but had to leave to get back to Knoxville by 9 Am Sunday Morning. I decided to pack my car that night instead of trying to rush Sunday morning. As I walked to my car outside on the decking, there was a group from the reunion sitting around a Glass Top Table discussing old times. Oh, how I wanted to be a fly under that umbrella, but alas, I walked by and loaded my car after passing pleasantries.

Early that Sunday morning as I was walking to my car to head for Knoxville, I saw the table again. Empty of participants, and on the dew covered table, sat a damp napkin wadded up next to an empty bottle of Scotch, a few empty glasses, and an empty pack of cigarettes, and one glass that had been converted to an ash tray, with lots of butts mashed into its bottom. This is what made me realize, any information I could ever share with my listeners and readers, would be ON THE OUTSIDE LOOKING IN.

The trials and experiences these Veterans endured, have had an impact on our society, and will continue to set the tone through the first half of the 21st Century and maybe beyond. For me to tell you some of these stories, and the lessons I learned have to be understood from the direction in which I deliver this information to you. ON THE OUTSIDE LOOKING IN.

Please read, learn and, enjoy this book.

"WHO WISHES TO FIGHT
MUST FIRST COUNT THE COST"

SUN TZU

FRENCH INDOCHINA

CHAPTER ONE

Setting the stage for the Vietnam War

Modern international law recognizes only three lawful **justifications** for waging **war**: self-defense, defense of an ally required by the terms of a treaty, and approval by the United **Nations**.

When Empires collide:

The **French and Indian War** began over the specific issue of whether the upper Ohio River valley was a part of the British Empire, and therefore open for trade and settlement by Virginians and Pennsylvanians, or part of the **French** Empire. The wealth to be obtained or maintained by the victors and the fate of the American Indians in that region were at risk for all.

The War for independence:

No single event caused the revolution. It was, instead, a series of events that led to the war. Essentially, it began as a disagreement over the way Great Britain governed the colonies and the way the colonies thought they should be treated. Americans felt they deserved all the rights of Englishmen. The British, on the other hand, thought that the colonies were created to be used in ways that best suited the Crown and Parliament. The revolution was different from most revolutions throughout History. Americans sought not to overthrow the British Government, but to separate itself from that government in order to better serve its citizens.

The War of 1812:

Conflict fought between the United States and Great Britain **over** British violations of U.S. maritime rights. It ended with the exchange of ratifications of the Treaty of Ghent.

It also established our power as a world Navy, and brought recognition from the world that had not yet been accepted universally. Many debates on a national level were concerned with world power. Do we maintain a strong Navy or let it go down in disrepair because we did not need it?

The Mexican War:

U.S. annexation of Texas in 1845 sparked the conflict. **Mexico** viewed Texas as a breakaway province and refused to recognize its 1836 secession. When **Polk** ordered forces south to the Rio Grande, entering territory claimed by **Mexico**, the **Mexican** army attacked them, justifying to **President Polk** the need to **go to war**.

I am sure Manifest Destiny and the desire to possess New Mexico, Arizona, Nevada, Utah, Colorado, and California were of interest.

The country in the eyes of President Polk needed to reach from coast to coast. How much would the world be changed if California, Arizona, New Mexico, Utah, and Colorado as well as Texas were part of Mexico?

Our soldiers at the time, had nothing to say about policy, and were mere tools used to accomplish the goals of President Polk.

The Civil War:

The **Civil War** started because of uncompromising differences between the free and slave states over the power of the national government to prohibit slavery in the territories that had not yet become states. The South believed the Constitution gave them the power to set policy on Slavery. The North believed the Constitution said all men should be free.

Many of the soldiers were emigrants looking for economic stability. In one battle, IRISH Soldiers from the north fought Irish soldiers from the south. Flying the same Irish battle flags, Standing next to the Stars and Stripes on one side and the Stars and Bars on the other.

No soldiers were setting policies. Merely following orders to do the soldier's job.

The Indian Wars

Although one side or group cannot take the whole blame for the **wars**, the mistreatment of Native Americans on their land and the expansion of America westward **were the main** contributing factors. Treaties were almost immediately broken, Presidential Policies kept changing, and the American Indian failing to unite as one, fell separately to superior technology, deception and greed. This led to the tragedies of The Trail of Tears, Wounded Knee, and the Little Big Horn to just name a few.

The Spanish American War:

On April 21, 1898, the United States declared **war** against Spain. The reasons for **war** were many, but there were two immediate ones: **America's** support of the ongoing struggle by Cubans and Filipinos against **Spanish** rule, and the mysterious explosion of the battleship U.S.S. Maine in Havana Harbor. Imperialism became the policy of the United States of America. With Manifest Destiny complete, Imperialism in the days of the Czars, and Victorian expansions and French and German approaches in the South East Asian geo-politics were inevitable.

During this same time the French were dominating control over an area known as French indo-China.

World War I

Now, up until just before the **U.S.** declared war on April 6th, 1917, the **U.S.** had desperately tried to stay neutral, but ties to Britain, propaganda, the sinking of ships by German U-boats, and a German attempt in the

Zimmermann Note to get Mexico to declare war on the **U.S.** pushed the **U.S.** to getting involved. Not many people are aware that Germany offered to restore the boundaries of Pre President Polk for their help in the Great War.

World War II

While **World War II** had been raging in Europe since 1939, the **United States** did not intervene until after Japanese planes bombed Pearl Harbor in 1941. As Japan had an alliance with Germany and Italy, both nations declared war on the **United States** on December 11th, 1941, four days after the Pearl Harbor attack. The end of World War II would set the stage for the two wars to follow in Vietnam. The Potsdam conference had already established the lines of conflict.

The Korean War

Today, historians generally agree on several main **causes** of the **Korean War**, including: the spread of communism during the Cold **War**, **American** containment, and Japanese occupation of **Korea** during World **War** II.... The **American** containment policy **is** often referred to as the Truman Doctrine, since **American** President Harry S. Trumen was president.

A line had been drawn, control of the Korean Nation was at stake.

The Vietnam War

The **U.S.** entered the **Vietnam War** in an attempt to prevent the spread of communism, but foreign policy, economic interests, national fears, and geopolitical strategies also played major roles.

And in return the war took a toll of its own in America.

Let's take a look at how it affected our soldiers in the field and when they came home.

This is the true purpose of this book.

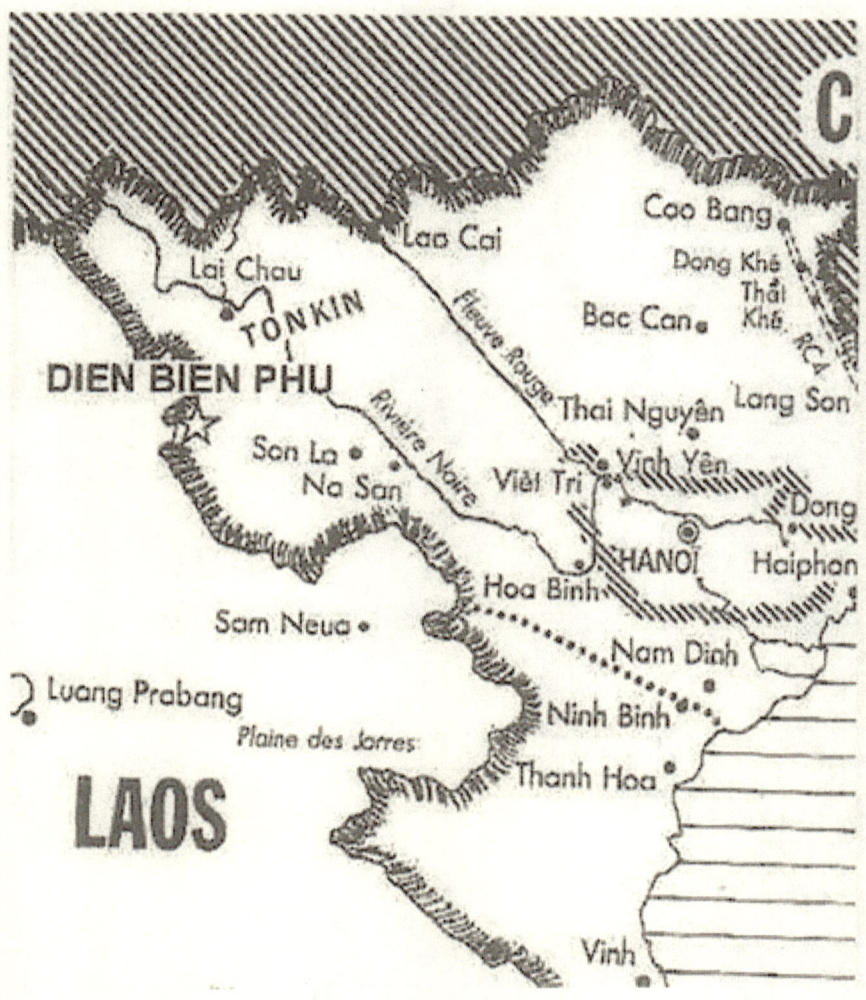

Now you know the location of Diem Bien Phu!

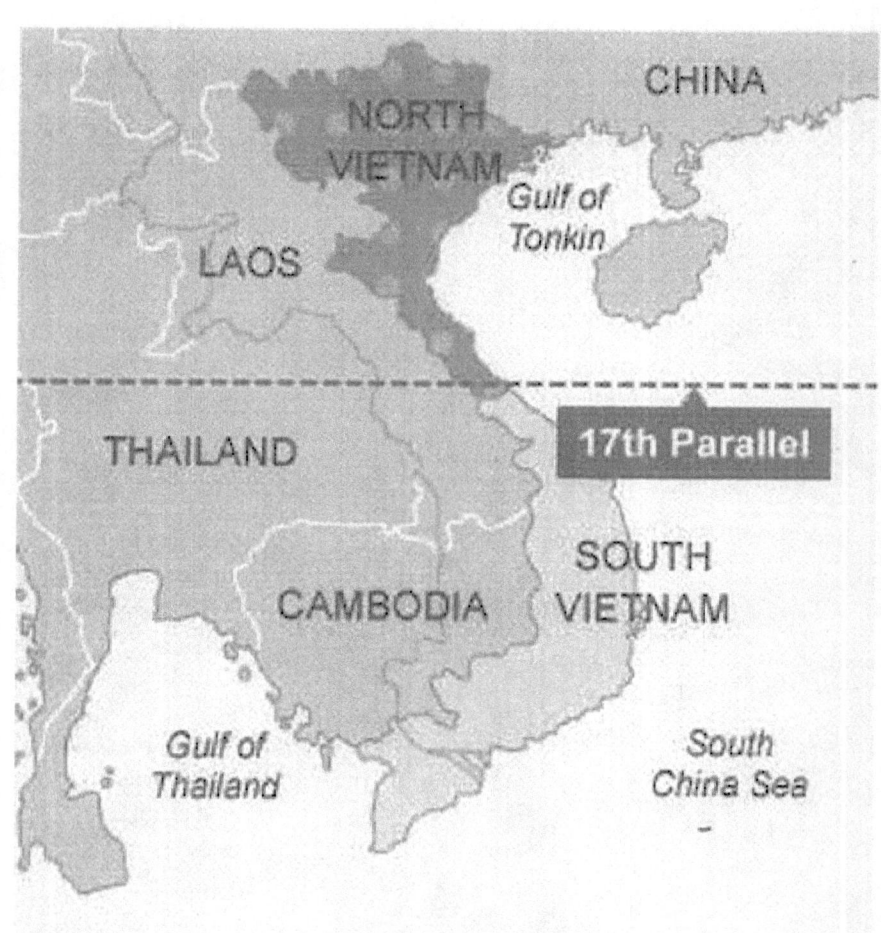

Vietnam after the French are expelled - Vietnam divided

CHAPTER TWO

Things you need to know

Vocabulary:

To understand the vocabulary, is to better understand the war and the soldiers who fought it.

The Vietnam War (1959-1975) was long and drawn out. It involved the United States supporting the South Vietnamese in an attempt to stay free from communism, but ended with the withdrawal of U.S. troops and a unified communist Vietnam.

Millions of Americans fought in the war, many came home with wounds no one could see.

As a former teacher I understand that there must be vocabulary development before a story can be best understood.

Let's examine some of the vocabulary of the Vietnam War.

I.e. A comparison of: The First verses the Second Indo China Wars.

The First Indo China War began the same day as the end of World War II.

Japan had recognized Vietnam as an independent nation and that was in direct conflict with agreements by the victors. France was to be returned as the dominant power in Indo China. It was preordained at the Potsdam Conference. HO Chi Minh felt differently.

The Second INDO China War began when France capitulated and Vietnam was split into two separate nations at the 17th parallel.

America chose the side they wanted to support, some say from fear of what would become the Domino Theory. Stating if one country falls others will follow.

North Vietnam and South Vietnam, Cambodia, Laos, Thailand, Burma, Indonesia, Malasia, the Philippines.

This list is not all inclusive: just a list to begin our journey.

Terms and Slang

Organized into persons, places and things.

ARVN Acronym for "Army of the Republic of Vietnam" (South Vietnam's army).

Boat people Refugees fleeing Vietnam after the Communist takeover of Vietnam in 1975. The refugees were called boat people because many of them escaped on small, leaky boats.

Charlie or Mr. Charlie Slang for Viet Cong (VC). The term is short for the phonetic spelling (used by the military and police to spell things over the radio) of "VC," which is "Victor Charlie." As I said earlier, My junior High School teacher marked my quiz as wrong when she asked me the nick name of the opposing forces in the early days of the war. My comic books called them Charlie. I got an X on my test. Good to know 50 years later it could have been marked correct.

Dove A person who is opposed to the Vietnam War. (Compare to "hawk.")

FNG: Fucking New Guy A new man in the platoon. Book knowledge and training but no on the job training. Dangerous addition to a group of experienced fighters.

Gook Negative slang term for Viet Cong. They were easier to kill if they were dehumanized.

Grunt Slang term used for an American infantry soldier.

Hawk A person who supports the Vietnam War. (Compare to "dove.")

Hanoi Jane: AKA Jane Fonda American Actress of a famous family. In her attempt to make Americans aware of their enemy, actually helped their causes in the war unintentionally, and became a hated figure of the war by Vietnam veterans all over the USA.

KIA Acronym for "killed in action."

Montagnard: primarily protestant and catholic central highlands Asians not used to being called Vietnamese, but many were very pro-American.

Some were not. Some people called them Vietnamese Hillbillies.

POW Acronym for "prisoner of war." A soldier that has been taken captive by the enemy.

MIA Acronym for "missing in action." This is a military term that means a soldier who is missing and whose death cannot be confirmed.

NLF Acronym for "National Liberation Front" (the communist guerrilla forces in South Vietnam). Also known as "Viet Cong."

NVA Acronym for "North Vietnamese Army" (officially called the People's Army of Viet-Nam or PAVN).

Peaceniks Early protesters against the Vietnam War.

Tunnel rats Soldiers who explored the dangerous network of tunnels that had been dug and used by the Viet Cong. These were not new tunnels and were very complex.

Viet Cong (VC) The communist guerrilla forces in South Vietnam, NLF.

Viet Minh Shortened term for the Viet Nam Doc Lap Dong Minh Hoi (League for the Independence of Vietnam), the organization established by Ho Chi Minh in 1941 to gain independence for Vietnam from France.

Vietniks Early protesters against the Vietnam War.

Places:

Boondock or boonies General term for the jungle or swampy areas in Vietnam.

Central highlands: a plateau in Vietnam predominately populated by Montagnards

Demilitarized Zone (DMZ) The line that divided North Vietnam and South Vietnam, located at the 17th parallel. This line was agreed upon as a temporary border at the 1954 Geneva Accords. There is also a DMZ in Korea.

Dien Bien Phu Battle of Dien Bien Phu was between communist Viet Minh forces and the French from March 13 - May 7, 1954. The decisive victory of the Viet Minh led to the withdrawal of the French from Vietnam, ending the First Indochina War. Setting the stage for America's involvement in the Second Indochina War, which began almost immediately after the end of the first Indochina War.

Gulf of Tonkin Incident Two attacks by North Vietnam against U.S. destroyers *USS Maddox* and *USS Turner Joy*, which were located in international waters in the Gulf of Tonkin, on August 2 and 4, 1964. This incident led U.S. Congress to pass the Gulf of Tonkin Resolution, which granted President Lyndon B. Johnson the authority to escalate American involvement in Vietnam. Some say these events never happened. Some say they did.

Hanoi Hilton Slang term for North Vietnam's Hoa Loa Prison which was notorious for being the place where American POWs were brought for interrogation and torture.

Ho Chi Minh Trail Supply paths from North Vietnam to South Vietnam that traveled through Cambodia and Laos to supply the communist forces fighting in South Vietnam. Since the paths were mostly outside of Vietnam, the U.S. (under President Lyndon B. Johnson) would not bomb or attack the Ho Chi Minh Trail for fear of expanding the conflict to these other countries.

HUE: A city in Vietnam with ancient history attached. The city of Hue was **the capital of a unified Vietnam from 1802 until the end of the WWII in 1945**. With its stately, tree-lined boulevards, Buddhist temples, national university, and ornate imperial palace within a massive walled city known as the Citadel, Hue was the cradle of the country's culture and heritage. As late as 1967, Hue remained an open city, unscathed by the various wars that since World War II had raged up and down the Indochinese peninsula.

Ia Drang: the first pitched battle between the US and the NVA both sides learning the value of attrition. 11:1 death ratio in favor of the US. The battle was made famous in the movie, WE WERE SOLDIERS.

Indochina: The term Indochina (originally Indo-China) was coined in the early nineteenth century. It emphasizes the cultural influence on the area of Indian civilization and Chinese civilization. The term was later adopted as the name of the colony of French Indochina (today's Cambodia, Vietnam, and Laos) Burma and Thailand are also part of Indochina but not French indo China.

Khe Sahn: Location of a battle in Vietnam, with the intention of drawing American forces out of the bigger cities right before the Tet offensive. Primarily a Montagnard area of inhabitance. Result: Indecisive; both sides claimed victory:, The siege of Khe Sanh was broken by ground forces on 6 April., Americans destroyed the base complex of Khe Sanh and withdrew from the battle area in July 1968., North

Vietnamese Army gained control of the Khe Sanh region after the American withdrawal., Termination of the McNamara Line. North Vietnamese lines of communication were extended further into South Vietnam.

Mekong Delta: The Mekong delta region encompasses a large portion of southwestern Vietnam of over 40,500 square kilometers (15,600 sq. mi). The size of the area covered by water depends on the season. Before 1975, Mekong Delta was part of Republic of Vietnam.

My Lai: a.k.a. Pinkville: a village where a massacre of civilians led to a turning point in the war against the American military at home.

American support for the war? The American Population could no longer separate the politics of the war, from the soldiers we sent to fight it.

THE PERFUME RIVER: the River near the City of Hue.

The World The United States; real life back home. Everybody else but Indo China,

Things:

Agent Orange An herbicide dropped on the forests and bush in Vietnam to defoliate (strip the leaves from plants and trees) an area. This was done to expose hiding enemy troops. Many Vietnam veterans who had been exposed to Agent Orange during the war have shown an increased risk of cancer. The soldiers saw the drums being unloaded by the helicopters and saw the barrels had an orange stripe on it. I.e. Agent Orange

AK-47 The AK-47, officially known as the Avtomat Kalashnikova, is a gas-operated, 7.62×39mm assault rifle, developed in the Soviet Union by Mikhail Kalashnikov. It is the originating firearm of the Kalashnikov rifle family. 47 refers to the year it was finished. **Preferred weapon of the Viet Cong, and North Vietnamese soldier.**

Bamboo whip: Spikes on a long bamboo pole, pulled back into an arc with a catch attached to a tripwire. When tripped, the spikes would be thrust into a soldier's chest at 100 miles per hour.

Containment US policy during the Cold War which sought the prevention of the spread of Communism to other countries.

Booby Trap: Retreating soldiers in most wars would leave a gift for their conquering opponents. The Viet Cong used broken bushes, palm leaves, sticks, spikes, grenades, wires and even souvenir memorabilia.

Cartridge trap: A single cartridge placed in a bamboo stalk, lowered into a shallow hole, on top of aboard with a nail detonator. The weight of the victim would push the cartridge onto the nail that would serve as a firing pin. Wounding the victim in the foot, taking other soldiers out of the battle to care for him.

Domino theory: A U.S. foreign policy theory that stated, like the chain effect begun when even just one domino is pushed over, one country in a region that falls to communism will lead to surrounding countries also soon falling to communism.

DRV: Acronym for "Democratic Republic of Vietnam" (Communist North Vietnam).

Flag bombs: NVA and VC loved to fly flags. Americans liked to capture their flags so many were abandoned by the VC and NVA and booby trapped.

Freedom Bird: Any airplane that took American soldiers back to the U.S. at the end of their tour of duty.

Friendly fire an accidental attack, whether by shooting or by dropping bombs, upon one's own troops, such as U.S soldiers shooting at other U.S. soldiers.

Grenade in a can: trip wire tied to a grenade in a can. Tripping on the wire pulled the grenade from the can to instantly explode. Could also be tied to cans on both ends.

Hootch: Slang term for a place to live, either a soldier's living quarters or a Vietnamese hut. Used a few times in this book as a helicopter of an officer, or headquarters for officers.

In country: Vietnam.

Johnson's War: Slang term for the Vietnam War because of U.S. President Lyndon B. Johnson's role in escalating the conflict.

Klick: Slang term for a kilometer.

M-16: Rifle used by most American Soldiers in Vietnam.

Napalm: A jellied gasoline that when dispersed by flamethrower or by bombs would stick to a surface as it burned. This was used directly against enemy soldiers and as a way to destroy foliage in order to expose enemy troops.

Operation Rolling Thunder: Designed to stop the spread of enemy supplies in Vietnam and to encourage the North to enter peace talks,

Pacification: or nation-building involved strengthening local government, rebuilding and goodwill efforts with the local populace so they'd support the efforts of South Vietnam.

Post-traumatic stress disorder (PTSD): A psychological disorder caused by experiencing a trauma. Symptoms can include nightmares, flashbacks, sweating, rapid heart rate, outbursts of anger, sleeplessness, and more. Many Vietnam veterans suffered from PTSD upon their return from their tour of duty. Also called Soldier's Heart and Shell Shock.

punji stakes A booby trap made out of a bunch of sharpened, short, wooden sticks placed upright in the ground and covered so that an unsuspecting soldier would fall or stumble upon them. Often smeared with urine or feces, or other poisons, stake pointing up for injury on the way down, and stakes pointing down to cause further injury coming out.

RVN Acronym for "Republic of Viet-Nam" (South Vietnam).

Soldier's Heart: PTSD is a relatively new name for soldiers suffering from Traumatic Stress long after the events of the war have come and gone. In earlier American Wars a Soldier would return from war and his personality would have changed. In the 20th Century the ailment became known as Post Traumatic Stress Disorder. I.e. PTSD

Snake Pits: carting Pit vipers in bags, the Viet Cong, the hope was that if an American found the pack and opened it, they would experience a deadly three stepper snake bite. Called that because the venom would kill a full grown man in three steps. These snakes would also be placed in tunnels, tied to a bamboo stake so it would be held in place until a tunnel rat would find it.

Spring Offensive The massive attack by North Vietnam's army into South Vietnam, begun on March 30, 1972, and lasting until October 22, 1972.

Tet Offensive The massive attack on South Vietnam by North Vietnam's army and the Viet Cong, begun on January 30, 1968 (on Tet, the Vietnamese New Year). An American military Victory, but a political defeat.

The Mace: Another trip wire trap. When released a heavy ball with spikes would swing down from a tree, killing anyone it hit.

The Phoenix Program: (Vietnamese: Chiến dịch Phụng Hoàng) was a program designed and coordinated by the United States Central Intelligence Agency (CIA) during the Vietnam War, involving cooperation between American, South Vietnamese and Australian militaries. The program was designed to **identify and destroy the Viet Cong.**

The program was in operation between 1965 and 1972, and similar efforts existed both before and after that period. By 1972, Phoenix operatives had "neutralized" 81,740 suspected VC operatives, informants and supporters, of whom between 26,000 and 41,000 were killed.

Eventually the CIA was forced to cancel the Program.

Tiger Traps: Trip wire would dump bricks and barbed spikes onto the head of the victim.

Vietnamese Catholics: Indo China portion dominated by France in their search for Empire. Brought with them their Catholic Religion and spread it through the land. Accepting and practicing Catholicism, meant acceptance into French Indo China society. and politics.

Vietnamization The process of withdrawing U.S. troops from Vietnam and turning over all fighting to the South Vietnamese. This was part of President Richard Nixon's plan to end U.S. involvement in the Vietnam War.

THE BUILD UP:

WASHINGTON (Army News Service, Aug. 3, 2015)—In early 1965, about 50,000 U.S. troops, mostly advisors, were in South Vietnam. By the end of 1966, that number had grown to 385,000 with the majority being Army and by that time, they were on the offensive, said Frank L. Jones.

Jones, a professor at the U.S. Army War College, authored a pamphlet, "Buying Time: 1965-1966," just published by the Army's Center of Military History.

The rapid buildup was not really part of the original strategy, Jones said. The U.S. advisors, including some 1,200 Green Berets, were there to buy time to train up the South Vietnamese, who would then carry the fight to the enemy on their own initiative.

Author's note: we need to remember, the nation of South Vietnam was a new anomaly. It was only 10 years old, war torn, with corrupt leadership, and disunity, and things weren't going well.

In 1965, President Lyndon Johnson's administration and military leaders became aware that South Vietnam was on the verge of collapse, Jones said. Insurgents controlled about half of South Vietnam, along with about a third of the population.

Furthermore, South Vietnamese forces were not showing a willingness to fight and many were deserting. There were even concerns that Saigon could fall unless more U.S. troops were sent in to bolster the country. The role was beginning to change from advice and assist to offensive action.

President Eisenhower's remarks to incoming President Kennedy,' "You may have to send troops", was coming true.

President Johnson, who was a senator during the Korean War, remembered how President Harry S. Truman had been castigated by the Republicans for "losing" China. "That stayed in his memory," Jones said. He didn't want Saigon to fall on his watch.

Furthermore, the U.S. saw the world divided into communist and non-communist countries. There were concerns that if South Vietnam fell to the communist north, other countries in Southeast Asia would follow. I.e. The Domino Theory

Back home, not a lot of attention was being paid to the rapid buildup of U.S. forces, sometimes called the "Americanization" of South Vietnam, Jones said. Johnson's "Great Society" and civil rights legislation, as well as the space program were taking much of the spotlight.

As the buildup continued, U.S. forces were joined by those from Australia, New Zealand, South Korea, the Philippines and Thailand. This was known as the "Many Flags" campaign.

Notably absent, Jones said, were NATO allies. They already had concerns about the Soviets to their east and were apprehensive about the new U.S. focus in Southeast Asia.

EARLY BATTLES

On Feb. 7, 1965, the Viet Cong attacked the U.S. base at Pleiku in the Central Highlands. This led to Johnson authorizing the use of strategic bombing of the North by the U.S. Air Force, an operation known as Rolling Thunder. A series of small ground battles ensued throughout the countryside as well.

Also that year, the newly-formed 1st Cavalry Division (Airmobile) was deployed to South Vietnam. While the helicopter had seen use in the Korean War for medevac and small troop movement, the strategy of moving larger formations by air really got its start in 1965, Jones said.

The concept of air mobility, or massive movement by helicopter, came about following the Howze Board studies, chaired by Gen. Hamilton H. Howze and overseen by Secretary of Defense Robert McNamara in 1962.

Besides airlifting Soldiers, the experiments carried out included using helicopter gunships and using heavier helicopters like the CH-47 to airlift artillery. The UH-1 Huey, a light helicopter, was relied upon to do much of the troop carrying and also serve as gunships. This was a major doctrinal change for the Army, Jones said.

In November 1965, 1st Battalion, 7th Cavalry Regiment, participated in the Ia Drang Valley Campaign, the most well-known battle at the time. The Soldiers were ferried into position using helicopters.

A reason there were fewer pitched battles than in previous wars is because the enemy, especially the insurgents, knew the terrain well and were elusive, Jones said. North Vietnamese Army troops would come in through Laos and Cambodia via the Ho Chi Minh Trail network and fan out below the jungle canopy, hiding weapons in caches. A lot of the work done by Soldiers at this time was locating and destroying these caches. Search and destroy.

The Army never officially entered Laos and Cambodia during this period, Jones said. This was a time of limited or restrained warfare. The Johnson administration didn't want to pull the Chinese and Soviets directly into the fighting and risk escalation into a larger conflict with the potential for nuclear weapons being used.

By 1966, Johnson became concerned that counterinsurgency, called "pacification," was getting short-shrift compared with applications of conventional force, Jones said. Gen. William C. Westmoreland, commander of Military Assistance Command, Vietnam, or MACV, began to pay more attention to "pacification" efforts. MACV controlled all U.S. ground forces in Vietnam.

Pacification or nation-building involved strengthening local government, rebuilding and goodwill efforts with the local populace so they'd support the efforts of South Vietnam. Today, as was the case then, these activities would be part of an interagency effort, Jones said.

One of the most under reported events of 1965 to 1966 was the massive logistical effort by the U.S. Army, Jones said. Sustaining such a large force, thousands of miles from home, was a huge undertaking.

Further, a massive engineering effort was needed to build port facilities and climate-controlled structures at various bases, he said. The U.S. Corps of Engineers was a large part of that undertaking.

The Soldiers doing the fighting and supporting the logistical effort were a mixture of enlistees and conscripts, Jones said.

Unlike the Korean War, the Army Reserve was not called up in 1965 and 1966. Johnson was concerned that should he do so, he'd lose backing for the war at home, as the military would seem to be losing control.

By 1965 and 1966, the protest movement had started, but it was still nowhere near in size to the protests that would erupt later in the war.

A number of company- and field-grade officers who served in Vietnam in 1965 and 1966 would later lead the Army in the late 1980s and 1990s.

Maj. H. Norman Schwarzkopf Jr. was one such officer who served in Pleiku and other areas advising and assisting the South Vietnamese, earning two Silver Star Medals in the process.

In 1991, by then, a general, he led coalition forces in the Persian Gulf War. Schwarzkopf advocated defeating the enemy quickly and with overwhelming force, which his troops did, liberating Kuwait in a matter of days. It was unlike his experience in Vietnam, Jones said.

CHAPTER THREE

The beginning of the Vietnam War

Ho Chi Minh second from right
General Giap third from right

Isaiah 21:5-9 ⁵They set the tables, they spread the rugs, they eat, they drink! Get up, you officers, oil the shields! ⁶This is what the LORD says to me: "Go, post a lookout and have him report what he sees. ⁷When he sees chariots with teams of horses, riders on donkeys or riders on camels, let him be alert, fully alert." ⁸And the lookout shouted, "Day after day, my LORD, I stand on the watchtower; every night I stay at my post. ⁹Look, here comes a man in a chariot with a team of horses. And he gives back the answer: 'Babylon has fallen, has fallen! All the images of its gods lie shattered on the ground!'"

For me, forty years before I published the Poem printed in the front of this book called, "I Never Was a Soldier", and for the years since that date. As I said earlier, I have been involved as a volunteer advocate with veterans of our American wars. I remember watching the old war movies of our WW II heroes, and playing with my army men in the yard, or in my bed room or living room. Never thinking of the toy soldiers or movie characters as real living beings, with families and struggles of their own after serving our nation. I guess I first heard the word Vietnam on the evening news reports probably watching either, ABC, NBC or CBS nightly news.

Maybe it was in late 1961 when President Kennedy announced his decisions to help the South Vietnam government. I did not know what had happened since World War II, much less what had happened in Indo-China in the most recent two thousand years that help form the region and the war we are discussing in this book. What harm could come of backing South Vietnam with some equipment and advisors? Was that the start of the war in Vietnam? Are wars caused by any one singular event?

In 1961 I was 7 years old. As I said in my poem, there were always soldiers when I slept in my bed. Being an amateur historian, I tried to look back into history to discover when the Vietnam War began. The further back I looked, the more war and turmoil I saw for the people of South East Asia. The Oriental Dynasties, the Chinese to the north for centuries, and the European colonialization during the European Age of Exploration from the 1400's to the Age of Empires in the 1800's. On top of that how can you avoid the impact of the powers to the west of Vietnam through the ages? Siam, Burma, India. Investigating these past events helped me understand the word INDO-CHINA. As a teen ager in the mid-1960's I wondered why the Peace Talks were in Paris, and how a Vietnamese waiter in French Restaurants could rise to be the leader of North Vietnam. All I knew was that he was a communist, with a long white oriental beard. And I thought of him as a villain. I knew nothing of all the super intelligent men who were in conflict over their goals and ideologies they wanted for this geo political region. Who were these men? Ho Chi Minh, Chairman Mao, Franklin Roosevelt, Eisenhower, Harry Truman, Stalin, Henry Kissinger, John Kennedy and what was Jane Fonda doing in North Viet Nam, and who were these soldiers who fought as ordered, and why was our nation unable to separate the policies of the war from those soldiers sent to fight? The Vietnamese people seemed to have been at war for a long time, with the French dominating their culture and economy up until France fell to Nazi Germany near the beginning of World War II.

That is why it was called French Indo-China.

The French lost control of French Indo-China in September 1940, during World War II the newly created impotent regime of Vichy France granted Japan's demands for military access to Tonkin following the Japanese occupation of French Indo China, which lasted until the end of the Pacific War. This allowed Japan better access to China in the Second Sino-Japanese War against the forces of Chiang Kai-shek. Most Americans at the time were unaware of the wars or why they were being fought. It was also part of Japan's strategy for dominion over this part of the world calling it the Greater East Asian Co-prosperity Sphere. These are all World War II events that had an effect on the French Indo China territories that soon became known as Laos, Cambodia, and Vietnam.

Thailand took this opportunity of weakness to reclaim previously lost territories, resulting in the French-Thai War between October 1940 and May 1941. The French Asian Empire established in 1862 was collapsing. They were ruling French Indo-China in name only. Real control belonged to the Japanese.

Who was Ho Chi Minh?

October 1930: Ho Chi Minh established the Indochinese Communist Party which was transformed from the Vietnam Communist Party in Hong Kong.

In 1941, communist activist Ho Chi Minh secretly returned to Vietnam after 30 years in exile and organized a nationalist organization known as the Viet Minh. I had never noticed the tie in to Ho Chi Minh and Viet Minh until recently. After Japanese troops occupied Vietnam during World War II, the U.S. military intelligence agency, Office of Strategic Services, OSS, aligned itself with Ho Chi Minh and his Viet Minh guerrillas to harass Japanese troops in the jungles and to help rescue downed American pilots.

What a small world it becomes when we start looking at how one event is connected to another. Many times when world leaders have a chance to correct political, tribal or economic issues, they choose to restore the status quo, or to realign the world according to the desires of the victors setting the stages for the next wars.

If you do not believe me, study the redefining of Middle East borders after World War I.

In March of 1945, amid rumors of a possible American invasion, the Japanese ousted the Vichy French colonial government which had been operating independently and seized control of Vietnam.

Biblical input FYI only!

Question: "Who are the four horsemen of the apocalypse?"

The first horseman of the Apocalypse is mentioned in the Bible in Revelation 6:2: "I looked, and there before me was a white horse! Its rider held a bow, and he was given a crown, and he rode out as a conqueror bent on conquest."

I do not believe the First Horseman represented the anti-Christ when it came to Japan. I do believe they were misled in their thought process that developed the cruelty and crimes against humanity that they committed. I also believe they were hell bent on conquest.

The second horseman of the Apocalypse appears in the Bible in Revelation 6:4, "Then another horse came out, a fiery red one. Its rider was given power to take peace from the earth and to make men slay each other. To him was given a large sword." The second horseman refers to terrible warfare that will break out in the end times. The story of Viet Nam is certainly not the end of time, but the warfare was terrible.

The third horseman is described in the Bible in Revelation 6:5-6, "…and there before me was a black horse! Its rider was holding a pair of scales in his hand. The third horseman of the Apocalypse refers to a great famine that will take place, likely as a result of the wars from the second horseman. The famine that followed in Vietnam was certainly contributed to by the events of World War II.

The fourth horseman is mentioned in the Bible in Revelation 6:8, "I looked, and there before me was a pale horse! Its rider was named Death, and Hades was following close behind him. The fourth horseman of the Apocalypse is symbolic of death and devastation. It seems to be a combination of the previous horsemen. The fourth horseman of the Apocalypse will bring further warfare and terrible famines along with awful plagues and diseases. And so it did.

That same summer of 1945, several of the Four Horsemen paid a visit to Vietnam. Severe famine struck Hanoi and the surrounding areas, eventually resulting in 2 million deaths from starvation out of a population of 10 million. Who would have known that? I didn't know that. I do not know if these deaths were counted in the total World War II deaths or not.

The famine generates political unrest and peasant revolts against the Japanese and remnants of French colonial society.

How could you blame the Vietnamese? They could not be as concerned about world events when they could not fill their bellies. They understandably would follow the leaders who offered solutions to their dilemmas. A reference to Maslow's hierarchy of needs says people will pay attention to their basic needs before considering higher needs like self-esteem and self-actualization.

Ho Chi Minh capitalizes on the turmoil by successfully spreading his Viet Minh movement. In July of 1945, following the defeat of Nazi Germany, World War II allies, including the U.S., Britain, and Soviet Union, held the Potsdam Conference in Germany to plan the postwar world. Vietnam is considered a minor item on the agenda, and in order to disarm the Japanese in Vietnam, the allies divide the country in half at the 16th parallel. Chinese nationalists were permitted to move in and disarm the Japanese North of the parallel, while the British moved in to disarm the Japanese in the South. If you were Vietnamese, would you see this as just another invasion of foreigners? During the Potsdam Conference, representatives from France requested the return of all French prewar colonies in Southeast Asia, and their request was granted. Vietnam, Laos, and Cambodia were once again to become French colonies following the removal of the Japanese.

According to Ho Chi Minh, this ruling could not stand!

It was time for the Vietnamese to determine the outcome and status of their country!

Most of the soldiers to fight in this on going drama were just glimmers in their father's eyes called the BABY BOOM!

About 30 days later in August of 1945, the Japanese surrendered unconditionally. On September 2, 1945, the Japanese signed the surrender agreement in Tokyo Bay, formally ending World War II in the Pacific. On this same day, Ho Chi Minh proclaimed the independence of Vietnam by quoting from the text of the American Declaration of Independence which has been supplied to him by the OSS:

"We hold these truths to be self-evident, that all men are created equal, that they are endowed by their Creator with certain unalienable Rights that among these are Life, Liberty, and the pursuit of Happiness."

Ho then declared himself President of the Democratic Republic of Viet Nam and pursued American recognition, but was repeatedly ignored by President Harry Truman. How could Harry Truman go against the POTSDAM conference? As far as he was concerned, the fate of Vietnam had already been decided by the victors of World War II. I am not sure Vietnam as a nation or the Vietnamese as a people were considered at the time.

Ho Chi Minh called his group The National Liberation Committee of Vietnam. One of Empirical Japan's last acts was to recognize Ho Chi Minh's new country.

There are several reasons, or shall we say causes of the war in Vietnam after World War II.

Reason 1: By taking control of Hanoi in 1945 Ho Chi Minh declared the independence of Vietnam as a nation. He had declared it was no longer part of the French Empire.

France disagreed and so did Harry Truman. It had been decided at Potsdam before the war had ended.

Is there any wonder that famine hit Vietnam so hard at the end of World War II? The newly declared country was invaded by victorious armies with the intention to disarm the Japanese Military presence in Vietnam at the end of World War II. September 13, 1945, British forces arrive in Saigon, and in the North, 150,000 Chinese nationalist soldiers consisting mainly of poor peasants arrive in Hanoi after looting Vietnamese villages during their entire march down from China. Then they proceeded to loot Hanoi. Ten days after that, in South Vietnam, 1400 French soldiers released by the British from former Japanese internment camps, enter Saigon and go on a deadly rampage, attacking Viet Minh and killing innocent civilians, including children, aided by French civilians who joined the rampage. An estimated 20,000 French civilians lived in Saigon at the time. Two days after that in Saigon, Viet Minh successfully organized a general strike, shutting down all commerce along with electricity and water supplies, and in a suburb of Saigon, members of Binh Xu Yen, a Vietnamese criminal organization, massacred 150 French and Eurasian civilians, including children. I am not sure when the body count started for the American/Vietnam War. Where and how do you determine the first death?

The American head of the American OSS mission was killed by Viet Minh troops while driving a jeep to the airport. It was later indicated that his death was a case of mistaken identity. He was believed to be French.

In 1946, France recognized Vietnam as a free state in the French union, and French troops replaced the marauding Chinese Soldiers in the Northern sections of Vietnam. The "Free State in the French union was not enough!"

Ho Chi Minh's Viet Minh negotiated with France, but the talks broke down, and amid the deteriorating relationship the Viet Minh went on the military offensive in 1946 to acquire independence. The French attempt to militarily wipe out the Viet Minh failed in 1947. A civil War in China was going on at the same time, and the eventual victor was Communist Red China under Mao Zedong. Forming the People's Republic of China.

In 1949, the same year as the Red Chinese Victory, the French agree to help build a national anti-communist army.

The Domino Theory was beginning to establish itself as a Philosophical battle between Communists and Non-communist theories and the governments representing these ideologies.

In January of 1950, the People's Republic of China and the Soviet Union recognize Ho Chi Minh's Democratic Republic of Vietnam. Each of these communist nations offered Vietnam weapons they needed to fight in their war of Independence. We need to remember that HO Chi Minh originally went to Harry Truman to ask for help and was refused. Franklin Roosevelt was pro Vietnamese independence, but The Potsdam Conference and the Geneva Accords would change the American position on Vietnam. By the end of 1951, French casualties in Vietnam surpass 90,000. The horsemen were still riding in Vietnam.

Seven months later, the United States military involvement in Vietnam began as President Harry Truman authorized $15 million in military aid to the French. Was this another thank you to Lafayette? Or maybe just one Ally helping another regardless of potential outcomes? Maybe a reaction to prevent another Korean situation? The American government was uneasy about the way things were going in Vietnam. American military advisers accompanied the flow of U.S. tanks, planes, artillery, and other supplies to Vietnam. Over the next 4 years, the U.S. spent $3 billion on the French war and by 1954, the US provided 80% of all war supplies used by the French.

France, in agreement with The Geneva Accords, granted Laos its full independence in 1953, and the Viet Minh forces pushed into the newly formed country. This would cause problems for our soldiers later on in the American participation of this war torn Laotian area.

Truman does not run for another term and Dwight D. Eisenhower is elected President of the United States.

Since the end of World War II we now had our second President involved in the Vietnam crisis.

After years of waging war on the French, General Giap, a master revolutionary/military planner, and the leader of the Vietnamese army. Used artillery and superior numbers to pound the French and shut down the only runway, thus forcing the French to rely on risky parachute drops for resupply at Dien Bien Phu. On May 1, 1954 the siege at Dien Bien Phu was over, and 10,000 French soldiers were trapped by 45,000 Viet Minh. French troops had run out of fresh water and medical supplies. Add to this the fact that the country of Vietnam was now split at the 17th Parallel, elections were never held. North Vietnam was Communist led by Ho Chi Minh, and South Vietnam was capitalist and led by a corrupt and weak president, Ngo Dinh Diem.

In 1954 Vietnam is split into two states at a conference in Geneva.

After the defeat of the French at Dien Bien Phu, the United States began direct aid to South Vietnam

Reason 2: War between the two nations broke out in 1958.

1959 the communist party starts military operations in South Vietnam

Again General Giap was in control.

His universal plan for warfare came in three stages.

Phase one: Guerrilla bands form in safe areas in the hills to establish bases.

Phase two: Guerrillas warfare attacks on enemy communications with extensions of power in villages.

We saw this in the movie, The Green Berets, starring john Wayne.

Phase three: Open warfare with conventional forces as demonstrated in the movie We Were Soldiers.

Reason three:

President Eisenhower agrees with the Domino Theory regarding Southeast Asia. He says that there are a row of dominoes set up. These dominoes represent countries in Asia, primarily South East Asia and when the first one falls the others will follow soon after.

Many believe this belief and support of the Domino Theory is the first step of America in its escalation of the Vietnam War.

Adding the French defeat at Dien Bien Phu, during the peace talks at the Geneva Convention. America, as well as France knew the French had lost control of French Indo China. The purpose was to end the hostilities in Indochina and the idea of portioning Vietnam into two parts at the 17th parallel was first explored. Even though an agreement was signed, not all parties, including The United States supported the agreement. Vietnam was divided at the 17th parallel until further elections could be held. Cambodia and Laos were allowed their independence. Elections were to be held, but South Vietnam's leaders refused to partake.

Even at the urging of Britain, France and the United States of America.

1. The elections that were held were reportedly rigged, and South Vietnam had a new leader: **Ngo Dinh Diem** born into a noble Vietnamese Catholic family at the turn of the 20th century. A staunch anti-Communist, he joined the U.S.-backed government, making himself president in 1955. He imprisoned and murdered hundreds of Buddhists, causing the U.S. to remove its support.

China and The Soviet Union Pledge additional support in 1955.

The ante is upped in the proxy wars of the super powerful and Vietnam was to be the game board and the battlefield.

Britain, France and the United States urge the leaders of South Vietnam to have discussions with the Viet Minh and the Communist North Vietnam.

In 1956 the French leave Vietnam, and The US Military Assistance Advisor group assumes responsibility from the French for training South Vietnamese forces. Is this when the American - Vietnamese war began? There was no declaration of war, just a co-operation agreement? The Soviets had the Berlin Wall and the Iron Curtain. The Red Chinese had been stopped in Korea, but no armistice, and now Vietnam was threatened by the communist agendas.

I was two years old at this time, but most of the non-commissioned soldiers who would be fighting, dying, and being wounded and becoming heroes and veterans, were already born. They were called baby boomers led by veterans of World War II and Korea and politicians with goals and ambitions yet to be learned by the general public.

1957:

Communist Insurgency begins to swell in South Vietnam. Over 400 South Vietnamese officials are assassinated. Thirteen Americans working for the US Military Assistance Advisor group an US Information Service, who had recently taken over the training of the South Vietnamese forces, are wounded in Saigon Terrorist bombings. Is this when the war started? Was it already underway?

If our soldiers and representatives are being shot at, is this war or not?

Must it be declared?

Reason four:

President Diem of South Vietnam was a weak and corrupt leader who refused to give the local peasants the lands they expected. Being Catholic, he did not like Buddhism, and treated Buddhists badly. The South Vietnamese population was rebelling and showing support for the Vietminh, and the National Liberation Front. Just as HO Chi Minh and General Giap had hoped.

1959:

The Ho Chi Minh Trail is open for business. It is used to infiltrate supplies and weapons into South Vietnam. Can one country declare war on another and no war be declared on the other side? At what point when an ally working in support of another nation finds itself at war with that nation's enemies? You could not have asked me at the time, I was only 5 years old.

John Kennedy was running for President. The veterans I have interviewed since 2010 were just kids themselves many still not even in high school when these events were occurring. The Happy Days lifestyle, Blue Suede shoes, and black and white westerns on TV were dominant.

1960:

North Vietnam imposes a Universal military conscription.

Hanoi formed the National Liberation Front for South Vietnam.

The South Vietnamese government dubs the Front, Viet Cong.

On top of all this someone tried to assassinate the President of South Vietnam in a coup attempt. He was the same guy who won the questionable election I mentioned earlier.

By this time, I am sure there were lots of organizations that would want him dead.

It sure does look like they were at war, but Eisenhower and Vice President Richard Nixon who was running against John Kennedy for President had not declared war at this time. Only co-operation with forces opposing those who would knock "free "nations down like dominoes is what I understood at the time. Of course I was only six years old. I was learning to read Alice and Jerry Books, and Dick and Jane readers. The older kids were going to sock hops, and Drive in movies. They were not being shot at, or killed in a non-declared war. I did watch TV, and I remember my dad, who was a staunch Democrat by inheritance of political philosophy, when I heard on the news,

January 20, 1961. John Fitzgerald Kennedy is inaugurated as the 35th U.S. President and declares in this speech:

"Let every nation know, whether it wishes us well or ill, that we shall pay any price, bear any burden, meet any hardship, support any friend, oppose any foe, to ensure the survival and the success of liberty. This much we pledge and more."

We now had our third President involved in Vietnam.

Is this when the war began?

Privately, outgoing President Eisenhower tells John Kennedy, "I think you're going to have to send troops." In May of 1961, President Kennedy sent 400 America Green Berets special advisers to South Vietnam to train South Vietnamese soldiers in methods of counterinsurgency in the fight against Viet Cong guerillas. The role of the Green Berets soon expands to include the establishment of civilian irregular defense groups made up of fierce mountain men known as the Montagnards. These groups established a series of fortified camps strung out along the mountains to thwart infiltration by the North Vietnamese.

All I knew was there was a movie called "THE GREEN BERETS" Later on I met a man who worked as an advisor for that movie, working primarily with helicopter safety.

One day my friend, Roger Phillips, a Viet Nam Veteran who fought at Doc To, and a client of mine. Gave me a Cross Bow with arrows and a quiver used by the Montagnards. You will learn more about the Montagnards later on in this book.

In 1961, 400 guerillas attacked a village in Kien Hoa province and were defeated by the South Vietnamese troops.

President Kennedy (JFK) sent Vice President Lyndon Baynes Johnson (LBJ) on a tour of Asian countries. He visited President Diem in Saigon. Now this is the guy that won the questionable election and had suffered a military coup and near assassination. LBJ declared Diem, crucial to US objectives in Vietnam and called him the "Churchill of Asia". What was he thinking? Would we help in the overthrow and possible assassination of a man LBJ called, THE CHURCHILL of Asia?

At age 7, how or why would I question that? In my studies as I grew older, I would have challenged that statement, but even the older kids were busy at the sock hop and drag races, dancing to rock and roll, and our parents were busy buying refrigerators, and washer dryers and buying 10-30 thousand dollar homes in a new phenomenon called a suburb.

Vietnam was a faraway place and insignificant in the lives of the Average American. Even the ones about to be called to serve.

1962

US Air Force begins using Agent Orange. A defoliant that came in metal orange containers to kill plant life so to expose roads and trails used by Vietcong forces. More on this soon.

The soldiers nick named it Agent Orange because of the orange stripe on the barrels they were off loading to spray the country side.

President Diem has a second coup attempt on his life and on his Presidency in South Vietnam. I wonder who did this. It is rumored that it was our CIA.

Along with some Vietnamese generals? The presidency of South Vietnam was contentious to say the least.

1962

Senate Majority Leader Mike Mansfield reported to JFK from Saigon that it is his opinion that President Diem had wasted the two billion dollars America had spent in Viet Nam.

Churchill of Asia?

1963:

Viet Cong units defeat South Vietnamese Soldiers in the Battle of Ap Bac. The Battle of Ap Bac was a small-scale battle early in the Vietnam War which resulted in the first major combat victory by the Viet Cong against regular South Vietnamese and American forces.

President Diem begins removing Buddhists from government positions and replacing them with Catholics. Remember the French are a catholic nation, and the Buddhists are primarily Asian. The Buddhists monks protest Diem's intolerance and his practices of keeping them quiet. In a show of protest, Buddhist monks began setting themselves on fire. In June of 1963, Vietnamese Mahayana Buddhist monk Thích Quang Duc burned himself to death at a busy intersection in Saigon. He was attempting to show that to **fight all forms of oppression on equal terms, Buddhism too, needed to have its martyrs.**

As a teen ager I remembered the Buddhist Monks setting themselves on fire, but I never understood why they did this to themselves. At the time I was nine years old, and seeing the burning Monks on TV. Now I know.

Our President Kennedy was assassinated, and now we had a fourth President involved in Vietnam.

With silent agreement of the United States, officers of the South Vietnamese military overthrew Diem, and killed the South Vietnamese president and his brother Nhu.

Again without elections, a new government was established.

So maybe the Vietnam War started when the French gave up control to the Japanese, but I did not know that when I was 7 years old. The Japanese weren't the enemy, so how did we get in the situation where we were coming to the aid of South Vietnam, and when did it change its name from Vietnam to South Vietnam, and why did they separate from North Vietnam?

So I guess the war did not start in 1940, but there certainly was a war going on in Vietnam at that time, but we as American People new it as the French Indo China. Now called the First Indo-China War.

When the Japanese surrendered, they gave up control of Indo China and the French "reappeared" and took over international affairs for the people of French Indo China and began reestablishing their laws and property deeds, taxes and speaking for the Vietnamese people through proxy leaders.

I did not know that when I was 7 Years old, I just knew that if America goes to war, we are right and we will win.

I did not know that the Vietnamese waiter, later to be identified to me as Ho Chi Minh had returned to Vietnam and had gained the support of the North Vietnamese population, and achieved power as a leader and asked President Harry Truman to help them be independent of the colonialization that existed before World War II. President Truman told him that power was to be returned to those in power before the war. Truman did not run for re-election and Eisenhower agreed to the Geneva Accords.

HO CHI Minh became an enemy of America and turned to the Communist powers that would help him free Vietnam of the French influences and colonialization.

This disagreement led the world to witness the siege of Dien Bien Phu,

And after a 55 day battle, thousands dead on both sides, France gave up its resolve to keep French Indo China as an economic sphere of influence.

Dien Bien Phu "was the first time that a non-European colonial independence movement had evolved through all the stages from guerrilla bands to a conventionally organized and equipped army able to defeat a modern Western occupier in a pitched battle," wrote British historian Martin Windrow, the author of "The Last Valley: Dien Bien Phu and the French Defeat in Vietnam." This process is exactly as General Giap planned it.

After the war, Vietnam's split into the communist north and the French-supported territory in the south proved tenuous.

But this was in May of 1954, and I had not yet been born. Did this event start the American/ Vietnam War?

Was this why President Kennedy wanted to send supplies and advisors in 1961? I don't think so.......

So what was it?

Maybe it was the 1959 North Vietnamese building of a supply route used to supply the communist insurgents in Viet Nam called the Viet Cong. The routes became known as THE HO CHI MIHN trail.

Or was it really the fear of the Domino Effect.

What price was President Kennedy willing to pay?

He died before we found out.

Some say the Fifth reason was the Gulf of Tonkin incident.

The news was full of descriptions of the event, how one of our ships at sea in the Gulf of Tonkin had been attacked.

Some say it never happened.

Congress believed it did.

On August 7, 1964, Congress passed the **Gulf of Tonkin Resolution**, authorizing President Johnson to take any measures he believed were necessary to retaliate and to promote the maintenance of international peace and security in Southeast Asia.

This is pretty important to our veterans who were to soon fight in this war.

How did LBJ change, modify or escalate that policy?

Who was Robert McNamara, and why was experimentation with helicopters such a driving force?

Maybe what really got us heavy into the war was February 6, 1965 when the Viet Cong attacked a US advisors compound at a place called Pleiku. Within hours, US Navy jets were hitting sights in North Viet Nam. By March, 1965 Operation Rolling Thunder was underway. American pilots were getting shot down. America escalated to 40000 boots on the ground, but by late 1965, the numbers had risen to 180,000 with 100,000 additional troops slated for 1966.

Maybe this was a good reason, if not the real reason?

Whatever it was, another war was provoked, and that brought millions of American troops into South Vietnam and ended only in 1975 with the fall of Saigon, after the deaths of 58,193 U.S. troops and as many as 3 million Vietnamese. Vietnam's long-deferred reunification followed.

"The ripples of Dien Bien Phu are still being felt by the veterans who fought and died. Since I am a non-veteran, I can only read the history books, and listen to the veterans who lived to share their lives, repercussions from the war, and their stories with us all.

From becoming early prisoners of war, witnessing the deaths and injuries of their friends, the invisible scars they came home to suffer, their personal injuries, and energy to advocate for their buddies and future warriors. These men and women fought bravely, and sacrificed for one another, and continue to do so today. I hope you enjoy the stories the people in this book share with us, and remember, if you were not a veteran of the Vietnam War, you must join me ON THE OUTSIDE LOOKING IN.

Those soldiers began arriving in December of 1961, many had been there unofficially for years, and within a month of arriving with the supplies President Kennedy had offered the French supported government of South Vietnam.

He also gave them the Green Berets!

And Barry Sadler and his song,

"THE GREEN BERETS

Fighting soldiers from the sky
Fearless men who jump and die
Men who mean just what they say
The brave men of the Green Beret
Silver wings upon their chest
These are men Americas best
One hundred men will test today but
Only three win the Green Beret
Trained to live off natures land
Trained in combat hand to hand
Men who fight by night and day
Courage take from the Green Beret

(Chorus)

Silver wings upon their chest
These are men Americas best
One hundred men will test today

But only three win the Green Beret
Back at home a young wife waits
Her Green Beret has met his fate
He has died for those oppressed
Leaving her this last request
Put silver wings on my sons chest
Make him one of Americas best
He'll be a man they'll test one day
Have him win the Green Beret!

They worked closely with the Vietnamese Hillbillies called the Montagnards.

Their tragic story is ahead.

No one knew of the time of captivity and emotional scars that went untreated.

The sickness that would manifest after they returned home when Agent Orange began to raise its ugly head. How our government would mishandle their care, and how many Vietnam Veterans would stand up and be counted by helping other veterans cope with the issues still occurring 50-60 years later. I hope the stories you will read in this book will help you understand the challenges we face today in the obligations we have to our veterans.

There seem to be two turning points of American policy.

How did the United States become irrevocably committed to large scale intervention, which we just discussed, and when did it become obvious that the United States would have to de-escalate.

The stories of the soldiers you are about to experience may help us all understand what happened.

Join me in the following chapters: The Shooting War is about to begin.

North Vietnam Capitalized on the photo opportunity showing
the large American Captive being guarded by a small Vietnamese
woman. It became one of their postage stamps.

CHAPTER FOUR

The Longest Held POW

The ordeal of William Robinson

Ho Chi Minh had said, "Since war was not declared that a pilot would
be a criminal."

War, children

It's just a shot away

Lyrics from:
Gimmie Shelter by the Rolling Stones

A soldier/pilot tells his story.

A recollection: (not mine!)

I would like to talk a little bit about the second prettiest airplane in the world is right behind me. The reason it is the second prettiest airplane is right behind it comes the Jolly Green Helicopter the prettiest airplane in the world.

After getting hit by a 357 millimeter shell while flying over North Vietnam in November 1967 my airplane burned for 7 ½ minutes I got out of it right into what I thought was elephant grass but it was 75 foot tall bamboo. I fell through there busted myself up some and about 2 hours later the second prettiest plane in the world, two of them showed up and I really didn't believe it. I didn't think anybody was stupid enough to come to a place that big. They brought in the prettiest airplane in the world which is an HH3 Jolly Green and I thought," you know, I am going to make it. "Harry Walker went into a hover over me put 135 foot of cable out and pulled me up. The guys covered for him, 4 MiG17's showed up and Harry would not leave me, he pulled me up. You don't know how wonderful that feels to think I was going to make it. I was 75 miles northwest of Hanoi in absolute Indian country. That is dedication beyond belief. They flew 8 hour missions you know your rear end gets real tired from doing that. They went into places they had no business being and all to pick up somebody and bring them out. Their dedication is beyond belief. I hope we never lose them.

The HH3 Jolly Green Giant Helicopter was not always available to our pilots. What you are about to read is a rescue involving the HH3 Jolly Green Giant Helicopter somewhere near the Vietnam Laos border. A pilot is down in the jungle, search and rescue forces are scrambled the Vietcong wait silently using the pilot as bait.

Some of the radio transmission was inaudible. This is what I could make out.

I have him in site (inaudible) prepare (inaudible) off my left wing. Circling very tightly around him.

Roger that! Affirm (inaudible) pickup he is hurt bad… hurt bad over

Roger I understand!

(Inaudible) this is Firefly we have you located we have you located a helicopter is going to land

(Inaudible) 1 (inaudible)

(Inaudible)Roger hovering over the survivor now! Negative! We are coming in now we are coming in now!

OK (inaudible)

Kingfish 1 Kingfish 1 this is Firefly 42 we have your parachute in site we have you in site the helicopter is close by!

Kingfish 1 what is your position to your chute

Kingfish is in his chute he says he has both (inaudible)

I think he was referring to the fact he could see two helicopters above.

Roger

(Inaudible)

Author: I think Kingfish1 was the downed pilot!

OK you are right over him he says.

Author: A rescue soldier was leaving the helicopter?

He is going out the door now (inaudible)

Roger

Firefly (inaudible)

Turn your beacon off turn your beacon off... (Inaudible) is on the ground going after the survivor!

(Inaudible)

Are you ready PJ?

I do not know if PJ was the pilot or the rescue soldier?

OK (inaudible) come and get us now come and get us now (inaudible)

(Inaudible)

Going over the survivor now

(Inaudible)

Roger

Go get him... (Vietnamese)... (inaudible).... you got the (inaudible)... (inaudible)... (inaudible) right behind you... (inaudible)... watch out the survivor is coming up... hold your hover hold your hover... survivor is coming up... hold your hover... about 5 foot below the aircraft hold your hover... hold your hover... hold your hover... hold hover... slightly to the door... survivor coming in the door... survivor is secure let's get the hell out of here... ok talk to me right now

That was in 1967 an actual audio of a rescue taking place. Our story begins in 1964 when we didn't have the HH Jolly Green Giant we had the HH43B a light weight helicopter designed for rescue and search but not for combat conditions.

In 1964 the situation improved with the arrival of the Kaman HH43 Husky also known as Pedro. Huskies were equipped with unusual counter-rotating blades giving them exceptional maneuverability. Although they were very effective within a small operational area, Huskies didn't fare well on long distance operations they had limited fuel capacity making trips deep into Laos very difficult. To extend their range some Husky crews actually carried fuel drums and a hand pump to provide their own in flight refueling. With only an M-16 for defense and without armor it was vital that the rescue be accomplished in seconds. By 1964 with the United States openly committed to the defense of South Vietnam 13 Husky units operated from 6 spaces in South East Asia.

An observer describes the HH43B

This is really thin metal it is like sheet metal there is no armor or anything. That is thin I can actually press it back a little bit.

No armor, small, slow and designed for peaceful extraction.

Something happened in one of these little copters. Something Heroic, and historic.

The President of the United States of America authorized by an act of Congress July 9, 1978 takes pleasure in presenting the Silver Star to Airman 1st Class William Andrew Robinson United States Air Force for gallantry in connection with military operations against an opposing armed force while serving as a helicopter mechanic in Detachment 3 38th Aerospace Rescue and Recovery Squadron Tan Son Nhut Airbase Vietnam in action in North Vietnam on 17 May 1965. On that date Airman Robinson flight mechanic of an air rescue service HH43B Helicopter participated in an extremely hazardous recovery of a downed pilot. The mission required a flight of over 200 miles mostly over hostile controlled areas. With complete disregard for his personal safety and despite heavy hostile fire Airman Robinson assisted in the successful recovery of the downed pilot through a most difficult hoist pick-up in a dense jungle area. By his gallantry and devotion to duty Airman Robinson has reflected great credit upon himself and the United States Air Force. That was in May of 1965 and in a way has nothing to do with the story that we are going to talk about today except that it happened 4 months before the events of this story.

I met Mr. William Robinson when I went with him to the McGhee Tyson Airbase and he pulled in to check in. They called him sir, Captain William Robinson. Mr. Robinson has the distinction of being the longest held enlisted Prisoner of War in American history. He lives in Madisonville, Tennessee. He was the crew chief on another mission in 1965 in September.

You had heard in the first section of this chapter about the time when he was awarded the Silver Star for going on such a mission. What you are going to hear about for the rest of the chapter is his last mission. Captain Robinson was a Prisoner of War from September 20, 1965 to February 12, 1973. That is eight Christmas's eight Thanksgivings, eight New Year's Eve's, seven birthdays and for a young 22 year old man over 400 Saturday nights. Captain Robinson considered himself the welcome committee for John McCain, he suffered starvation, daily beatings, sickness, he suffered the death of his fellow POW's he became the subject of a North Vietnamese postage stamp. This is his story. The day you got captured can you tell me about that day? From the time you woke up... you woke up a free man and went to sleep a prisoner of war, a POW.

This is his story: his words:

We had 3 different crews so each day we rotated and the crew that was on active then we had a back-up crew and a crew at rest. That particular day was my turn to be the primary crew and we had the two airplanes, essentially 4 pilots you know 2 or 3 for each airplane and a crew chief for each airplane which was 2 and 2 paramedics which made it a crew of 4.

Sometimes there was flight engineer. In the beginning the crew chief was also the maintenance guy and so later on they separated it and made a crew chief and a maintenance person. We did a combination of both at that particular time. Each shift the first thing we normally did was to go out an prep our airplane and get them prepared for flight Removing all the slip covers Et cetera so it is ready for when we need it. The pilot would come out and do his pre-check so that if the whistle blew then we just load up and move on. We made sure that all the equipment that we desired was on board and the power unit was standing by so it was just a normal... everything was normal at that point.

We were stationed in NKP Thailand. Nakhon Phanom it is in the northeast corner of Thailand it was 7 miles from the Laotian border so Laos was considered the combat zone seven miles west. We covered the combat zone. Laos Cambodia and Vietnam

This was in September of '65. We had been over since April and we were scheduled to go back in July but again this as most of those who have ever been in the military know that what happens is that they never necessarily know. You do what you have got to do with what you have and then you move on and hopefully when we were scheduled to get new airplanes then we were scheduled to go home in July. When the new airplanes came over they had mechanical problems so we were extended for the duration. The duration included our being shot down.

I was over North Vietnam when we got shot down.

Looking at a map of North Vietnam we were down in the very thin portion…

Laos is north of Cambodia. Laos if west of North Vietnam and Cambodia is west of South Vietnam. I was about 40 miles south of Vinh it is kind of the narrowest spot where the countries merge together. It is a narrow spot there and just south of Vinh in the jungles out there was a downed pilot. He had been on a bombing mission earlier and when he pulled off the target he took enemy fire and had to evacuate the airplane. We were aware of the policy that Ho Chi Minh had said, "Since war was not declared that a pilot would be a criminal."

It was reemphasized real quickly after we were captured. We were called piratical airmen caught while committing grave crimes against the heroic peace loving Vietnamese people. Even though they extended some humane policies we would never be classified as Prisoners of War.

According to the North Vietnamese?

Right, we were referred to as criminals. The rescue techniques we were using you might say they needed polishing. What happened was once we were notified that the pilot was down, the airplane was already prepped and we had an approximate area where he was down. We loaded unnecessary fuel to make it and to give us search time Et cetera. We were fortunate that he had made it a few miles away from the target so we weren't concerned about "being over target" trying to locate him. Because of the procedures they wouldn't allow us to get airborne until he was physically contacted on the ground either visual or they would confirm that they had a pinpoint location through different means of the detectors and things like that sent out a signal so they knew where he was. They had to make sure it wasn't an enemy that had gotten ahold of his equipment and so they had to have several verifications. They wouldn't even let us get airborne until that and sometimes that took anywhere from 45 minutes to 2 hours. Then our flying time at 60 miles an hour meant 10,000 feet they just weren't very fast. So it was probably pretty close to 3 to 3 ½ hours before we arrived on target once we were notified of the pilot down. At the same time we weren't the only ones looking for him and so that created a certain amount of intensity you might say that we wanted to get there before they did. Later on they improved the system procedures with a new airplane. They had in flight air crews and they could dart in, pick up a pilot and be back out before anybody knew about it. That was an improvement over what we had but once we pulled in the area we had the combination of you had to have an escort airplane a top-cover airplanes all kinds of different things involved. We had A-1 E's and as we pulled in and set up our grid they had been talking to the pilot and we were pretty much in the same loop and we had to find him on the ground. As we were descending down to pick him up then we started picking up small arms fire and of course we could maneuver around it that wasn't a big deal. Unfortunately the A-1 E's that were there to suppress any ill intentions by the enemy you might say they took some hits in the rocket pod and one of the airplanes caught on fire and so the transmission of the radio is inaudible and we were receiving ordinance from the local area. So, they had to peel off and go out to the ocean to drop their rocket pod they weren't authorized to dispose of them there even though they had been shot at. I guess it was kind of the mismanagement of the war being managed in the basement of the White House which created a lot of tension. At the same time this is happening you know these are all split second decisions that had to be made. We got a fix on the pilot and we were descending down to pick him up and of course choices have to be made you know do you wait... which we didn't... we were below fuel which means we had just enough to get home and so we would not have... we couldn't climb back up to wait and then come back down again without accepting the idea that we would crash before we could get home.

So naturally once you looked into the eyes of an American sitting on the ground in enemy territory… there was no choice in your mind except to make the rescue and as we pulled into the hover and we got him in the sling which is hanging about 90 feet below the airplane and no other way to describe it all hell broke loose. Whether they were just waiting and waiting for us to become a stationary target because in order to make a rescue you have to be a sitting duck. Without our A-1 to support us then we had no defense what-so-ever. We immediately took hits and crashed landed and within a few feet where the pilot was standing.

All of us were captured including the pilot. One did escape, they didn't really know how many were there… there were 3 of us stayed together and the one when we got out of the airplane we dispersed and then 3 of us joined back up later and the 4th one didn't join back up with us and we learned later that he made it into Laos and was captured there. After 2 years in captivity he was killed during an escape attempt. So we all four got out of the airplane safely and made it into the jungle. We were hoping to be able to travel at night but unfortunately we were probably out numbered 200 to 1 because they had all the little small hamlets and villages in the local area out beating the bushes trying to make sure they located everyone. Two reasons: one they were looking for us and two they were looking for anything they could find off the airplane so…

Believe it or not a helicopter is an airplane. They both have wings except the wings on a helicopter rotate.

We were treated like a prize trophy. You see the great white hunters. You see they kind of throw the deer over the hood of the car or the truck and you know they put it on display and we were paraded among the locals. They were allowed to spit upon us, kick us and slap us around whatever they felt comfortable doing. I wouldn't say they were hospitable at all. You would think they would have refrained from anybody shooting at us but I mean they pretty much had their way with us you know with the sticks and shovels and what other things, they had rifle butts. They weren't allowed to fire a shot but they were… anything you might say that might raise the crowd's spirit they were pretty much allowed to do.

At that particular time I was just worried about surviving. You know like I said, everybody was nervous. You could physically see the guy holding a rifle on you that he was physically shaking because by this time there were other American airplanes overhead and their mission was to blow up the airplane that was kind of an unwritten rule. A written rule was that we need to get far enough from the airplane that if we did crash they could get in there to blow it up so they couldn't retrieve any of the sensitive data on board the airplane. So when they started bombing the local area the natives got a little restless. When you are looking down at the business end of a weapon you could easily feel like your minutes were numbered.

We did not have anything to eat until the next day. They brought us… by the time things settled in we were just the last thing in the world they thought about… they did give us some water of course. We were exhausted because when we were being escorted out of the jungle we didn't have the luxury of using our hands… our hands were tied behind us we were hog tied like you would cattle. You were trying to make it out of the jungle with your hands tied behind your back. They had actually ropes on our legs where we couldn't walk but you couldn't run.

After the helicopter was shot down the crew including Mr. Robinson and the pilot they were trying to save were captured and paraded around from village to village so that the locals could see who was dropping bombs on them.

There is no other way to describe it. The local villagers were kind of pissed off. You know we were dropping bombs in the local area where these military people were operating. Our guards were just military and they were sent down here to take us to Hanoi and once we got in their hands you might say the pep rallies and all this other stuff that was going on came to a halt. We were just displayed for the pep rallies and everything was just to benefit the locals that were involved in the helping to capture of the ugly American's. Once we started to Hanoi we were pretty well isolated from the general public. We weren't on display after that. We had no scheduled pep rallies we had to attend.

Other than the ones we were captured with it was probably a month later before we saw other Americans. I could hear them but we were always behind closed doors and but once we got into the Hanoi Hilton complex and I got a message from Lt. Colonel Robbie Risner but never saw him because he was captured, too.

I never saw anything other than a captured American from that point on.

He was Lt. Colonel Robbie Risner when he was shot down and he retired as a General.

James Robinson "Robbie" Risner (January 16, 1925 – October 22, 2013) was a Brigadier General and a fighter pilot in the United States Air Force. During the Vietnam War, Risner was a double recipient of the Air Force Cross, the second highest military decoration for valor that can be awarded to a member of the United States Air Force, awarded the first for valor in aerial combat and the second for gallantry as a prisoner of war of the North Vietnamese for more than seven years. He was the first living recipient of the medal. Risner became an ace in the Korean War and commanded a squadron of F-105 Thunderchiefs in the first missions of Operation Rolling Thunder in 1965. He flew a combined 163 combat missions, was shot down twice, and was credited with destroying eight MiG-15s. Risner retired as a brigadier general in 1976. At his death, Air Force Chief of Staff General Mark A. Welsh III observed: "Brig. Gen. James Robinson "Robbie" Risner was part of that legendary group who served in three wars, built an Air Force, and gave us an enduring example of courage and mission success… Today's Airmen know we stand on the shoulders of giants. One of 'em is 9 feet tall… and headed west in full afterburner."

I was in the Hanoi Hilton complex at that particular time. Most of the time the Hilton complex we were only using 30% of it. So we were using things like the Udai Village and Heartbreak Hotel and then they set up later what we call Little Vegas. Also a prison camp within a prison camp you might say it was different cells. Another jail we referred to as the Zoo which is about 5 miles away but still within the city limits of Hanoi. This had been an old film studio that they took and turned into a prison camp.

We were put in 5 X 8 cells. You could see other Americans but you weren't able to communicate with them. You didn't get good views of them but we had to develop our own communication which was a tap code and we tapped through the walls. Basically we took the alphabet and we dropped the K and made it into a block of 25 so what you would do first is you would tap to identify the row you wanted to be on then you would tap that letter that you wanted on that row. For instance a B would be first you would identify the row would be 1 tap and then you would identify by 2 more taps to identify the first row second letter. If you wanted to send an R essentially it was the fourth row the second letter so it became our primary means of communication and we were using it 7 ½ years later when we left. It was... it served us well in different ways. The good part is if somebody got out he would sweep in code we called it and mainly in the beginning we just passed names and all we ended with God bless you or God Bless America. So these are the kind of... you might say the spiritual guidance we got on a daily basis if someone got out a tap or if somebody tapped on the wall and we felt that if an end would come the most important thing was to be able to make sure that we had a full accounting of numbers so that we could insure that everyone was accounted for. That was the main intent we did pass other information as to what was going on and some of the questions that the Vietnamese were asking which basically in the beginning they started out being different. They would slap you around a little bit but they were trying to be on your side. They were trying to point out that we were wrong and that they were right. We were the aggressors and we really didn't understand what freedom was because they were the freest people on earth. They claimed that they didn't pay any taxes and the government supported them you know. Of course out of the their kindness they worked 10 days a month for the government to repay them for all their services but they never paid any taxes. So we did listen to their spiel but after a while... we pretty much argued with them a little bit. Some of that came back to haunt us later when we were in consultation in the beginning... then later when the hammer did fall and they reminded us of all the nasty things we had said.

I never thought about going insane... I guess I never looked too far forward and never looked too far back. Today is today and well we will deal with this. I didn't... I guess you might say that I as well as the others we had a certain amount of confidence in ourselves. We knew that we came from the greatest country on Earth and we were backed by the greatest military on Earth and so we felt kind of comforted in knowing that we were American's.

I was about 22 days past my 22nd birthday. I turned 22 on the 28th of August and shot down the 20th of September so that is 22 or 23 days.

I had a girlfriend but I knew it was already on the skids because I didn't come home on time you know. So when my folks got the Dear John then I pretty well accepted it at that point.

Yes I got Deer Johned. Well my folks didn't send it to me they just kind of ignored it and they just said well since Bev is not writing no more then somebody else wanted to say hi so...

I got a few throughout my life there sometimes you might get 2 or 3 at one time then you might not get another one for a year. Letters were coming from my parents my folks wrote most of the letters, I guess, all the letters that I received. Sometimes they would send some photos and they would include family members. Other times they sent them but I never received them so... it was probably on an average 10% of what was sent actually ever reached us. In many cases it was 0% that reached anybody. Later on they allowed the families to send packages because the rules to the International Red Cross. It was one of those deals where they were not getting involved unless they were allowed to visit the prison camps and of course the Vietnamese weren't going to allow that to happen. They just insured the world that we were being treated as Prisoners of War even though we were being classified as criminals. The hardest time we went through was in '66 when they took a group of American's and marched them through the streets of Hanoi and it backfired on them. So Ho Chi Minh, in trying to recover, assured the world that those who needed medical attention were cared for, and Hanoi was continuing to extend the lengthy and humane policies. Then he made a statement that all of us who asked forgiveness of our crimes would be forgiven and allowed to return home when the war was over.

The prisoners in the Hanoi Hilton were beaten and tortured and finally some of them would give up information. It was decided within the ranks that it was better to give in when you can control it than it was to give information when you could not control it. The prisoners knew that they could not leave until the one who had been there the longest was sent out first. First Lt. William Andrew Robinson United States Air Force was held as a Prisoner of War in North Vietnam from September 20, 1965 until his release February 12, 1973. For this he received a Prisoner of War metal. He also received the Bronze Star with a combat V for Valor. The North Vietnamese interrogators and guards kept constant pressure on Mr. Robinson through harassment and intimidation and cruelty from which they hoped to gain information and cooperative participation in their propaganda exercises. He also received the Legion of Merit his ceaseless efforts by continuously showing resistance to an enemy who ignored all international agreements on treatment of Prisoners of War. Despite the harsh treatment through his long years of incarceration he continued to perform his duties in a clearly exceptional manner which reflected great credit upon himself and the United States Air Force.

On the Freedom Bird, there was a ceremony for the non-commissioned officer promoting him to an officer and a gentleman.

Only officers got off that plane.

Captain Robinson travels to air bases to give talks on how to behave if you are a soldier and become a prisoner of war.

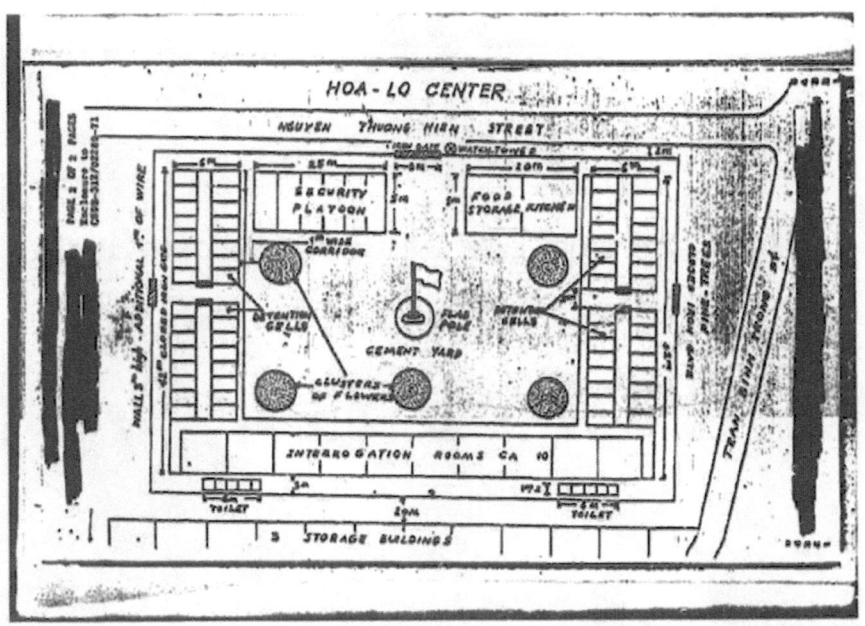

This is a hand drawn picture of a prison camp in Hanoi

CHAPTER FIVE

IA Drang and the need for debriefing

Ia Drang, The opposing nations and their warriors face off to learn how to fight each other.

"There's battle lines being drawn
Nobody's right if everybody's wrong!"

Lyrics from: For What it is Worth
By: Buffalo Springfield

The Battle of Ia Drang was the first major engagement during the Vietnam War, between members of the U.S. Army and the People's Army of North Vietnam. The two-part battle took place between November 14 and

November 18, 1965 west of Plei Me, in the **Central Highlands of South Vietnam**.

Ia Drang Valley to many, this marks the beginning of the U.S.'s Vietnam War in the days of President Lyndon B. Johnson's ordered troop build-up. Much of the force Lieutenant Colonel Moore was leading into the jungle had never been combat tested. The North Vietnamese, however, both knew the dense terrain and had been fighting Western nations in it since the beginning of the French Indochina war in 1945. The location of the battle, far into the jungle from any roads, meant troops had to be airlifted in. The idea was that whole battalions could be dropped and complete their mission on the ground, calling in artillery barrages, helicopter support, and bombing sorties (including napalm) as needed, guided by coordinates given from the battalions' radio operators.

For this purpose, the Air Cavalry was born.

Upon getting an idea of the U.S. air mobility tactics, Colonel Nguyễn Hữu An is quoted as saying "Move inside the column, grab them by the belt, and thus avoid casualties from the artillery and air." He knew he had to get his troops as close as possible to the Americans, to mix into their lines if they were to avoid direct bombardments.

During the nights of the battle especially, large groups of North Vietnamese would attempt to sneak as far up as possible and then charge the U.S. lines. This tactic would be seen in Vietnam, again and again, including in the Tet Offensive.

In the early morning attacks of the second day, Charlie Company was taking fire from advances on three sides of their position. More than 100 enemy troops were found dead around one foxhole after the battle.

The U.S. military was not yet prepared to deliver news of dead soldiers. Telegrams were thus dispatched via taxi cab driver to families, informing them of their loss. Upon noticing this, Julia Compton Moore took it upon herself to go by the houses of those under her husband's command and console the grieving widows and children.

Only after Mrs. Moore complained about this to the Army did they set up teams of one officer and one chaplain to deliver the heartbreaking letters from then onward.

Even with an 11:1 kill ratio, there were still many American dead and wounded.

One man had a viewpoint not shared by many during the early days of the war.

He was Private JL Tucker.

This is his story.

JLTucker a Vietnam Veteran. Mr. J.L. Tucker who served in Vietnam from 1965 till 1966.

For those of you who follow the history of the Vietnam War it was 1965 when it really started heating up and there was a battle there and even a book written about it, We Were Soldiers in Ia Drang Valley. There were some other little hamlets around there. Plei Me, Pleiku and An Khe: base camps.

Before we get started I just want to let you remember that I am not a Veteran so there is sometimes I can't fathom some of the things some of the Veterans have experienced, I can't share them with you. You have to hear them from the Veteran's themselves and we really appreciate the ones who share their stories. To know that they didn't just go to Vietnam then come back home and go back to normal lives. They went to Vietnam and experienced things that changed their lives and that they have carried with them ever since that happened. That is what we are going to be experiencing.

To give you an idea what the story is going to be about, we are going to take an army clerk... supply clerk in Vietnam, who is used to doing paperwork and used to doing whatever had to be done by a supply specialist. He heard that they need a volunteer... not a volunteer but several volunteers and this soldier volunteered to do whatever he had to do on that mission that day. What happened to him on that mission what he experienced, what he saw what he felt and again how he carried that with him for the rest of his life. JL Tucker who is a Veteran from the Vietnam War had a very special and disturbing experience in Vietnam.

Mr. Tucker was raised in Hillsboro County, Tampa, Florida.

He did not finish high school.

Went into the Army at 17?

His parents agreed to his enlisting.

He did not know where he would be going or what he might be doing?

This is his story. His words:

When I was raised we had a large family so when we got 16 if you wanted to quit school you could. You weren't encouraged to quit but you wasn't encouraged to attend either. I had to go to work to help support my family. When I turned 17 I went to Tampa to the recruiting station and volunteered for 3 years back then we hadn't even heard about Vietnam.

I never considered anything but the Army.

I was sent to Jacksonville while I was inducted then they sent me to Ft. Jackson in South Carolina for basic training about 8 weeks. After the 30 day leave I went back to Ft. Jackson to be trained as a personnel specialist.

I went home on my 30 day leave.

I never did wear my uniform in town I wore it around the house.

So, after training and leave, I was sent to Korea for a year and I served a turn there. Then I went home again. I got a 30 day leave and went back home. Still wearing my uniform?

I had orders to report to Ft. Benning, Georgia and I became part of the 383rd transportation detachment which was attached to the 17th Aviation Company with the 1st Air Calvary Division, but at the time it was the 11th Air Assault. We were training, didn't know it to start with, to go to Vietnam.

I was 19 years old here were lots of 17-19year old boys there.

So I got trained and then they said pack your stuff we are heading out?

Yes by then we knew. Next Stop Vietnam. We were training because this was the first time helicopters had been used as a primary way of getting troops in and out of battle and of course I was trained to drive trucks. We had to do 20 mile marches and all that. Then we got orders to deploy to Vietnam. It became the 1st Air Calvary Division.

I did not know very much about Vietnam. I knew we had advisors there.

I never located it on a map.

Never looked. Ok so, hey Mom I am going to Vietnam be back soon?

I think I had 8 months left to serve.

We left America in August of 1965

It was only 2 or 3 months before the Battle at Ia Drang.

We arrived by sea and I think August 14, 1965 and...

I had turned 20 in the army.

Most of my enlistment time already served

I arrived in Vietnam and I started out as a supply specialist. I ordered parts for trucks, aircraft and we got off the skiff the next morning and helicoptered into Pleiku. It wasn't very far from Cambodia it was in the Central Highlands.

I started out being a supply specialist but it changed. Because I volunteered to go from Pleiku... usually flew in a CV-2 aircraft to An Khe. A lot of times there would be supplies loaded on the conveyor rollers to be dropped in for the troops in battle. So we would land at Pleiku and I would do paperwork down there for division for 2 or 3 days while we were getting the convoy ready to go back to Pleiku.

There was no battle then but anywhere you went in Vietnam you were in danger. Like on the highway going from An Khe to Pleiku the hillside was full of caves and snipers would come out and harass you and shoot at you. We had the floorboard of the truck full of sand bags because there was danger of running over a land mine and we were trying to save our feet and legs.

I volunteered for whatever they needed me to do. I had a helper in the supply room so when I was gone he took over. So I was a supply clerk and supply specialist going to 2 or 3 different fire bases. There were Base Camps in Vietnam and we went to the base camp and then out from there like a spider you would have landing zones fed by the base camp?

Well I am not sure about how many miles but the Ia Drang Valley and Plei My and Pleiku wasn't very far apart I am not sure exactly how many miles. And those were landing zones?

Landing Zone Albany and Landing Zone X-ray, but Plei Me was a Special Forces encampment it came under heavy siege and was nearly over-run. I was there just south east in Pleiku.

Plei Me was an encampment of Special Forces.

I would fly by aircraft down to An Khe and do paperwork for 2 or 3 days and then I would volunteer to drive on the trucks a 2 ½ ton truck back to Pleiku but there was a whole column of different supplies and ammunition, fuel all kinds of stuff.

No IED's they didn't use IED at that time.

Just land mines there were a lot of land mines.

I had an office but we also had guard duty a couple times a week and 3 of us would be in each bunker… a concrete bunker. One man would be on top of the bunker, one man would be resting and one man would be on the M-60 machine gun manning it.

That wasn't volunteerism, then we had to do that.

This is just something that has to be done. We did whatever we were asked.

When they needed somebody to do something, I just did it.

Officers walked in and said we need volunteers and you didn't ask you just said I will go?

I was a supply specialist… not a combat soldier.

I wasn't a trained infantry man I hadn't had combat training, just basic training.

I maintained everything and kept it running.

One day somebody came in and said we need a volunteer and up went my hand.

Now this is where the helicopters come in.

I was sitting on my bunk and we were taking a lunch break it was about 12:30 I will never forget it and we had just got back from Pleiku with a convoy. Now you readers bear with me because a lot of times I get emotional when I talk about this but I prayed all week for the Lord to help me get through it so they can hear the story.

They came over the PA system that we had incoming casualties and they needed some volunteers down at the tarmac which is part of the landing zone it is a parking area for the air craft.

We ran to the tarmac.

About 1:00 there was the sound of a Huey and it came around facing us and set down turned around and set the skids down and he opened the doors and there were maybe 6 to 10 dead I don't remember but they were all KIA no wounded. We unloaded them...

The door was opened from the inside.

We didn't know what we were going to see or what to expect?

We were looking for wounded but they were all KIA they were all killed there was nobody left.

They were just lying in the floor of the helicopter.

All their heads in one direction on that one.

We didn't know where they were coming from and we didn't know what it was going to be when they opened the door. We unloaded those bodies and it was bad enough that then after they carried those bodies up to the big tent we had set up to put them in a big Chinook CH47 Chinook... that is the helicopter with a wing on both ends. Yes, a big transport helicopter came around from towards the Ia Drang Valley facing us. Turned around and set his wheels down and there was blood dripping off the... between the hinges on the ramp and we let that ramp down and all we seen was just unimaginable... it was within 30 minutes of the first one landing.

So first we saw a Huey helicopter come in that is the helicopter that just has the one blade that goes around in a circle. It has a supply compartment in the back and what we called a Medivac?

We had Medivac Slicks which wasn't armed and then you had your gun ships. It was a slick. It had just come off the battlefield. We knew there was a battle going on. The Chinook came in right behind it. We could see blood dripping out of the crack where the ramp went up and the pilot let that ramp down and there were bodies just piled in the back way up to the door gunner.

We came to find out later on all together there was 155.

We unloaded that one and I went up to the tent to start cleaning them up so I don't know if another one came... I don't think one could have held all 155.

It was... devastating. I didn't let it affect me as much at that time.

At that time no we had a job to do.

Everybody there was volunteering there were no officers there so two of us would get up... we started at the back and two of us would get up there and place the bodies on stretchers... now these bodies were just piled because it was a hot landing zone. This would have meant they were under heavy fire and they just had to throw them in there... didn't have time to put them on litters. In fact they had 20 on litters and then the helicopter prepared to take off and they put an M-16 in the pilots face and told him he wasn't going anywhere. They loaded it and here they come and like I said when he put that ramp down you just can't imagine what a sight that was. Very devastating... at the time we had a job to do so, we just organized ourselves and the birds were landing and you knew you needed to take them to a tent.

Two of us would get up there in the copter at a time, but you would get physically ill so you would have to get back off and two more would take your place. You couldn't stay there long because... our noses had the stench of death you just can't get over the stench of death... those bodies had been out in the hot sun for a couple of days and they were decomposing. It could have been anything from a small bullet hole in the head to body parts.

We determined the small holes in the heads were executions. That is usually a sign of execution yes... because during those battles the enemy would come up on wounded and just shoot them between the eyes to kill them.

Militarily did they have any other choice? They could have taken a prisoner but a wounded soldier was still a threat.

To them they didn't care, life meant nothing to these people. If they came up on a wounded American soldier they would put a gun to their head and kill them they didn't take prisoners not in this particular instance. I helped unload the Huey and the first Chinook and it took us a while because like I said you would get physically ill and have to get off and they were placing the litters… we put them on litters or stretchers. They were placing them on things we would call goats they were just a little cart with a little motor on the front. They would haul them up to this tent and then when we got them all off the helicopter I went up to the tent… we went up to the tent and the rest of the afternoon and all night that night and till about 10:00 the next morning we worked on their bodies… just to get them cleaned up and in a body bag. We put them in body bags. A horrific 20 hour day. With no relief.

It was just us volunteers… you know it was odd that night there was such a hush in that tent it was very quiet no crying no yelling no screaming we were just murmuring between our partners we had to work in a two man team and it was just a strange quiet and dignified.

We were identifying bodies. They had dog tags and it seemed to me we put one in the bag with them and the other one on the bag… I can't remember. They had dog tags. There were 10 of us 5 teams of two.

I don't know any of their names can't remember them they were all part of my youth but I can't remember the names. I can't remember any of the names.

So after that 10:00 the next morning, well you know all night long we wore masks and you had to keep putting stuff on it so you wouldn't get ill and when we got through we just went to our tent and just sat on our bunk

No one came in to talk to us about it?

We were all volunteers, not a unit so there was nobody in charge of us volunteers. We became a unit but none of the officers were in there it was just us that volunteered to do that job.

Author's note:

When you read the book We Were Soldiers or you watch the movie they talk about how ill prepared the military was and the communication to the families and things like that. It sounds to me like they weren't prepared for the casualties, either.

When they went in I think it was the 1st and the 5th Regiment or Battalion and the 1st and the 7th. When they went into X-ray they didn't have any idea of how many enemy was even there… there had been no recon or anything like that so they had a big mountain there called Chu Pong Massif and it went from Vietnam over into Cambodia. These people would come down the Ho Chi Minh Trail they called it and they would just cross over into Vietnam whenever they got ready. But there was… it turned out they were between 2,500 and 3,100 enemy killed I think it was about 4,000 on that mountain and they had no idea. I think when they went into to X-ray there was about 400. 400 American soldiers but they didn't have any idea how many enemy was there. Of course these numbers are only guesstimates.

That is where Freddy Owens said he lost 200 and something of his friends that day. Before the Battle of la Drang was over, 305 Americans had been killed along with an estimated 2,000 North Vietnamese troops. American officials declared the Battle of the la Drang Valley a victory. The service members killed in the Battle of la Drang are remembered on Panel 3E of the Vietnam Veterans Memorial.

Casualty notification

The U.S. Army had not set up casualty-notification teams this early in the war. The notification telegrams at this time were handed over to taxi cab drivers for delivery to the next of kin. Hal Moore's wife, Julia Compton Moore, followed in the wake of the deliveries to widows in the Ft. Benning housing complex, grieving with the wives and comforting the children, and attended the funerals of all the men killed under her husband's command who were buried at Ft. Benning.[58] Her complaints about the notifications prompted the Army to quickly set up two-man teams to deliver them, consisting of an officer and a chaplain.[85] Mrs. Frank Henry, the wife of the battalion executive officer, and Mrs. James Scott, wife of the battalion command sergeant major, performed the same duty for the dead of the 2nd Battalion, 7th Cavalry.

At this point, as author, I am not sure if there had also been any planning for Post Traumatic Stress Disorders, as an outcome of battles yet to be fought in Vietnam.

It was still called shell shock, soldiers heart, battle fatigue. Now back to the story.

I was a PFC Private First Class JL Tucker. There were some E-4's and E-5's. No one took charge. We just each did what we had to do.

When we were done working at 10:00 we all went back to separate tents. We went back to our bunks but, we didn't go to sleep there was no sleep and for days it was just a nap here and a nap there you couldn't sleep.

Nobody talked to us about what had happened.

All I remember was those soldiers. But I am sure that some of the other helicopters probably went somewhere else because total kill was 305 Americans and 250 wounded and 1 Air Force pilot killed and that was among all the landing zones.

There was the one that got shot down in the movie I guess I don't know maybe not there was one that got shot down in the movie a helicopter. I think there were several that got shot down.

Bruce Crandall and Ed Freeman they was flying the… they helped fly the force in. They could only go in 60 at a time. Then they would have to go back and get 60 more.

They constantly went in under withering fire.

It was 4 or 5 then they would have to go back and get more till they got the whole 400.

Do you think those soldiers knew what they were flying into? Even Colonel Moore at the time he was a Lt. General when he retired... they didn't know that... he asked before he went but they didn't have any idea how many were there.

They were hoping to get them all in before they started how many were they hoping to have in?

Well about 500.

Of the 500 men in the original column, 150 were killed and only 84 were able to return to immediate duty; Company C suffered 93 percent casualties, half of them deaths. Despite these numbers, senior American officials in Saigon declared the Battle of the Ia Drang Valley a great victory.

But first they had 60 then 60 more came in which meant 85 or 90 then 60 more came in and they didn't have 180 when the third thing came in but maybe 120.

They kept bringing them in and the Platoon they call it the Lost Platoon it got separated and they were... they lost most of their men. They got a few of them out

We weren't hungry when we were done and had no debriefing.

We were isolated from the other 10 men

Well there were one or two of them in my tent but...

We never got together to talk about what we had been doing? We never did.

Nobody asked.

Nobody ever asked.

Author's note: There is a reason they call it Post Traumatic Stress Disorder.

It takes time to manifest.

When I came home it was a few years before it affected me of course I was young and out partying and drinking and it didn't really affect me. You didn't talk about it back then and I think around '90 I really started having real problems.

That is 25 years later, but it had been sneaking up on me the whole time I just didn't know it.

Well it wasn't guilt I didn't do anything wrong.

No we didn't do anything wrong

It was rage… if I had to identify what it was that was affecting my behavior.

Rage, anger, anxiety, aggression and sadness

I did not know who to have those feelings for. Did not know who to direct it at?

No just sad over what had happened… over what had taken place

Just sad. I just stayed anxious and depressed all the time.

I started getting lost and started crying a lot and didn't know why. I would get lost out on the highway tears just rolling down my cheeks so I was telling my doctor about it and he said you sound like you are depressed I am going to send you down to the mental health center to be evaluated. I saw a therapist down there and she… after I seen her for 10 weeks, she said, "Mr. Tucker, you have Post Traumatic Stress Disorder due to your service in Vietnam because you have answered all these questions." I started seeing the psychiatrist but she never done me any good she never really talked to me.

Back then they weren't trained. PTSD was just something that was starting... although it had gone all the way back to WWII shell shock all the way back to WWI as shell shock and in the Civil War it was called Soldiers Heart and it goes all the way back to the Achilles in the Greek Wars. You know if you look at the things in the books things that Achilles said, he had Post Traumatic Stress Disorder but he let his rage out in being a great warrior and he would release it by killing the enemy. I didn't have anybody to kill.

I didn't have anybody to kill.

Didn't have anybody to blame?

And they said I had depression?

Yes anxiety, panic attacks, sadness, loneliness and isolation. I started drinking real bad and I guess to cover it up.

I never blamed myself but years later I was... my youngest daughter encouraged me to go to a clinic... the VA clinic in Knoxville, TN and seek help. I went over there and I was assigned a psychologist Dr. Richardson.

Author's note: Thank you JL Tucker, for going through that for all of us.

JL Tucker and what a story you have sir. You volunteered to step into something that you carried what is it 50 years

Forty Nine years and all he did was raise his hand and say I will help you with that.

And the process of identifying them and those kinds of things and had no coaching or counseling after that you just reported back to duty and went back to work and brought all those memories home with you.

Those memories changed his life?

"Yes, forever."

JL Tucker explained, "After I went through all the years of anger and drinking I drank for a long time being sad and depressed I wound up going to see Dr. Richardson at the VA clinic he was a wonderful Christian man.

I was not married until after my time at war.

Dr. Richardson talked to me for 1 hour and he said, "You know JL, I am not going to put you on medicine. I don't think you need that, but I know what you do need and there is a group of men called Legacy Peer Support Group and it is all Vietnam veterans. Then it was all Vietnam Veterans, not now, now we have veterans from all the wars since Vietnam. He urged me to go see them and meet with them... still it was 6 months before I went. But when I walked in that room I just felt love that they had for one another and immediately I felt loved. I just fell in love with that group.

That group Legacy Peer Support Group and that is a group dedicated to...

Talking about your problems and getting it out in the open, helping each other...

They are all Vietnam Veterans?

I think we got one or two that are Iraqi Veterans now.

So it is starting to grow and build?

Oh yes it has sprung from one group to two groups and then they got one in Sevier County and one in Blount County... is that right Howie?

"Yes." You will hear more from Howie later in Chapter 16. Anonymous Soldier.

"OK so what is your roll in that group now?"

Well there are three parts to it there is the Legacy Peer Support Group and Vet to Vet Tennessee which I was asked to become the Vice President of and I accepted and then the other part is the Knoxville Veteran's Mental Health Counsel I am not sure what my role is in that.

Author's note: That is a group that I have had the pleasure of being a part of.

I was introduced to the group by Freddie Owens and Ed Junod.

I dedicated this book to those two men. Al JL Tucker and Howard Jenkins deserve equal billing.

I provided them office space to get started, and attended several of their initial formative meetings as a non-veteran volunteer.

I asked Mr. Tucker, "So how do you take your experience in Vietnam and apply it to what you are doing today or do you?"

He replied, "Well I don't know how to answer that… I take what I learned and I apply it to helping others."

Like right now we have a bicycle drive going to give to our Veterans that are on the street are homeless or maybe live in a half-way house so that they… they get into the Veteran's Treatment pool if they qualify… so we are very involved in collecting bicycles so they will have a way to go look for a job. We found out they were walking one to two miles a day just to put in a job interview and that was just intolerable. The rest of the Vet to Vet Tennessee and Legacy decided to start collecting bicycles so I have been heavily involved in that. Now I think they are collecting clothes also… good used clothing. Some of these vets have their families with them so we donate bicycles all sizes it doesn't make a difference what.

Do these Veterans know who you are… do they know your story?

Oh yes… not the ones off the street don't but the ones in Legacy do.

Do you know their stories?

No... I do the ones in Legacy but not the ones off the street. Now Howard he is a mentor aren't you Howard?

Yes

He knows more about that.

In the Veterans Court?

Veterans courts have spread across our nation.

The Concept is to be sure a veteran suffering from PTSD has a veteran judge and a veteran lawyer.

It does not forgive his transgressions, but allows him access to an understanding group of people.

Many times a veterans court can help get the perpetrator back on his job, or even be sure if he is on medication, the medications do not stop because of incarceration.

Yes.

So you guys for the past couple of weeks we had interviews and for 6 weeks before that we were talking about the Veteran friendly congregations and the Veteran's Courts and you guys are part of the push behind that.

Yes.

And your role in particular, what is your role?

Well my role is to get out and do whatever needs to be done like the bicycles and the clothing. Of course we have a business meeting every week before the group meetings start. I listen to Ed and Freddy a lot there they do most of the talking and I just do like I did in Vietnam I just do what I was asked to do.

Where do you think this is going to go… where do you want it to go?

Well I am a lot better than I was when I joined that group but I am not a coward. I don't want to be 100% cured, because I don't want to leave this group. Reaching out to these Veteran's that don't know anything about PTSD. Veterans need to know and they are learning that through us.

A mother's story about her veteran son.

Well she called very concerned about her son he had been a heavy drinker for years he was totally disabled and drawing benefits from the VA. He had started drinking whiskey and she was really concerned about his health he had a full heart attack, lost all his teeth and is just in sad shape and she asked me what she needed to do about it. I said you need to encourage him to see a psychologist. I said is he getting VA medical care and she said yes I said he needs to see a psychologist. She said what will that cost him I said it won't cost him anything so anyway I gave her our website and she was going to give it to her daughter because she didn't want to make her son mad at her. She was going to check the website out.

Author's note:

His problem was not unique to him. In several of my interviews even with the World War II Veterans they talked about the drinking problems they had when they came home. I had one even say that after he talked to a minister his drinking left him. I looked at him and said you're drinking left you? He said yes sir my drinking left me so OK if we have a Veteran out there that needs help you can go to. You can also go to tnvhc.org on the internet. JL wrap us up here.

I would like to take this time to say a few words about my youngest daughter Christy Pond whose has got into this bicycle drive she has done an excellent job working very hard at it she has taken it to heart to help get bicycles to these Veterans and Legacy loves her and appreciates what she is doing and so do I. She is a great young lady.

JL we want to thank you for your story and your service to our country.

Troops fighting at Ia Drang

CHAPTER SIX

Freedom Bird and the Pointman

Tom Mercer with his prize!

Mr. Tom Mercer is a Vietnam veteran and he has a story to tell. I learned about Tom, a.k.a Pointman from one of my listeners to my radio show, THE VETERAN NEXT DOOR. You are about to read Tom Mercer's story. There are a lot of things that happened in Vietnam that a lot of us don't know about. You are going to hear some of it today from what I think is probably a gentle reluctant warrior.

This is how it started:

Tom, "I was in Apopka High School in Apopka, Florida, right outside of Orlando in 1966. Of course I always wanted to be in the army before I got involved in the war in Vietnam So I joined." When I got out of high school we had heard a little about the Vietnam War. We knew where Vietnam was, but we didn't know what the war was about. Once I got out of high school I didn't want to get drafted, because I thought they could send me anywhere they wanted, so I went down, me and a few of my buddies and joined. I joined to go airborne, which I did. Why? I don't know."

I went to Fort Gordon, Georgia for basic training then to Fort Benning for jump school after that. I had a thirty day leave, and then I headed to Oakland, California and from there on to Vietnam. I went with a group I was assigned to the 173rd Airborne Division and we all went to Oakland, California. We landed in Long Binh at the 90th Replacement Center. "That is where they assigned you to the unit you are going to be serving in."

Author's note:

I had to ask, "Tom, now the 90th Replacement Center it sounds like you guys were inventory."

He replied, "We were."

I had to get this straight. It seemed to me that soldiers could be sent to Vietnam and positioned where needed. "So you came in as trained soldiers and you didn't know what unit you were going to be in or what division you were going to be in you were just... somebody would look at you and go, "OK this one is ready to go, ready to fight" is that what you just said?

That is probably pretty close to what it was for me. I thought I was going to be with the 173rd but they kept calling people's names out and all the guys I went over with were put with the 173rd, but they took me and a few other guys and put them in the Big Red One which I didn't know the difference at the time. I just knew I was in Vietnam.

Tom had trained and bonded with soldiers, sent with them to Vietnam and was separated when it was time to go to battle. I asked Tom, So did you ever see those other guys again."

"No I never have seen them again and"... Tom Paused a little choked up.

I tried to break the silence, what I understand from what I read in the book they separated you all and...

Yes, they did go to the 173rd but the majority of my friends from jump school were wiped out in a battle. Similar to the one described below in song.

8th of November
Big & Rich

Said goodbye to his momma as he left South Dakota
To fight for the red, white and blue
He was nineteen and green with a new M-16
Just doing what he had to do
He was dropped in the jungle where the choppers would rumble
With the smell of napalm in the air
And the sergeant said look up ahead
Like a dark evil cloud
Twelve-hundred came down on him and twenty-nine more
they fought for their lives but most of them died
in the one-seventy-third Airborne
On the eighth of November the angels were crying
as they carried his brothers away
with the fire raining down and the hell all around
There were few men left standing that day
saw the eagle fly through a clear blue sky
1965, the eighth of November
Now he's fifty-eight and his pony tail's gray
But the battle still plays in his head
He limps when he walks but he's strong when he talks
About the Shrapnel they left in his leg
He puts on a gray suit over his Airborne tattoo

And he ties it on one time a year
And remembers the fallen as he orders a tall one
And swallows it down with his tears
On the eighth of November the angels were crying
As they carried his brothers away
With the fire raining down and the hell all around
There were few men left standing that day
Saw the eagle fly through a clear blue sky
1965
The eighth of November
The eighth of November (eighth of November)
Said goodbye to his momma as he left South Dakota
to fight for the red, white, and blue
He was nineteen and green with a new M-16
Just doing what he had to do

"Caught in the action of kill or be killed, greater love hath no man than to lay down his life for his friend."

Not a direct quote, but a reference to:

John 15:13

That is all I know about them. I found that out coming into a later story.

Advancing to a new topic to relieve the silence from the teary eyed veteran, "OK so after you arrived with the Big Red One tell me about your first day there what was going on?"

"Well, at the 90th Replacement Center of course they assigned me to the Big Red One and they told me and a couple of guys, that we were going to be in a unit that sees a lot of action so just be careful and listen to what people tell you. They put us on this deuce and a half which is a big ole truck like a cattle hauler, and took us to Zeon which was my base camp to Charlie Company which was a part of the 1st 18th... 1st Battalion 18th Infantry of the Big Red One. I was assigned to Charlie Company so they took us in there and gave us our weapons our M-16's which didn't work very well, our claymores and grenades, and smoke grenades. Then we had a little… I call it a little camp… they take you out on ambushes and take you out on patrol to teach you how to work when you get out to the field. Most of it we forgot and learned the real way to do it once we got out in the field, OJT. (On the job training. We learned from the guys that had been there for a while?

Exactly, the old timers we called them. (Six to eight months in the field.)

For the readers out there Tom is also a musician. He has produced several songs about his buddies in the fields of Vietnam. Tom met somebody named Mac during one of your first days in there.

"Right, Sergeant Mac was my squad leader. He had been there 6 months and he was wore out too. But, he had it together and he taught me the right things to do.

I believe you wrote a little song about Mac didn't you?

Yes I did."

Ode to Sgt. Mac

My first day in the field, the guys looked all worn out
Mac said it won't be long, you'll see what Nam's about
The old timers shook their heads-as they were looking at me
Mac told is to saddle up,- Pointman is OC.
Mac was six foot three- had a real thick mustache.
I did not want to piss him off- or give him a case of the ass.
Mac said pay attention-going home is your main goal
Then I saw the good man in mac-his story will be told.
Mac would lead us into hell, at the battle of Loc Ninh
We kicked the devils ass- and made it out again
But things do not always workout, sometimes you lose your friends
And the war keeps on going-will it ever end?
Lessons learned every day-you never give back
The things about surviving- like we got from Mac.
Then I saw the good man in Mac

And his story will be told!

Tom, tell me a little about the relationship between the FNG which is the Fucking New Guy and the guys who had been there for a while.

When you first get to 'Nam you got a brand put on you. (FNG) and a lot of the old timers they didn't like to hang around with you all the time because you didn't know nothing and the FNG's did a lot of stupid things. They thought they had to remember everything they were taught back in the states or in the little camp I told you about. They taught us the right way and the old timers taught us exactly what to do and how to do it. So, for them to hang around us they thought it was putting their life in danger.

I felt I was no longer an FNG right after the battle of Loc Ninh in 1967.

The **First Battle of Loc Ninh** was a battle during the Vietnam War that occurred As a part of his strategic preparations for the Tet Offensive in early 1968, General Võ Nguyên Giáp began attacking isolated allied bases in the fall of 1967 in hopes he could draw US and Army of the Republic of Vietnam (ARVN) forces outside of several major South Vietnamese cities. The battle was considered a US/ARVN victory with the United States claiming more than 850 PAVN/VC killed.[4] The PAVN/VC had failed to capture Loc Ninh or inflict severe casualties on US forces with Allied losses of only 50 dead. The battle did, however, succeed in drawing Allied forces away from the population centers and into the remote border.

Tom continued his story.

I noticed and found out then you can really get killed if you didn't pay attention to what was going on. We were stuck in a battle for 5 days and a lot of VC were killed and NVA and a lot of our guys were wounded and died. I knew then that I better get it together.

I saw in your song that you sang a verse in there about Mac and he said point man is OC what does that mean?

OC is a guy, Johnny O'Conner is his name. Mac was picking somebody to be point."

OC was experienced. He was colorblind and for some reason he could see in the jungle better than a person who wasn't colorblind. He was good and he taught me how to walk point.

OC was not always point man. He walked a lot of point before I got there and then he was one of the best in Charlie Company at the time. Mac just wanted him on point this day because we were… in a hot LZ and we were in a rubber tree plantation and Charlie Company was picked to go out on the patrol. Lima Platoon, which was my platoon, 1ˢᵗ Squad had lead so he wanted his best guy up front.

"At that point I was still an FNG?"

It was about half and half FNG to experience field soldiers. That is why they had that six month rotation because if you took everybody out of the field at one time you had all new guys coming in so they tried to keep everybody there on a six month rotation.

It was after the battle of Loc Ninh that I felt I was no longer an FNG?

"For sure, Loc Ninh like I was saying it was a bad battle. You had to keep your wits about you, and you had to be alert and after that I was always alert. Jonny O'Conner as I told you a while ago saved a lot of people's lives that day. If you don't have a good point man there is going to be a lot of people getting hurt."

I needed to know, so I asked. "So what is the role of a point man?"

Tom answered me this way, "A point man is the first guy in line on everything and usually he is one of the first people who is going to get shot at. Sometimes they let him go past and a second go past then they hit the radio and the officers and stuff. He is out there by himself. A point man has to watch in the trees to his left, to his right. He needs to look for signs of booby traps and he is usually out there 15 to 20 feet ahead of everybody.

He is by himself and when the shots go off he has got anywhere from 3 to 5 seconds to decide if he is going to live or die. A lot of point men didn't make it… it is one of the worst jobs in Vietnam. Anybody will tell you that.

So many questions were running through my mind, "I saw in your book and(by the way Tom has written a book with contributions from many of the soldiers he served with in Vietnam called "Dog Faced Charlie" we will tell you how to get a copy of that book here in a few minutes.) Tom when I was reading that about the point man some of the soldiers would rather have been point men as being back in the back with everybody else, tell me about that.

"Exactly, some people who are hyper and when they got it together would rather be upfront where you know what is going on. If you are in the rear, you don't know what is going on up front, and all you can do is keep your head down and duck. That is why I started walking point. I wanted to be upfront and see what was going on and be in the action. I guess my youth and stupidity came out in me.

I didn't think of Tom as stupid, I admired his courage. I asked if he ever worried about mortar fire.

He responded quickly, "Oh yes he had to worry about everything!"

In the back, you just don't know what is going on because everybody went forward with the lieutenant. Everybody with the radio, and you had no idea what was going on except what was being passed back to you by word of mouth. So all you could do was turn towards whatever direction the activity and noise was coming. To see or hear an order and that is all you could do was look until you saw them coming at you. Friend or foe. Up front man you were where the action was, you were up there because the VC and NVA knew that point men were usually some of the best soldiers in your platoon or your company or your squad. It was a rough job.

What made you decide to take point?, I asked.

"I had a revenge mindset, for my friend who got killed. I will tell you about that later but I just wanted to be up front, I wanted to be in the action. My dad said I was losing it. I don't know but I just had to be upfront. I wanted to be there."

Exploring other topics with Tom, I asked about some items he brought into my office one day. One of them was a little clear packet full of Vietnamese money."

"Can you tell me a little bit about this money?"

"Yes, he replied, "some of this money was taken off NVA's up in the highlands around Song Be and some off of some VC and NVA at Loc Ninh.

"You didn't just take it off of them? I asked.

"No, we did it the old fashioned way", we had them caught on an ambush or on a patrol and we got it after they were KIA.""

For those of us not so savvy on the lingo, I replied, "So you are throwing some initials at us NVA that was the North Vietnamese Army?"

Readers! I WANT YOU TO KNOW WHO THEY WERE FIGHTING! "That was not the Viet Cong?"

General Giap's plan was being implemented.

"Right."

These were the professional soldiers. Trained by General Giap. The third stage of his military plan we discussed earlier.

"Right, these were the bad guys." The VC were bad, too. These guys were smart and they had better weapons. They were better trained, a lot better. They got paid and I can't pronounce half these words that are on here but there are some 20 cent ones and some 2 dollar ones and some of them are from Hanoi.

Remember earlier when I was trying to tell you about me as a 10 year old who saw the Viet Cong as bad guys? I know now that these North Vietnamese soldiers were not necessarily bad meaning evil, but bad meaning they had to be reduced to a level that made it easier to kill.

This is why they were given nick names like Gook, or Charlie, or VC.

There is one question I had for you I think I read in your book, you all (your company) killed a Russian advisor one day.

"Yes, we did."

My curiosity was building, "Was he with the Viet Cong or NVA?

Tom answered, "He was with the NVA on this one here. They kept it really hush hush because I was all excited about it and I said, "I think we killed a Russian." Come to find out he was a military advisor he may have been Russian or East German. I think it was Russian he said he was about 6'1" or 6'2" had the blond hair and a brand new AK47. He could have been East German but maybe Russian."

Then, another item you gave me was a piece of paper that had a copy on it looked like a ticket. Can you tell me a little bit about that ticket you found in I guess you found lots of them in the jungle.

"Yes these little pamphlets that the VC or the NVA would hand out around the villages it says here, they wrote, an end to the war American troops". Go back to America do not fight the Vietnamese who are struggling for independence and freedom. That is in American on the opposite side is in North Vietnamese.

So this was propaganda that you would find laying around?

Right we would find it all over the place.

After studying the actual history to prepare for this book, I have to agree, that maybe we Americans were involved in a Civil War in Vietnam and that the struggle for "Independence" was a true statement, with the ends justifying the means. Assassinations, Murders of tribal leaders, indoctrination and brainwashing, and intimidation were tactics being used by the Viet Cong to convert the peasants and local populations. We called it winning the hearts and minds, and our tactics were different in almost all cases. More on this later.

So not only did TOM Mercer have to try to protect himself from getting killed, he had to deal with propaganda and those kinds of things. One day he was in a rice paddy.

Tom perked up, "Oh yes, it was kind of right outside of a rice paddy in the wood line, but during the TET offensive right outside of Saigon on Tu Doc. We were working that area, on a long patrol and we had a company sized patrol. Colonel Phillip McClure was our Captain at the time, and a great guy. We had been chasing these guys and we would see pieces of clothes laying here and a piece of their hardware laying over here. All they ended up was with their black shorts and their little Ho Chi Min sandals made out of tires and tubes. We did this off and on and they would stop and ambush us. Then they would take off and we would pull back and call in strikes finally we would see blood trails bleeding off every one of them so we knew we were getting to them. We had no body count as of yet, but we knew we were hitting somebody. We came to this little berm that was about 8 feet high. To the top of it and there was a VC or NVA I think it was a VC standing there with his AK-47 above his head hollering "chu hoi" and he was all excited. I mean all he had was his black shorts on and his AK-47. So I got the interpreter and my Captain called up to me and says, "Please do not shoot that guy. We need information!" So I said, "All right!" We were really ticked off at him. He, or his buddies had wounded a couple of our guys! So the interpreter came up, and they were really rough with him. He was a Viet Cong who had done a "chu hoi" himself, and we made him our interpreter. He was good and he hated the Viet Cong. He started asking questions all of a sudden the new prisoner jumped back and throwed his rifle down into the rice paddy and started talking this crazy language I couldn't understand. So we did the same thing you know I didn't know what we was aiming at but we were aiming at the water. About that time he says he is telling us to back up. My heart was really throbbing you know I was ready. Then three or four more guys raised up out of the rice paddy and they was breathing through bamboo stalks they had in their mouths. They were in the water about 3 feet deep but they were hiding there. If we had of messed with that guy they would have shot every one of us. We got them up and made them sit down in the water and got their AK's away from them. The leaches... they must have been getting eaten up with leaches. They were tired and dirty and they were ready for this war to end so we ended the war for them and took them to my Captain McClure, Colonel McClure now he retired a Colonel. He was so mad because we had captured them and that is what he had told me to do but we had to drag them around all day because he couldn't get a helicopter in where we were.

So wait a minute Tom there were three men sitting in three feet of water with straws in their mouth, in their underwear holding on to AK-47's that when they came up out of the water their guns would have worked? Oh yeah an AK-47 they were good weapons. I hate to say it but if we would have done that with an M-16 you were out of luck.

Tom explained, I carried an M-14 so it never jammed.

I knew about the M-16 issues from my friend Glenn Palmer. So I asked Tom, "You mentioned that a little bit, but what was the difference between the M-14 and the M-16?"

Tom taught me this, "The M-16 was a new type rifle, we were like guinea pigs because a lot of people like at Doc To and up in the A-Shau Valley from the 101st and people up there even the marines... poor marines they had a lot of M-16s and when we found them dead, their weapon had a round jammed in the chamber. M-14's just didn't work like that, it worked. It was heavier but most of our point men and rear security and flankers used M-14's."

"So that was your weapon of choice?" I asked.

"Right, Tom said sheepishly smiling, a lot of them we had to go out and steal them off deuce and a half's and leave an M-16 and take the M-14's."

April 1968

Tom Mercer was involved in an ambush.

We were on an ambush and we had a NDP set up. A NDP is a Night Defensive Perimeter and it was battalion sized so there were 4 companies out there including our LRRP units. The LRRP's had gone out and they came back and said there were VC tracks everywhere. There were signs of movement all up and down the road so we picked a spot and we went out to it. We had a new E6 who was in charge at the time of my platoon or my squad. He didn't know what he was doing. He was too old to be in the field to start with anyway. We went out there and we got all set up. He couldn't figure out what to do. We set up in this ambush. We got in our spot. We set up our claymore mines, first. We kind of went around just to make sure we were there by ourselves. We got a phone call from the CO... we heard the mortar rounds going off then we got a phone call from our platoon leader saying you've got VC coming your way. Again your heart just starts just a throbbing. This was about 4:00 in the morning so you have been getting just a little sleep maybe a couple of hours anyway. We had new guys and old guys there so we split them up.

So at this time I wasn't an FNG anymore.

You had some in your unit?

Yes and I was mad. Well the enemy started coming our way. We could hear them. It had gotten louder and louder so I told the guys to get ready. They come down the road and they split and got out about 25 or 30 yards from us and set up their own ambush but they didn't know we were there. They were expecting the men from the Company to send up a patrol and chase them out which we don't do stuff like that. We are American soldiers. We are not stupid. We didn't do that. So it went on for about an hour and a half or two hours like that. Maybe an hour and a half because it was about 4:15 or 5:00. The enemy soldiers got up and walked out to the road and they walked out and stumbled over my guys' claymore mine and that is when everything broke loose. He blew his claymore and killed a couple and they started firing but they didn't know where we was at. We hadn't fired any small arms weapons yet we exploded our claymores but we didn't want them to know where we were. Then they started shooting so much toward where we were and we had to open up with our machine guns and our M-14's and M-16's. We killed 2 with the claymores and then we found 2 or 3 more and a Russian advisor the next morning. The Lieutenant sent the rest of a platoon out to get us. We were tore up. We were messed up I mean nobody killed but we had some wounded. We were scared to death no matter how long you have been there if you have been in a fire fight you are scared if somebody says he is not scared he wasn't in the same Vietnam I was in.

"Rocket Day"

Another Tom Mercer Experience.

Lai Khe was probably the most rocketed base camp in the country except for Khe Sand during the siege. At times, the camp would receive incoming rockets three times per day and twice per night and there was a sign at the main gate reading: 'Welcome to Rocket City'.

An Anonymous soldier remarked about Lai Khe:

Why would I ever want to go back? I got there Jan.15, 1968, 2 weeks before the Tet Offensive. I was on a 50 cal. On top of a VTR without a shield. Wounded in a rocket attack, had guys from my unit blown away in pieces, went out with Col. Patten on a search and destroy with 10 days left to go in country. Found 2 tunnels and a land mine. Rotated back home. Proud of all my Brothers. Some PTSD, but I deal with it. Scars on my legs and lungs. I have no animosity towards the people or their country. I don't need closure, I got that the day I left. Lai khe truly was ROCKET CITY. Why would I want to go back???? I've been around the world at least 6 times, and in the Far East. While there are beautiful places in NAM, there are NONE more beautiful than back here in the USA. Why would I want to go back?

We were stationed in a place they called a rocket belt which was 12 miles outside of Lai Khe and was General Keith Ware's Division Headquarters. He was a big guy, and a Medal of Honor recipient, great guy. He had been getting hit by rockets every day. These rockets were 6 foot 1 inches 122 mm Russian made rockets and they did a lot of damage. They made a big hole and a lot of shrapnel. General Ware picked Charlie Company and our battalion to leave the NDP and head out and find these rockets he said, "I was getting >Blankety Blank" tired of them.

Author's note: By the way, I do not believe he said "Blankety Blank".

A lot of people were dying each day and a lot of people were getting wounded. Charlie Company got picked to go. Lima platoon got picked for point platoon and I got picked for point. I wasn't an FNG no more, but I was still a Private. We headed out and we walked for a few hours and we had a scout dog with us his name was Fritz Fritz was later killed by a mortar round. The VC hated scout dogs because they were good. We walked and walked then we stopped and sent out some clover leafs. A clover leaf is like a patrol outside of a patrol you go out and just check it out. I made it out to about 4 or 5 hours, I guess. We came to another spot and the dog just sat down. His hair raised up and he just sat down and just not growling loud, but he was looking at his trainer and just going "GRRRRRRRR" like so. The handler said, "Tom you need to have the Lieutenant check this out there is something out here." The Lieutenant didn't want to do that. He said, "we have got to keep moving." I didn't want to but I did one more time. So we moved on and nothing happened but they had us in their sites the whole time and we were right on the edge of an open field and the woods kind of staying in the wood line and away from that open field with big elephant grass about 4 or 5 feet high which is a scary and an eerie feeling. Anytime you are walking point you have always got to listen to your gut. When something is going to happen you get this funny feeling in your stomach and mine was getting worse so we came to this open spot and the dog sat down again and the scout dog handler said, "Tom you have got to check it out." I told the Lieutenant I passed on the information but he said we have got to keep going. I refused to go. I said I am not going out there and none of the guys behind me is going to go.

About the time he was going to pick somebody else to go out they opened up on us. They were about a squad of VC, but you know when there is only 3 or 4 of us right there in that area there is nothing you can do. One guy got hit in the hand and they were trying to kill the dog and trying to kill the point man, ME! And the other guy, There was three of us. Kenny Gardellis, Rusty Little and the scout dog handler which I can't remember his name and Fritz the dog. Well these two guys got knocked down, Kenny jumped on top of a wounded man to keep him from getting hurt any more than he needed to be and that was a heroic act to me. He should have gotten a medal just for doing that. The scout dog man jumped on top of the dog. I only had one place to go because they had taken all the cover so I just ran toward where the VC were and I was shooting at the time I was running. I guess they thought I was crazy. Anyway we killed one VC and one rocket got fired before we killed the VC. I can still see that picture of the tail just going left and right but it was headed right to Saigon and we got a message on our l radio. The rocket had just hit Lai Khe outside of Saigon close to our commander's (Keith Ware's) Headquarters Group. That is when I charged the VC. I didn't really think I was charging the VC. I was just trying to get to one log behind some coverage where I needed to be. It turned out that is where the gook was. The VC were laying behind that log. We shot and got him and they kept firing and as they were firing they must have been running they didn't hit no more people. We captured 3 more rockets, one more rocket went off. We didn't have no body killed then. General Ware came out to the field in his helicopter with his white German Shepherd and Fritz fell in love with that white German Shepherd. I called that love in a war zone. This is when he took me to the side and talked to me. I was nervous. He said, "Don't be nervous, and don't worry about it. He was a great guy he had a Silver Star, he pinned the Silver Star on me and promoted me from a Private to an E5 out in the field. He took the wounded guy back in his chopper to the headquarters hospital. The next morning we woke up and we were sitting ducks. They had us zoned in and they knew where those mortar rounds were going to come. The next morning as we were lined up to go to the chow line those mortars started coming in and my machine gunner took a direct hit and it killed him. We had about 8 or 9 guys wounded and it was just a bad time to be a soldier in Vietnam for the next 10 or 15 minutes. The mortar rounds arrived as fast as they could drop them in a tube they were bringing them in on us. I couldn't get back to my bunker so I got behind a tree and I was just hoping for the best. That is my story of Rocket Day. We just had some good people and good leaders.

August 2012, I went to a reunion of the USS Indianapolis that was the 65th year reunion for the sinking of the Indianapolis and now this week I have learned about another soldier Tom Mercer who has set up reunions for his group. One thing that I learned while I was in Indianapolis for the Indianapolis reunion was that the wives do participate and the wives do get involved. What you are about to hear is a dissertation from the wife of our guest Mrs. Joyce Mercer.

I will begin this story with a little history of Tom and myself. We met over 23 years ago and have been married for 22 years. Tom is a very caring and wonderful man always putting everyone before himself. He is almost too nice and polite to a fault. I know he wouldn't think twice if he had to risk his life for me or any other family member or friend for that matter. I consider myself very lucky to have found a wonderful man to spend the rest of my life with. Prior to the first Charlie Company reunion Tom never spoke about his experiences in Vietnam. If I asked a question he would respond with a short answer. It didn't take me long to figure out not to bring up the subject. During the course of our marriage there are little things that Tom does that I couldn't quite understand. I have since found out most of it is due to Vietnam. For instance I noticed Tom doesn't like to go to bed until he is absolutely exhausted and usually he falls asleep in his chair. He has a terrible time sleeping and has to take sleeping medications most of the time. If it were up to him he would stay up all night and sleep during the day. Tom is also very fidgety while driving or sitting. You can never ease up on him and scare him because you are likely to get your head knocked off. Tom has a lot of nightmares and sometimes will talk in his sleep and call me the General. I don't know if he is dreaming about Vietnam or dreaming about the present. There are times he will be very quiet like he is real deep thought about something. I know he is thinking about Vietnam. I could go on and on after talking with some of the other veteran's wives I have come to find out that many of these men have the same Vietnam symptoms it is so sad. Unfortunately I have to admit I really didn't know what Vietnam was all about at the time I was 18 years old and a working single mother taking care of my baby daughter. I didn't have time to stop and think about world affairs because it was all I could do to be a single parent. I didn't realize how bad and senseless this war was until many years of being married to Tom. The realization for me actually began by visiting the traveling wall in September of 2008. For many years the thought of Tom finding the men he served with in Vietnam was a far-fetched idea to him. Little did he know a visit to the traveling wall would be the beginning of the first reunion for the 1st of the 18th Charlie Company? This all began with an article I had read in our local newspaper about the wall coming to our town in late September 2008. I mentioned it to Tom because I knew he had always wanted to visit the real one in Washington, D.C. Tom was so excited and called our best friends Jim and Carol Gavial to join us. I distinctly remember it was a warm evening and about 40 people were walking around Tom immediately went to ask an attendant how to locate some of his friends who had died. Tom walked to the wall with all of us by his side. Within a few minutes he discovered his best friends name Jerry Tucker and immediately broke down crying. We all felt his emotion and followed with our tears. After walking for a while and looking at names it was time for the memorial service to begin for the fallen soldiers. Neither of us had attended one of these services and we didn't really know what to expect. While we were sitting waiting for the service to start there was a cute little boy with his mother handing out key chains made with beads consisting of the South Vietnamese colors. He handed them out to all the men waiting for the service. Later we learned that this little boy had lost his father in the Iraq war several months earlier. That evening on the way home Tom mentioned that he would like to find some of the men he served with. Little did I know this was going to be the mission for the rest of his life as soon as we arrived home Tom turned on the computer and started. Luckily we have a program for our business that can locate people provided we have good information. The first person he looked for was Kenny Gardellis a young man who became his best friend in Vietnam in 1967 through 1968. Tom never knew whether Kenny made it home alive. When Tom left Vietnam for home Kenny was on R & R he never knew whether any of the young men he served made it home alive. I know this weighed on him all these years but he never talked about it. As luck would have it Tom found an address and phone number for Kenny he was so excited and almost speechless. Ironically Kenny lived in a little town outside Asheville, North Carolina and only 1 ½ hours away from us. Tom immediately picked up the telephone and dialed his number. I had to go to another room so Tom couldn't see my tears of joy. Kenny's girlfriend Tracy answered the phone and I heard him ask to speak to Kenny. He explained to Tracy that he had served with him in Vietnam. Kenny got on the phone and Tom was so excited and couldn't believe he was actually talking to him after all these years. I remained in the other room until I composed myself. I could hear plans being made for all of us to meet in a restaurant in 2 days which couldn't come fast enough for Tom. The initial meeting with Kenny and Tracy who have since married was likely something out of the movies. I can remember Tom was so nervous and couldn't wait to see him. Once we arrived at the restaurant he immediately recognized Kenny and they couldn't stop hugging each other although after 40 years had passed it wasn't hard for Tom to note it was his best friend from Vietnam. We all tried to hold back the tears. That was the beginning of the 1st of the 18th Charlie Company reunion in the making. Tom told Kenny of his idea of trying to find the other guys and Kenny with no hesitation offered his help. When we left the restaurant that evening Tom couldn't stop talking about how happy he was to finally find his best friend from Vietnam. I was so happy for him once home Tom turned on the computer and spent endless hours trying to find the men that he served with. There was also many hours on the telephone every time Tom found someone he called that person and immediately called Kenny. After several months the reunion date and location were set. Another man Tom served with Doug Goddard lives about 45 minutes from us. Doug and his wife Caroline also offered their help with the first reunion. The date was to be April 30 – May 2 2009 in Gatlinburg, Tennessee. Everyone put in a lot of time and effort to make this first reunion a huge success. I believe there were 38 Charlie Company members who attended many brought their wives or girlfriends. As the reunion approached Tom was extremely nervous although he had spoken to all these men by telephone he would soon be seeing them for the first time in over 40 years. We could hardly wait until we arrived at the hotel. Doug and Caroline did a great job of preparing the name badges which helped tremendously. Doug actually had a picture of each soldier when they were in Vietnam along with his name beside the photo. The reunion was a huge success and a lot of tears were shed. I realized all the hard work and effort was worth every minute I also realized how much people thought of my husband and what a good genuine person he is. After the reunion Tom told me he would like to write a book on his experiences in Vietnam. My immediate thought was, "Oh no here we go again!" Once we arrived home Tom was back on his computer typing away.

Over several months until the wee hours of the night he had the idea not only to write a book but to include his army buddies as well. Tom contacted the other men and most of them seemed very interested in writing of their experiences. It took well over a year for Tom to compile all the stories born this book and mail it to the First Division Museum in Wheaton, Illinois for editing and publishing. I have to admit after the first reunion I thought it was the end of Tom being so consumed with his Charlie Company's Swamp Rats, I was so wrong. Now he was on another Charlie Company mission there were times I became annoyed with Tom for spending so much time on Charlie Company but I realized how much it meant to him. It was great therapy for Tom it seemed that he talked much more about his experiences in Vietnam. We recently attended our third Charlie Company reunion which was held in Orlando, Florida May 11 – 13, 2011 it was a huge success. It is special that the wives and or girlfriends also attended. The first year we decided the wives should be invited which turned out to be a great idea. At first we thought if the wives didn't actually want to sit in the meetings they could go shopping or find other things to do. Little did we know that the meetings would turn out to be so interesting the wives attended every single one we have a great group of people and everyone is bonded very well. The first reunion was a little awkward because no one really knew each other and the men also had to get to know each other all over again. By the third reunion this had all changed I had no idea the effect this senseless war made on so many of the men I met at the reunion. It is so sad to see them sitting at the tables looking at actual pictures from Vietnam and all of a sudden they break down in tears or I see them talking to each other and all of a sudden tears roll down their cheeks and they hug each other. When I witness things like this I immediately tear up and can't imagine the pain they have gone through and will go through for the rest of their lives. I find it so awful they never received the great receptions and home-comings when they arrived home. Now the soldiers that come home from their tours in Iraq and Afghanistan have huge receptions and parades, not that I begrudge them in any way, but it was so unfair the way the soldiers were treated when they arrived home from Vietnam. So many times they were called names and things were thrown at them how awful. In my mind their home-coming reception is every year we have the 1st of the 18th Charlie Company reunion. I look at these proud brave veterans that have such a special bond between them I am so happy to be married to one of these veterans who sacrificed it all for our country. I am also happy to have been involved getting the 1st of the 18th Charlie Company together after all these years.

The Army's version of Rocket Day:

Tom Mercer's Silver Star

April 10, 1968 the Silver Star, the Republic of Vietnam for gallantry in action while engaged in military operations involving conflict with an armed hostile force in the Republic of Vietnam on this date Sgt. Mercer then Private 1st Class was serving as point man for his company on reconnaissance in the force operation Northwest of Lai Khe. As the lead element proceeded into the clearing of this jungle it was suddenly subjected to intense automatic weapons and small arms fire from fortifications defending a rocket launcher site. Although this movement was restricted Sgt. Mercer observed that a comrade was pinned down in the clearing and unable to move to a move advantageous position. With complete disregard for his personal safety Sgt. Mercer ran through the hail of hostile rounds toward his companion and simultaneously fired at the Viet Cong enabling the wounded man to reach a secure location. He exposed himself again in this insurgent's barrage breaking the area as he repeated his actions and helped another soldier to safety. Sgt. Mercer then directed his men's devastating fire on the enemy forcing them to retreat leaving behind one dead Viet Cong and two rockets. His exemplary courage, outstanding leadership and selfless concern for his comrades were instrumental in saving soldier's lives and significantly contributed toward the successful of the encounter. Sgt. Mercer's unquestionable valor in close combat against numerically superior hostile forces was in keeping with the finest traditions of the military service and reflects great credit upon himself and the 1st Infantry Division in the United States Army. By direction of the President as established by the act of congress 9 July 1918 in the United States Army message 16695 dated 1 July 1966.

You know the Vietnam War was never really explained to our children the way it should have been explained. We had a real problem and we still have this problem today that we as a nation have never been able to separate this unpopular war with the soldiers we sent to fight it. We want to take a minute to welcome home all of our Vietnam veterans every chance we get. Tom if somebody wants to get in touch with you what do they do?

Well you can get on my email site: pointmantom@aol.com

And they can talk to you about ordering the book DOG FACE CHARLIE, and or his wonderful CD. I have really enjoyed listening to the CD and so will you!

CHAPTER SEVEN

It's just a Thang

It ain't me, it ain't me
I ain't no senator's son, son
It ain't me, it ain't me
I ain't no fortunate one

Lyrics from Fortunate Son
By: Creedence Clearwater Revival

Today I am visiting Vietnam with an old friend. A couple of months ago I was walking in the park down by the Holston River in Knoxville, Tn. A young red headed boy was on a bicycle, one of those bicycles with the goose neck handlebars. He came up and he was aiming right at me and slammed on his brakes and slid. He didn't know me from Adam, I looked at him and I said I know who you are. He said, "How do you know that?" I said, "You have got to be Henry Carson's grandson." He said, "How did you know that?" and I said, "you look just like he did when I knew him about 55 years ago, you have got to be him." Turned out he was and I asked him where his granddad lived and he said across the street down on the corner. I said well I need to renew my contact with that man and I went to see him and today's story is about Henry Carson's life in Vietnam.

Henry Carson

I went into the Army in July of 1966 right out of high school, East High School in Knoxville, Tennessee?

I didn't join, I got drafted. I had planned on going into the Navy. Me and a friend of mine decided we were going down and join and he said I don't want to go in the Navy I want to go in the Marine Corps. I said well I really don't want to go into the Marine Corps so I didn't go with him, Bob Corn. Bob Corn was from Knoxville here we went to school together, great guy. Bob joined the Marines and it wasn't but just a short time after that I opened my mail box and there was a letter inviting me to be in the Army.

I started out going to Fort Campbell?

Yes, they sent us to Nashville on a bus. We picked up more troops and of course they swore us in at Knoxville over on Central Avenue. I never will forget that morning when I got my brother-in-law to drive me over there and I told my brother-in-law I said this old car belonged to me you can have this car. I said I probably won't need it no more I will just give you this car. He drove me over there and dropped me off. They lined us all up there and swore us all in. It just took a few minutes and had everybody line up they swore us in and said you are in the Army now.

First I was at Fort Campbell then I went to Fort Sam Houston?

Basic training at Fort Campbell, Kentucky and as soon as I got out of there they sent us straight to Fort Sam Houston in Texas at least they sent me. There wasn't many from our graduating class from boot camp that went to Fort Sam Houston but there was a handful of us.

We were going to be medics?

Yes, they said that after they inducted us and sent us through testing and all that they advised us that they wanted us to be medics. They said they thought we were suited to be in the Medic Corps.

So after Fort Sam Houston they sent me to Fort Polk?

Yes, after graduation from Fort Sam Houston, Texas they was going to send me to Vietnam right then but they changed my orders. Now they sent me to the 565th Medical Detachment in Fort Polk, Louisiana. They wanted me to work in the emergency room there. I went there and worked with the 565th and it was just a short time after that I did get my orders to go on to Vietnam. They had a good program at Fort Sam Houston and it was fast you didn't have time to slow down for anything it was just train, train, train, train and train.

At Fort Sam Houston those were college classroom type setting environments. You go in to sit down and study then you go out in the field and put it to application. You work and some of us got an opportunity to go to Brooke General and do a few things up there you know minimal tasks at Brooke General but some of us didn't. They were teaching us through the whole process how to deal with every kind of medical emergency that you could encounter in any condition.

Author's Note:

Speaking of teaching something else you need to know Henry Carson was in elementary school at Robert Huff Elementary School where my mother taught. The first time I met Henry was when my bicycle had broken down and my mom had asked Henry to come fix it for me.

I have had an admiration for Henry since that day.

Henry Carson's Vietnam Story

You learn to do a lot of things in Vietnam. First of all you can live on a whole lot less sleep than you think you can. When I got into Vietnam as the plane landed they was firing rockets on the 44th Replacement and they had a staging area there they called a bull pen. They got all the troops and herded us into a fence lot. We were all trying to get a place to get down and get under cover they were blowing the place up when we got there.

That was at the 44th Replacement in Vietnam down south and it was hot. We were used to temperatures at Fort Polk, Louisiana. We thought Fort Polk was humid and hot, bugs and mosquitoes and everything. That was a cake walk compared to Vietnam. When I got off the plane over there the heat was so bad it would just take your breath. You know I was a pretty good sized fellow when I went over I weighed over 200 lbs. actually I weighed 230 lbs. that is what I weighed when I went over to Vietnam. I was a pretty good chunk of a fellow then. I came home I weighed 167 lbs. Of course being red-headed and fair complexed I don't do very well in the sun and heat. I was dark and sandy and the sun had really worked on me I was weathered.

I was in lots of fire fights and battles. And one helicopter crash?

Right near Hue. About 60 or 70 miles I guess above Hue in that neighborhood but we didn't stay there very long that was our base camp. The 3rd of the 187th, the 101st Airborne to us we were the "Rakkasans". We just stayed there long enough to get geared up, get equipment and I was assigned right away. I was assigned out in the field when they flew me out of there they flew me right to the A Shau Valley and it was just one of those things where it was let's go and you are out of here. Now the A Shau Valley they talk about the A Shau Valley in the battle movie "Hamburger Hill".

The A Shau Valley (Vietnamese: A Sầu) is a valley in Vietnam's Thừa Thiên-Huế Province, west of the coastal city of Huế, along the border of Laos. The valley runs north and south for 40 kilometers and is a 1.5- kilometer-wide flat bottomland covered with tall elephant grass, flanked by two densely forested mountain ridges whose summits vary in elevation from 900 to 1,800 meters. A Shau Valley was one of the key entry points into South Vietnam for men and material brought along the Ho Chi Minh trail by the North Vietnamese.

The A Shau Valley was a big boundary of a real harsh wilderness and jungle and it is almost impenetrable in places. You have to blow a hole to get a bird on the ground. There was a lot of activity there. The Ho Chi Minh Trail was up in that area and you had a lot of infiltration of supplies and troops. You know the 3rd of the 187th the Rakkasans is the actual unit that stumbled in there on the Hamburger Hill incident. That was my unit and that had happened just previously before I got there. I was a replacement is one of the reasons I ended up being there. I was a replacement. An FNG. When they dropped us off the bird there from Camp Evans in the A Shau Valley of course the guys that took you out there they are seasoned they have been there a while and one of the sayings they have and I guess it just burns in your memories, "it's just a thang man, I see you when or if you get back." That is just one of those things you don't know if you are going to make it back or not but… it's just a thang. I never will forget they flew us out there and they bumped us out and they told us, "it's just a thang man, see you if you make it back."

They said that in the movies a lot, "it's just a thang."

It helps you get through it when you are in a fire fight or a battle or some of your buddies and you know being a medic immediately you found yourself exposed to the environment that if something goes wrong I am the one who is going to be here to help. It becomes reality right there when the first fire fight or the first battle you go through it really hits home closer than any training you can learn here. When something goes dreadfully wrong an explosion or a stray bullet or whatever, immediately the first word you hear is "medic! Help!" You know and you learn to pick up on some of those phrases that people get in those conditions. Like it is just a thang man you know I worked on people that has had bullet wounds and mine explosions and all kinds of situations and you know you kind of stir them up a little bit and give them some hope by saying, "hey man it is just a thang you will be alright it's just a thang." You know the troops they want to hear you say you are going to be alright. They want to hear those words. They know the situation many of them do but if you can have some reinforcing words that are realistic then you need to try to share those at those times. You know, I met this friend of mine and we keep in touch constantly over the years. We nicknamed him "Swamp rat" and he calls me "Hillbilly" and we keep in touch. It has been a good friendship over all these years and from time to time we will call each other but you know we went through a lot of real bad locations, we went through up in the DMZ up in Laos and the Cambodian border all up the fire bases all up through the valley. We have been through all kinds of situations together and he was a radio operator and you know he is my other hand in a situation. If I have got people hurt, people injured or there is something going on hey I got to get a MEDEVAC in here. I have got this going on here I need this or that. You know he was right there he could radio in your MEDEVAC and get it in there and no matter how hard you try to do your job there is so many other people out there that has to do their job to make yours work.

That was before the helicopter crash. You will learn about this soon enough.

We left the Hamburger Hill area after several weeks up in that area working it.

We were on a team that went out and we moved all the time. Our little team, we would go out and set up and we would bunk in somewhere. You know, then we would move 3 or 4 times during the day. At night time we would move just right at the edge of dark then it would be part of our team who would go out and set up Claymores and set up an ambush. The old man, or the Captain, he would have his CP or Command Post wherever he elected to be. Of course I ended up staying usually with or near that area because if something happened I had to have communication right then. If something was going down I had to be able to make a decision if we needed MEDEVAC's or if we needed whatever. Of course the other radio operators were busy folks on air support or anything like that we needed.

How did the soldiers treat the medics?

They was good to us, we were soldiers together. We wouldn't separate. We was in the same trenches together, we carried our own loads. They tried to do things to help the medics you know, but we wanted to pull our own load. I knew I carried a can of 60 ammo for one of the gunners because he couldn't handle all the weight. I had a ruck sack, an aid bag and that can of 60 ammo I carried for him that is what you do you help each other. No matter what the situations are, if our goal was to move so many clicks this day, or if we were going in there to support somebody. I was a medic, true, but I was a soldier first. The limits that you go for one another there are no boundaries.

It's just a thang man.

I was a ground medic not a helicopter medic. But I spent time on helicopters or in a MASH unit either one. I had experience in all 3; I actually worked in Vietnam on all 3 at different times. Of course the rear area the MASH type setting I didn't like very much there was something going on all the time but I basically spent most of my entire time in the field.

It was a little less than 12 months; it was just a one year tour.

Its in a little place called Phong Dien. ETS meant Enlisted Time Served. It was monsoon season. They had lots of bad weather and actually some bad things had happened there. We still stayed on the same type mission we still went out and patrolled in the A Shau Valley and all up in that country. Then they pulled us out of there and put us in a place down near Phong Dien. It was just rice paddies, villages and all kinds of stuff. They sent us on patrol and the patrol they wanted us to go on was out in this area that had a lot of booby traps and a lot of mines and we had a lot of problems right there in the few days that we had been there. We had a new medic come in and he came with us there and I told him I said, "Why don't you just stay here in the rear area today you are new and you kind of hang loose here." They had their own RTO that day.

Radio operator they had their own RTO and Swamp Rat was the radio operator and we were a team we were a real team together. He wasn't going to be on that patrol and the other RTO of course I knew him but the medic he was green as a gourd. I told him to just hang back and it is just a thang man I will take this one. We got out on that long patrol and one of the guys I think there were 16 of us and he hit an 82 mortar. That mortar went off and it killed Sgt. McCarley. He was right behind... third one back and it killed him and mangled up some other guys and blew a big hole in one of them's chest and it hit me and it knocked me down. Anyway there were two guys left that could actually walk.

It was a booby trapped 82 mortar. There was two guys that could actually move. You know, everybody else was either hurt, shot, crippled up. I couldn't even move from my waist down. Big chunks of shrapnel had gone through my legs and stuff. I couldn't move and I was trying to crawl and I got some help and I got to the Sergeant and he was in horrible shape I mean the concussion was so strong that it blew smoke charges off his chest. Didn't even pull the pins just blew them. He was burned up and he had a big chunk of metal through the side of his head and he was just barely alive. I was doing all I could to get him an airway. I got him an airway established and he would go in and out of consciousness... he would just lose it and I got down to the point I was trying to save his life.... I had to cut his throat it was completely blocked. I had to get him over where I could get some of that blood out of him and try to keep an airway so I got him open enough to get an airway established and I knew this wasn't going to work. He was too far gone and of course I did ventilations and everything on him as long as I could but he just didn't make it, he was in really bad shape. Our radio... the radio operator... he had a PRC25 radio and a big chunk of metal went dead through the middle of it. There we were stranded, had two people who could walk, no communications what-so-ever, and I was trying to maintain, I had a guy with a chest wound. I got him stable and got him where he was going to be OK. I had some other guys that were maimed up pretty bad and I got them all what I could do with. I just wore these two guys that could walk out dragging me around to each wounded soldier. It was getting a while before dark and I thought we are going to be stranded out here sure as the world. I told these two guys that could move, I said, "anybody that can lay down fire, get your position and just get ready to lay down fire because the Gooks will be back and they will check this explosion. They know what is going on. They will be back, so we will just lay down a perimeter as best we can. Way off in the distance I seen a helicopter and I told one of the guys if you got a red smoke pop it and they had a red smoke so they popped that red smoke. In just a minute you can see that helicopter. He was a long way off, you could see him start making a move he started making a circle. Once he started making that circle I knew right then hey they got us.

Yes somebody knew where we was at. That red smoke if you go on an LZ that is a hot LZ somebody is going to throw a red smoke and that tells all the pilots and everybody, hey this is a red hot LZ. You signal with smoke. You screen with smoke and you guide helicopters in with smoke but that red smoke signal when they saw that was a hot LZ over there they knew something was going on. So they made that big circle and it wasn't but just a few minutes everybody in the world was buzzing in there in helicopters. MEDEVAC's and the old man come in his loach and we got everybody loaded up and I was the last guy on the bird out of there but we was fortunate to have made it as much as we did but we did lose a man there, a good man.

"The old man came in there on his loach" what does that mean?

That is the Battalion Commander he came through there on his loach.

That is a small 2 seat bubble face type helicopter. They... if something really goes down the Battalion Commander he will get on a loach and fly out. He was really conscientious about what was going on. But I was hit and I hadn't even cut my trousers or anything at that time I knew I was losing blood but I wasn't losing a lot. My right leg was mangled up but I knew it hadn't hit the femoral artery I was losing blood but I wasn't going under or anything like that. I knew I was not going to bleed to death even though I had blood everywhere. I knew it wasn't an artery. I hadn't even looked at my own wounds I just didn't even cut my trousers I just figured it is just a thang man. I believe I will get out of here if they get me back to the 18th Field Surgery they can check it out and see what it is. They did. They got me on a bird. They flew me up there and they landed it at the field unit there and they knew who it was. They was trying to ask me what happened and everything. I was trying to explain to them by the time they got me from the landing zone into the unit. They had done had all my clothes off of me. They just had everything jerked and cut off of me. You got to do that. You just got to cut everything away and the guy that was checking my legs and everything out there it was real obvious you could see a great big hole. You could see the muscle of my leg sticking out and everything. He said you know what we got to do? I said yea I know I know and it was just a few minutes you know they already had me hung and strung and everything. They had the IV started and everything and he came over there and he said let's do a countdown here and he said give me a count and I think I made it to 9. I woke up... they knew me there they knew who I was and they were giving me attention trying to find out what was messed up and what wasn't. They come back after the surgery and told me they said there were some pretty good chunks of metal you took and they said we got most of it but we couldn't get it all. They said there is some of it we can't get. They did what they could and...

Yes, it's still in there.

About half way down from my hip and knee on this side and I got a piece on the other side there but it is still in there.

I don't know if I set them off or not in airports, but if you x-ray me you will say what is that?

It's a souvenir.

Yes a souvenir but you know that was a bad experience.

I do not know if I was scared more in the helicopter burning or the fire fight?

Well you are scared in all of them. There is not a situation that you are going to go through when you start hearing an AK rack rounds or if you start seeing things just start to unravel in front of you, you are going to be afraid. But you are going to do what you have got to do, you are going to go the distance no matter how far it is you have just got to do it and you are not going to let up. I did find out some things I didn't really know about myself. In a bad situation or something like that is probably my calmest time on focusing on what I am doing. If something really bad is going on I just found out that I focus real intently on what I was doing. After it was all over and after everything is said I couldn't tell you my name. That is when it really hit me and during a situation like that sure I am scared, sure I am if somebody says they are not scared in those situations they are lying.

You are about to hear how five soldiers got by with a little help from a friend.

Well, there was a fire base above us that was getting overrun up there and the word come down that we was going to CA out.

What does that mean CA out?

CA equals Combat Assault. They are going to fly you in. They are going to get you in either by blowing an LZ out of there or repelling you in or whatever it took to get you in to get those guys some support. Anyway they mustered a bunch of us to the helipad and we was waiting on the final organization of that thing to come together where we would get on a bird and get the heck out of there. You know we saw this bird coming and we knew it was in trouble and of course the helipad was on a little ridge and had a ravine on both sides of us and had a perimeter, wire and mines and everything all the way around it. I mean it was a guarded helipad. The bird was in trouble and I am sure as the pilot got closer to the helipad he knew he had more trouble because he had a whole helipad full of troops and no place to go. The bird you could tell it was smoking and it wasn't stable you could just tell there was something going on. The pilot had enough courage about him to try to take that thing out over the ravine and crash it. He knew he couldn't fly it any further it was in too bad of shape. I saw it go down in the ravine and then go straight up nose up and then it just fell straight backwards, tail rotor first. Down in the bottom of that ravine it was muddy and marshy with constantina wire and claymores and strip flares and stuff set up everywhere. I see the bird start to go up. Me and a fellow from Detroit big tall black fellow his name was Joe and he dwarfed me he was a big man. We took off running and here we went we ran as hard as we could we got to the marsh and got over that constantina stuff that was a pain in the battute. We got to the bird… I got to the bird first and I crawled up in it and it was screaming, the jet was screaming and it was smoking and stunk it was just a wad of twisted metal. I got to where I could pull some of the people out of there I think there were 5 people. One of them had a broken arm, the other had an eye out and the 60 caliber caught one of the guys in the stomach and ripped a big place in him and I think he had a broken leg. It was just all kinds of problems. Anyway I was able to get them freed up enough to slide them back to where I crawled in and Joe could reach them from there. He would grab them and snatch them out of that bird. As he could snatch them out…

Was Joe "Swamp rat"?

No Swamp Rat was Mike Portly from Louisiana Joe was a fellow soldier and Joe was such a big man he carried an M-60 machine gun and he took 2 webbed pistol belts and made a special sling and he carried that thing in that sling he was a monstrous man. I have seen him many a time fire that thing just standing up shooting it. He could really handle that assault but anyway he was grabbing those people and pulling them and sliding them out to where the people could get to them and they got them over to the edge of the ravine and I knew the bird wasn't too stable because the jet was still screaming and the smoke was so thick in it you couldn't hardly see or breath in but I was trying to get them out of there and get out myself. I was afraid that thing was going to blow up. I got out of it and started trying to wade away from it and I hadn't gone just nowhere and that thing went "woooooom" and it burnt the hair off the back of me and I mean it really if I had been in it I wouldn't have had a prayer but I was fortunate the Lord seen a way to get me out of there and get away from it. That thing finally blew.

Author's note:

I heard that sound WOOOOOOOOM once when a gas grill flashed with gas, but I think Henry's woooom was louder.

We got everybody out of there. They couldn't have gotten out on their own?

They was pinned, they were trapped. They could have never made it out of there I don't see any way any of them could have the way the bird was all mangled up and they were in such bad shape I just don't see how anybody could have gotten out of it without help.

They had to be pulled out.

Had to be physically pulled out, just like the guy with the broken arm and his eye hanging out and everything he was just totally out of it you know. The guy had with a machine gun caught him and ripped him up he was in bad shape. They just couldn't have made it out of there.

I do not know whatever happened to them?

I did run across one of the guys that was in the bird. He was a co-pilot and it was just by accident later on I run into this guy and he made it ok. He had some injuries but the rest of them I don't know what happened.

Don't know their names?

Don't know their names don't know… I am sure they all lived they was in bad shape but I am sure they made it ok.

Here is how Henry Carson was rewarded.

Department of the Army Headquarters 101st Airborne Division Air Mobile awarded a soldiers medal. Carson, Henry Private First Class Company A 3rd Battalion 187th Infantry awarded the Soldiers Medal date of action September 13, 1969 theatre Republic of Vietnam. Reason: for heroism not involving actual conflict with a hostile force in the Republic of Vietnam on 13 September, 1969. Private Carson distinguished himself while serving as a medic in Company A 3rd Battalion 187th Infantry as his company was in a staging area on fire support base rendezvous Private Carson spotted a UH1H helicopter attempting to land. It was immediately apparent to him that the aircraft was having mechanical difficulties. On the 3rd attempt to land the aircraft crashed on a hill across from the staging area. Immediately Private Carson gathered a small group of men and led them down to the now burning aircraft. Though the aircraft was burning and rounds were exploding from the heat of the fire Private Carson continuously ran back to the burning aircraft and pulled the dazed and wounded personnel to safety knowing that the aircraft could explode at any time and kill them all. He would not leave the area until all the people had been retrieved from the aircraft and brought to safety. Through his brave and courageous actions he saved many lives and kept others from being injured. Private Carson's personal bravery and devotion to duty were in keeping with the highest traditions of the military services and reflect great credit upon himself and his unit in the United States Army by authority of and direction of the President of the United States under provisions of the act of congress approved 2 July, 1926. There were only 101 of the Soldiers Medal handed out in Vietnam. The first medals were awarded on October 17, 1927 to John Burns and James Martin for heroism during a fire and to James Wilson and Cletus Burnett for saving people from drowning. Noteworthy recipients of the Soldiers Medal include Colin Powell who was awarded the decoration during his 2nd tour in Vietnam when he was injured in a helicopter crash and despite his wounds rescued 2 comrades from the burning wreckage, Henry rescued 5. In 1998 three soldiers were awarded this medal for their intervention in the My Lai massacre including threatening to fire on their own army's troops to make them halt their murderous rampage. In 2001 following a terrorist attack on the Pentagon the US Army issued an unprecedented number of these awards 28 to personnel who risked their own lives to assist their fellow comrades in the wake of the attack. Many kids get a senior trip out of high school Henry Carson's senior trip was Vietnam. He learned to be a medic as well as a soldier he learned to deal with the injury and war. My mom first introduced me to Henry Carson as the go to man to get your bicycle fixed all of Robert Huff Elementary School alumni and East High School alumni should be proud that Henry

Carson represented them so well in Vietnam. Who is Henry Carson literally he is the Veteran Next Door.

Criteria: The Soldier's Medal is awarded to any person of the Armed Forces of the United States, or of a friendly foreign nation who while serving in any capacity with the Army of the United States, distinguished him/herself by heroism not involving actual conflict with an enemy. The same degree of heroism is required as for the award of the Distinguished Flying Cross. The performance must have involved personal hazard or danger and the voluntary risk of life under conditions not involving conflict with an armed enemy. Awards will not be made solely on the basis of having saved a life.

Add to that his heroism in the jungle when he was wounded He deserves a bigger medal. Much bigger.

He still has shrapnel located near his heart.

CHAPTER EIGHT

M-16 and Ben Het

From rifles to artillery to paintball guns

First we are going to learn a little bit about the weapon that most of the soldiers in Vietnam carried. It was the M-16 rifle.

The rifle that has equipped the American soldier for over 40 years. M-16... type semi-or fully automatic assault rifle... country of origin United States... caliber 5.56 by 45 millimeter... cartridge capacity 20 and 30 rounds... muzzle velocity approximately 3281 feet per second... rate of fire 700 to 950 rounds per minute...

There are a lot of people around the planet not breathing anymore because of the M-16. It will do its job.

It was great we had lots of fire-fights where there were lots of orange tracers going that way and green tracers going this way and it became kind of the quintessential rifle of Vietnam... everybody had one.

During the 1950's the US military was searching for a light weight modern assault rifle which could replace the semi-automatic M-1 and its selective fire counter-part the M-14. Eugene Stoner an engineer at the Carmelite factory came up with a workable design.

What Gene Stoner does is he cuts out lots of the pipe-work and creates a much simpler gas system that reloads a smaller lighter round the 5.56 mm round.

Because the weapon fires 5.56 mm you could carry twice the amount of ammunition for the same weight of a 7.62. In some units, soldiers were carrying 1500 rounds of ammunition and that was the standard.

Despite being lighter than the older, bigger hitting rounds, the 5.56 were still capable of causing untold damage.

Because of the particular ballistics of the 5.56 bullet it tumbles when it hits flesh and it causes immense wound damage. Because of this the weapon is good enough to stop an enemy soldier when you fired at him.

The weapon Stoner designed to chamber the new ammo stemmed from work he was conducting with high speed alloys. Usually used for jet engines and jet parts he began to realize that they could also be used to forge new weapons.

It looked very space-aged for the time it was a weapon that had not only aluminum alloy forging that would then be milled or machined, but also had plastic parts on it. So it was not very popular among the traditional crowd.

In Vietnam the M-16 got a chance to prove its worth on the battlefield.

Stoner and the ArmaLite Corporation convinced the US high command they should try fielding some of them in Vietnam to see how they performed. This is called Project Agile. Project Agile is a great success and the soldiers who are using them love them it is simply known as the black rifle, sort of sounds kind of sexy.

But in 1965 the Vietnam War escalated, American troops poured into the jungle and almost immediately problems with the M-16 began to emerge. With alarming regularity the weapon was jamming and young soldiers were dying as a result. When it went to Vietnam it went with a reputation that it never needed to be cleaned and consequently no cleaning kits went with it. Well, it does!

Wary of a scandal the American military began to issue new orders to their troops in Vietnam.

The United States Army looked very closely at this and designed specialized cleaning kits, and even printed a comic book called PM Magazine... Preventive Maintenance Magazine with women soldiers in t-shirts telling the soldiers how to strip their sweet 16 and this type of thing. When these new rifle cleaning kits and training were sent to Vietnam the rifle began to build a reputation as an excellent jungle carbine.

Post-Vietnam the M-16 is still going strong.

Soldiers originally carried a weapon that needed to be serviced a little bit and the US Military sent service technicians to fix those guns or re-build them. We have also got to talk about a little town in Vietnam called Bin Het. It was near the Cambodian border and the Laotian border. If you saw it from the area you would think it was just little a mountain area, you wouldn't think that the soldiers lived and worked in underground bunkers. When they had to cross the camp they sprinted or crawled on their bellies to avoid shelling. US Military was trying to hold on to Bin Het with a staff of about 200 Americans, artillery and Special Forces soldiers. They had to help with about 500 Vietnamese guerrilla fighters they were surrounded by about 10,000 Vietnamese forces located about ½ mile away. You had to go in by helicopter because the roads to Bin Het were blocked, mortars rained down almost daily and you might get bit by a rat a bite from one meant 21 rabies shots in the stomach. The soldier's job was to locate the enemy's guns and direct US planes and guns to fire on them. They did that with something called crater analysis which you will hear about later. The soldiers hugged the ground until the shelling stopped and hoped it didn't hit them. You never worried about the bullet with your name on it you worried about the big blast that was addressed "to whom it may concern". The real problem was the North Vietnamese soldier was only 500 yards away constantly. These are the conditions the soldiers met when they were in Vietnam when they had a gun that wouldn't always work and sometimes they were positioned way out away from the protection of the American infantry guarded by local soldiers and surrounded by the enemy.

Our next Vietnam veteran is Mr. Glenn Palmer. He developed and owned Palmer Pursuit Paintball Shop in Sacramento, California… His primary job in Vietnam was as a gun service tech.

Yes that is close enough… an armament technician.

Glenn started out by saying, "the only way to be in the military is to get into the military.

When I joined I was going to high school, the Vietnam War was commencing its growing stages and I was in ROTC in high school and I was really good at it. I was the consummate soldier if you will, even at that age. So, it was just kind of natural… although my whole family on my dad's side was all navy I was in Army ROTC so I signed up to the Army.

One of my uncles… dad's brother or half-brother actually he was just about 14 months older than I am and he was in Vietnam as a Navy Corpsman. He was working with a Marine Unit on riverboats down in the Delta and was killed there just about 2 or 3 months before I went into the Army.

My mom had a little resistance to that fact. Oh yes she didn't like the idea of me going into the Army at all but as long as I promised to stay out of combat… she knew I wanted to be a combat soldier, but so long as I promised to stay out of the combat jobs and get into a support job she would sign for me. I was only 17 when I graduated. I agreed to that in all faith and honesty.

I did… but opportunities came up later that I volunteered to go to Vietnam because I have a talent that I could help with the M-16 issue. I am 3rd generation… at least 3 generations… a long line of gunsmith's in my family. Several of my dad's brothers were involved in gun smithing as was grandpa and my dad of course. It was just kind of came natural for me I was already a wiz bang with guns by the time I was 15 or 16 years old. I knew I could help with the issues with the M-16.

So, a 17 year old boy convinces his mom it is OK for him to join the military with the Vietnam War going on. They didn't put you right into Vietnam; tell us a little bit about your military experience before you went to Vietnam.

Actually I signed up for the Army over Easter vacation before graduation. I was sworn in just 2 weeks out of high school, basic training in Ft. Lewis, Washington. Went from there to Aberdeen Proving Grounds in Maryland for small arms repair school it was a high end 3rd 4th echelon high depot level stuff. As far as the service every kind of small arm that the military had, small arms up to and including recoils, rifles, mortars and everything else. I managed to come out the honor graduate out of that, got a promotion to E-4… Spec 4, first shot at AIT and they sent me to Alaska. Although I had been volunteering for Vietnam they didn't want me to go they actually wanted me to stay and teach but I am no teacher so they sent me to Alaska and I was building national match stuff for military rifle and pistol teams for a few months. They wouldn't accept my transfers to Vietnam so I cut short my initial enlistment, re-enlisted and chose duty station Vietnam. That is how I got there.

When I first got there I was assigned to a unit that was doing the re-build actually. What I wanted to go in the military for they had a conversion process going on for the M-16's to cure the problems and converting them to the A-1's. I ended up in a shop doing the housings on them. All the ones that were in country had to be worked on when I first got there I was basically in a unit that was supporting 173rd Airborne out of Quin Yon in the central coast area of South Vietnam.

It was on the coastal region as opposed to later I ended up on the Western border inland in country. I went from the M-16 rebuild shop there basically when we finished up with the 173rd they sent me out to Pleiku which was into the highlands up into the central highlands closer to the Western border for an armament shop up there which was supporting the busiest artillery or artillery regiment in country. I was still an armament tech with small arms training but ended up working on big guns, artillery and tank turrets and stuff more than anything else.

You had to replace those barrels after 300 shots. Full charge they were high powered shots and you know a lot of power behind those things and the barrels were only good for about 300 rounds they start burning out inside and metal fatigue.

What were we shooting at? Well at that point in time at Bin Het we were shooting where we weren't supposed to be. Most of our rounds were going into Cambodia and Laos at a time before we were supposed to there.

What was over there was the Ho Chi Minh trail. The primary function of the artillery battery at Bin Het was to interdict on the Ho Chi Minh Trail.

The Trail is kind of a multi-trail bit when the battery first went out there. The Trail was just on the other side of the border a few miles away. They kept moving it as we got closer... as we got closer they moved in and out to where they were... we were only a couple of miles from the border, the Trail anywhere from 2 – 10 miles 2 – 15 miles inside Cambodia and Laos is where their ammo was going.

The North Vietnamese were not just letting us shoot at them without throwing something back. They had beat upon Bin Het for a long time. Matter of fact they need to get rid of us. There had been a long siege since February of 1969. The camp was notable for being the site of a tank battle between the US Army and the Peoples Army of Vietnam. One of the few such encounters during the Vietnam War.

Bin Het was a Special Forces camp located almost 300 miles northeast of Saigon, six miles from Cambodia/Laotian borders and was attacked by thousands of North Vietnamese soldiers using artillery and mortars. Defended by about 250 American Soldiers and about 450 Montagnard. A four month siege. Billed as the American Dien Bien Phu by the North Vietnamese it was important to keep the supply roads from Dak To and Kontum open or reopened as required. Casualties among US Artillery men were high and Glen Palmer was one of the replacements.

*Stars and Stripes Thursday, June 26, 1969

SAIGON (UPI) – American B52 bombers unloaded hundreds of thousands of pounds on NVA Troops concentrations threatening the Allied Specials Forces camp at Ben Het, military spokesmen said Wednesday. The B52s struck in two raids Tuesday night and early Wednesday, dumping their bombs on targets in jungles about three miles south and two miles north of the Special Forces camp, 285 miles Northeast of Saigon. Reverberations from at least 180 tons of bombs rolled over the beleaguered outpost, which sits near the South Vietnam's, Cambodian and Laotian borders.

Tuesday, Military spokesman reported Allied troops at the Special Forces Camp were resupplied by truck convoy but remained under pressure from NVA gunners. They said there had been continuing battles with NVA troops in the jungle. A spokesman reported that at least 183 NVA soldiers were killed around the outpost in a series of firefights on Monday.

I didn't get out there till July. They had beat up on Bin Het hard and then even after the siege was over every time they wanted to do something or move stuff down the Trail or get a spot to where they could beat up on another camp or whatever they had to come beat us down first so hopefully we wouldn't be firing support against whatever they were doing. It was a constant thing for the bulk of the time I was there.

Actually when I went out there it was the start of the monsoon season. When I first went out there it was all wet and muggy like I mean we are talking mud because of the vehicles and tracks and just the ground had no vegetation on it, and on the fire-base and the mud was 3 or 4 feet deep. We had to walk around on steel plating every place.

The problems the M-16 rifle was having?

The biggest problem with it is it just had no tolerance for dirt or any corrosion on the ammo or that sort of thing a few little odds and ends. The M-16 was prone to sticky cartridges in the chamber when you shoot them. It couldn't extract it so couldn't put the next round in so you were a dead duck in the water with the gun. Dead guns cause dead soldiers.

It depends on the type of jam for the most part. Throw it down and grab another one. In a fire-fight somebody is going to be down and not be able to use their weapon so you grab theirs. But that was like I said, "the gun got notorious early on. The military just thought it was a cleaning issue. They came out with new manuals and cleaning tools or what have you. Then they came out with the conversion for the A-1 which was largely just a matter of changing some tolerances, make them a little less susceptible to the problems with dirt or grit, hard chroming which we called stellite of the liner of the barrel. It was a barrel liner and internal parts such as the bulk carrier. Changed the gas tube configuration a little bit, recoil buffer the first attempt that was even before the A-1 was the forward assist a little latch that you tried to pump it close in case stuff was around the chamber. With a cartridge stuck in the chamber that forward assist didn't help matters any? There were 17 parts involved in the conversion and a lot of it… some of them didn't have to do with jamming but stupid little things like the original flash suppressor was good at getting caught up in the brush so they put one with a ringer on the front of it.

In those days many of the combat soldiers if they had a problem with the M-16 often tried to carry an AK because it was… it had a reputation for just never fouling up. Although the Chi Com versions of them were kind of dangerous. The AK is what the North Vietnamese soldiers were carrying?

And they carried it because it could get dirty and those kinds of thing but it wasn't as accurate and didn't have the long range abilities.

It was a little sloppier so it wasn't quite as accurate per se but as far as a marksmanship went but they were real durable. They rattled and had a very distinct sound.

Yes built sloppy they would work when dirty. You could throw them in the mud, pick them up, shake them off and keep on shooting. The M-16 wouldn't tolerate that. I mean it was a finely made rifle, it is! The M-16 is a very fine gun but it just wasn't well suited for jungle warfare.

Yes but it is with all the improvements... it is still the same basic format but a whole lot different gun.

In the shop I was in we got guns in by the carnex load just racks and racks and racks of them we would get 100's of them at a time and get a whole unit's rifles in and we would exchange them with units that we had already re-built. We would go through those then carry those to another unit and take their old guns and work them through that way.

I modified my own M-16.

I increased the rate of fire a little bit more than anything else when I did mine it was more like what they are today. The older ones were about 700 rounds per minute mine was about 900 with the recoil buffer and gas tube changes and that sort of thing but I was a gunsmith that is what I did.

OK always tinkering on the gun. Let's talk a little bit about your personal experience in Vietnam as far as fear and the sense of danger or things like that you bring home with you that sometimes you wish you could shake.

Never shake it... you learn to live with it and to kind of shut it off but you never really shake it. It doesn't go away.

If the North Vietnamese were dropping mortar rounds I had read a little story about you could tell where the mortars were if you measured the angle of the hole or something like that?

Actually it is called crater analysis which actually I did some of that. I was the one who was stupid enough to go out and do it in the rain and figure out by looking at the angle that the round hit the ground you could dig down into the crater and actually find a fuse or enough of the round to tell first of all what kind of round it is and then there was some other hardware that we could stick down into the hole that you could get an alignment and actually measure the angle that it hit the ground and the direction in which it came from by putting a compass along this wad that is stuck in the ground. Once you knew what it was, the direction it came from and the angle it hit the ground then you could calculate back fire. The control center could then calculate back just to pretty close to where it came from. Then, we would transfer that information over to the big guns and start shooting back at them.

Oh absolutely matter of fact the attack on Bin Het was pretty much focused... pretty much the same thing that they had done to the French at Dien Bien Phu some years before. General Giap's soldiers overwhelmed and kick them out and took over. But that was in the northern part of the country we were down south and they needed to kick us out of there before they could own Kontum Province.

I replaced a wounded technician. I had been with the unit at the support unit and Pleiku just a short period of time actually when he got wounded. I had been out there one time to help him. I don't know it was about 3 weeks before he got wounded. When he got hit it was within just a few days they were looking for somebody to take his place I said well I will go. I have been out there. So I took my box of tech manuals I needed some help with the big guns the hydraulics and that sort of thing on the big guns that I wasn't as familiar with. Took a few books with me and jumped on a helicopter and went out.

I was on a transport helicopter, a Huey Slick. We had door gunners. They were hauling wounded out and replacements in and all we were flying along probably 1000 or 1200 feet or so I guess making tracks getting out to the fire-base and we took some fire. The first indication was the bump bump bump on the outsides sounded like hammers hitting the machine, hitting the helicopter. The pilot put it into a dive headed into the deck and was doing all kinds of evasive maneuvers and hell I... far as I knew we were crashing. Scared the hell out of me that was my first experience with getting shot at then because I couldn't do anything... if I had been on the ground at least you can shoot back. But up there I was without any means to do anything and the door gunners were busy shooting at the ground although I don't know if they could see anything but... then we were only 10 or 5 miles from the fire-base when that happened. We got to the fire-base and landed and just about the time the bird set down we started taking mortar fire on the fire-base. First it was machine-gun fire then mortar fire?

We don't know what machine gun or small arms fire it was 3 or 4 rounds was all that hit the chopper on the way in. It sounds like hammers hitting on a garbage can hitting on that bird. I mean everybody knew we were shot at but... the worst part of the thing was one of the incoming rounds as we landed pretty close on the other side and those of us that got out on the left side of the helicopter we ran around and put 3 of the guys back on it that came out there with us. They got wounded by mortar rounds that was my

What happened to me when I got back from Vietnam? I still had time in service left and actually I was supposed to go to flight school but they canceled the flight school while I was home and sent me to the 82nd Airborne Division Ft. Bragg, NC to work on some of their sophisticated weaponry that they had on a new tank.

Actually it was the targeting system for a new tank supposed to be an amphibious tank that they had that was fired both conventional and wire guided missiles. The targeting system supposedly I was supposed to not work on them and I had to learn it was all OJT when I got there.

On the job training. There I was with the 82nd Airborne. But, things changed. The military just wasn't going the way I had expected and when I was not allowed to go to flight school that kind of turned me off to the whole concept of career training. Then there were other things that took place I got into sport parachuting I never did go to jump school but I got into sport parachuting while I was at Ft. Bragg. I got onto the demo team and I stayed in the Army. I could have been on the Golden Knights but that wasn't in the cards… there were things I had to do that I didn't want to do in order to make that work. I just said to heck with it and got out.

Then I went to New Jersey? I took a job… I was in transition… project transition going to school learning a civilian job for a couple of months before I got actually discharged. I took a police science course which was actually police academy and I ended up when a recruiter came down from Trenton, NJ and maxed their test and he said do you want to work I said I have never been in New Jersey before, I get out of the Army 15th of May on the 1st of June I am ready to go and June 1 I was sworn into the Union City New Jersey Police Department.

Glenn Palmer was a cop in New Jersey. Then involved in the paint ball industry working or becoming a master of the paint ball gun?

1984… taking my son fishing we drove by a paint ball field. I had heard about it very briefly then it was The National Survival Game. When we saw the paint ball field I said I gotta check into this. It is something I am going to be good at. I did… by the time I played just a couple of times I was hooked and it was my gun smithing background it was natural for me to start tinkering with the guns. It just kind of blew up from there. It was all a matter of solving problems early on what were the limitations we had… when was I the most vulnerable… how many times did I get shot while I changed the CO_2 cartridges so I came up with a quick change. We needed better efficiency so I figured out how to make them get 30 shots instead of 10 out of a 12 gram and just kind of went from there. When I come up with the quick change unit I put a little ad in the magazine and a lot of people wondered what I could do with their equipment and I told my (inaudible) who was in the over-head door business doing garage doors and I was managing the commercial department of a garage door company and I said I gotta... I am a single parent and need to be home with my son and this is a perfect opportunity so I gave him my notice and set about doing paint ball equipment.

Author's note:

I played a little paintball myself. I had a playing field called Splat-1 Adventures. You were one of the guys on the west coast and I was in the Appalachians playing paint ball and running a small field and you were the guys that were making my equipment obsolete every 10 days.

To stay competitive I had to keep retooling my paintball gun fleet. But anyway everybody knows you in paint ball as a player and as a super machine shop operator for paint ball and your family has grown up in the paint ball business. But you all do something else that I admire a lot. You are a motorcycle rider and you are member of the Patriot Guard.

Yes, Patriot Guard riders formed at the end of '05 fall of '05. Pretty much a Veteran's motorcycle group but you don't have to be a Veteran to join. There was a group of crazies out of Kansas that were protesting at military funerals made... their thing was that our soldiers are dying because it is God's wrath upon America for tolerating homosexuality. That was their thing. But, more importantly they were really causing misery for the families of our fallen and American Legion riders got together and said this just can't stand so they started a group called the Patriot Guard riders basically designed to be a counter to the protesters to make sure that they just can't bother the families. A bunch of flags and loud motorcycles keep the protesters from being heard basically is all it boils out to. There is about 200,000... over 200,000 of us nationwide now from all walks of life every aspect and it is Patriotguard.org is the best way to learn about them. There are too many of us from Vietnam that came home to a real ugly situation and it just that can't be allowed to ever happen again.

Tell me about the note in one of your emails that said you had heard a newsman make a statement right after I think the first Iraq war can you tell me a little about that?

Everybody was tuned in to what was going on in the first Gulf War and there was a ticker tape parade in New York after a bunch of the guys came home right after you know it was a 100 hour war. It was one of the new anchors and I can't remember which one it was but had made a comment, "I bet there are a bunch of Vietnam veterans who are sitting at home asking what they did wrong. What did I do? Why didn't I get this kind of reception when I came home?" I was sitting there crying, YES! Crying!, what did we do? Up until then I had been pretty much in a shell. I hadn't even talked about Vietnam. It was embarrassing too many people were disrespecting us! It was awful hard. After that it was a different story. I didn't mind talking to people, I sought out other vet's and just kind of tried to make it all better. Then the Patriot Guard Riders come along and I ride with a lot of my brothers and sisters. Veteran's from Vietnam or anybody who has served in the military pretty much that rides a motorcycle is pretty much involved in the Patriot Guard Riders.

The healing process is ongoing it will probably be going on for generations but, we need to hear your stories and I appreciate your spending the time to talk to me about what is going on. We had a problem during Vietnam we had a population at home that had a hard time separating the individual soldiers doing their duty from the actual politics of that unpopular war.

The people who gained by dissing the American soldier I think most of them will go down in history as it won't speak very well of them.

Mr. Palmer said, I have had a lot of those people apologize. As I have met them over the years in my travels.

I said to Glenn, "You soldiers from Vietnam are going to have to tell your stories so that we know what you did and what you went through."

Glenn said, "We do now".

Yes, Glenn. I've got to wrap up here but I sure do appreciate your talking to me I think this has been a great interview.

My pleasure my friend.

We are going to be talking again real soon.

I am always up for that I will talk to you any chance I get.

I know you are a good friend to veterans.

Educate me on history.

That is a long story, too.

The Patriot Guard Riders mission statement says this:

> The Patriot Guard Riders is a diverse amalgamation of riders from across the nation. We have one thing in common besides motorcycles we have an unwavering respect for those who have risked their lives for America's freedom and security. If you share this respect please join us. We don't care what you ride or if you ride what your political views are or whether you are a hawk or a dove. It is not a requirement that you be a Veteran, it doesn't matter where you are from or what your income is. You don't even have to ride the only prerequisite is respect. Our main mission is to attend the funeral services of the fallen American heroes as invited guests of the family. Each mission we undertake has two basic objectives show our sincere respect for our fallen heroes, their families and communities, shield the mourning families and their friends from interruptions created by any protestor or group of protestors. We accomplish the latter through strictly legal and non-violent means. To those of you who are currently serving and fighting for the freedoms of others at home and abroad please note that we are backing you. We honor and support you with every mission we carry out. We are praying for a safe return home for all.

When a soldier goes to war he doesn't set political policy or military strategy or tactics. As I have heard, "His is not to reason why only do or die." When he comes home salute him, hear his stories, share his pain and thank him.

It's the least we can do.

Ear Plugs required!

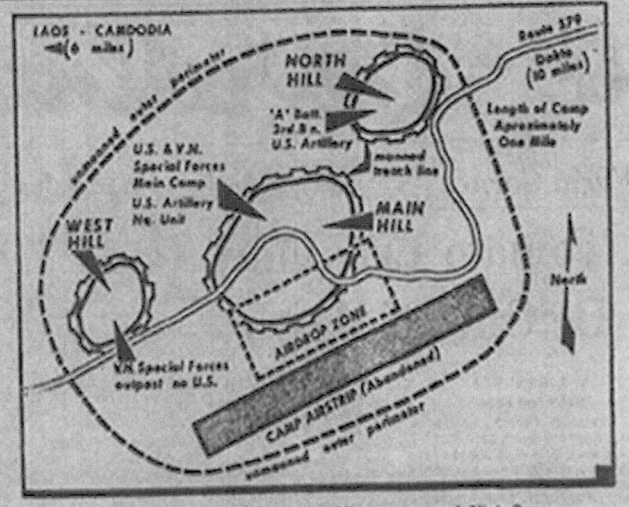

12—DAILY INTELLIGENCER JOURNAL, LANCASTER, PA., SATURDAY, JUNE 28, 1969

Ben Het Supplied By Air

SAIGON (AP) — U.S. and South Vietnamese pilots, threading through monsoon storm clouds, maintained an aerial lifeline into embattled Ben Het Friday, slashing at enemy gun positions and dropping supplies by parachute.

The Viet Cong's clandestine radio boasted that the Green Beret camp still is surrounded, with the U.S.-advised South Vietnamese forces there forced into a "desperate position."

The U.S. Command in Saigon considers the Ben Het campaign a major test of how the South Vietnamese handle themselves against the North Vietnamese and the Viet Cong. The Saigon government has expressed hope South Vietnamese forces can take on more of the fighting to relieve U.S. troops, 25,000 of whom are due to leave by the end of August.

NOT UNDER SEIGE

The 700 defenders of the hilltop outpost—Vietnamese civilian irregulars, Green Beret advisers and American artillermen—probably would agree with the enemy's assessment of the situation. Allied spokesmen have stated that the frontier camp is not under siege, but the only supplies delivered there since Tuesday have been by air drop or helicopter.

Although figures were not available for Friday, U.S. Air Force twin-engined cargo planes dropped 40 tons of supplies into Ben Het Wednesday and Thursday. At the same time, fighter-bombers protecting the slow cargo planes hit enemy positions with 17 tons of bombs, napalm and rockets.

Map shows Ben Het, the Green Beret camp under siege by North Vietnamese and Viet Cong.

CHAPTER NINE

The Beast was out there!

Excerpts form the book written by
General James E. Shelton USA Retired

The Beast Was Out There:

This is a direct quote from a book called "The Beast Was Out There" by
General James E. Shelton USA Retired and it is related to a Vietnam event
that happened in 1967.

It is a weekend. It is Saturday morning your family, your wife, children and your parents are driving to another city to spend the weekend with friends. The weather is not too good, it is a hard drive but the family has made the trip a number of times before. You found yourself in this position before. You have to work this weekend but you hope to be able to join the family before the weekend is over. You leave for work early in the morning. While at work you receive a phone call there has been an accident all in the car are either dead or seriously injured come to the morgue to identify the victims.

That is a civilian correlation to what happened October 17, 1967 to one of our military leaders who was my guest on a Sunday morning radio broadcast and is also going to be the topic of our show today. What would you do? If you were in that situation? You knew them all, you loved them all, you know maybe half of them are dead and half of them are wounded but, you don't know which ones and now you are getting ready to go find out. I had a co-host that day. You know him he is Mr. Tom Mercer, you read about Tom earlier in the book, and he introduced me to General Shelton.

The battle of Ong Thanh was in Vietnam and it occurred on October 17, 1967. That morning there was a little over 20 helicopters loaded full of men maybe 8 men in each helicopter going off on a mission. On that mission I have heard different numbers. On the internet I found that there were about 142 to 155 in the stories and in the book on other internet sites I heard there may have been as up to 160 American soldiers. The battle was in Ong Thanh Stream Binh Duong Province, South Vietnam. The winner of the battle depends on who you talk to. Most people say it was a Viet Cong victory. The belligerents were the United States vs the Viet Cong not the North Vietnamese Army but the Viet Cong. Representing Stage two of General Giap's master military strategy for victory in Vietnam. The Units involved were the 1st Infantry Division "The Big Red One", the Second Battalion, 28th Infantry Regiment and they were up against the 9th Division 271st Regiment plus the Rear Service Group 83, and what is called the C1 Company so approximately 155 to 160 American Soldiers vs 1400 Viet Cong. The casualties? You know when I started the story I told you about a car wreck and you don't know who is dead and who is wounded and besides that they didn't say who wasn't hurt, but there were 64 American dead, 2 missing and 75 wounded. We are not sure of the exact number it says unknown US claim was 103 dead. So that is what we are talking about. The situation that lead one man to write a book and to carry his personal campaign on to find out exactly what happened and making sure that if he could prevent it from happening again he would do so. So Tom Mercer is helping understand the battle involving his fellow Big Red one brothers who were the soldiers of A Company and D Company?

They were about half strength there was a B Company and a C Company. I understood that B Company was working on supplies and C Company had gone off on another mission.

So we have A Company and D Company walking in single file up a mountain, not a mountain but up a jungle trail.

It wasn't heavy jungle overhead. The canopy wasn't heavy but you couldn't see more than 30 or 40 meters ahead of you. I believe A Company was in the lead.

They walked into what is called an L-shaped ambush. An L-shaped ambush is a deadly ambush. If you happen to walk into it you are in trouble. But you never know when you are walking into something like it, or that there is an ambush even there. An L-shaped ambush is where the enemy is lined up in front of you and either down one side to the left or to the right and the side that they don't have men lined up on they have booby traps and a couple men over there just in case like the 2nd or 28th had gotten away or got out they would be waiting on them. They had snipers up in trees, big booby traps up in trees and machine guns all over and they were good.

The American soldiers' kind of thought they were going into the jungle, they were going to be the ones opening up the can of whoop-ass right?

They thought they were going to go in and beat the Viet Cong up.

They did not know what was ahead of them. They didn't know really what was out there. They knew something was out there because they had been following some people who had come in and out and back into the jungle which is a bad thing to do anyway.

In the book THE BEAST WAS OUT THERE authored by General Shelton and who was previously a major in charge of those men before they went into battle. Actually it was a couple weeks before they went into the battle he got transferred out and became S3for THE BIG RED ONE.

S3 Brigade Staff Mission:

1st Information Operations (IO) Command operations staff (**S3**) serves as the principle staff section for all matters concerning training, operations, plans, force development and modernization.

These men of the two companies, though he had been in battle with them were not quite his kids but they were his boys?

Yes indeed most officers think of them that way, as their children because if something happens to them they have to explain why and they better have an answer.

So we have an Army Major who had taken care of these young men and had watched them get hurt and watched them go into battle and watched them and had developed a comradery with those men.

When he went back to the rear he was in charge of radio communications with the field, the Battalion Commander and the Company Commander. It was his new responsibility to keep track of everything that went on.

He was on the radio listening to the battle?

He was devastated as he listened to the battle. It tore him up.

Sure it did because those were those were his boys... when they were calling out the names of the dead and the wounded he knew them.

I can see now why he wanted to start that chapter out with the Twilight Zone how everybody that he knew and was close to all of a sudden were in a battle where they weren't coming out alive. He felt glad that he was alive but he felt bad that he wasn't out there with those guys. You always think that maybe you could have done something, which I don't think would have been possible.

There was nothing he could do.

He wanted to, but was powerless to help.

Inside the book he talked about wanting to take over command on the radio, but the Battalion Commander at that time was not going to allow that. He kept command of the battle.

I asked Tom Mercer before we went any further what is it about battlefield situations that develop all the comradery because I could see it with him and his friends when I attended one of his reunions in Nashville, Tennessee. I spoke of it in the prologue. It is life-long isn't it?

Yes it is, well if you don't have it out on the field during a battle you got problems because if nobody likes you, you could be the one getting shot, and you just don't give people a lot of crap and you become real good friends. You are not out there for medals, you are not out there for the recognition, and you are out there to stay alive and make it home and help your friend make it home. That lasts a long time even if you haven't seen that person for years you've always got him in your mind and what you did or what he did to help you stay alive. So it is very important.

These guys were the "Black Lions"?

Yes the "Black Lions" 2nd of the 28th

What was your unit called?

The 1st of the 18th "Dog Faced Charlie's" "Swamp Rats"

OK "Swamp Rats" then the "Black Lions"

They were a great unit they were great they were good so it was just something that happen.

"Just a Thang" as it were.

They simply walked into a spot where nobody was going to walk out or not many walked out.

You know 20 helicopters flew 160 men in, before the day was over they only needed 5 helicopters to bring them back.

You can just imagine the looks on the faces of the helicopter crews that didn't go into the battle but sent all these men out that morning.

It had to take a toll on each and every one of them.

That is amazing, so it was a Tuesday morning October 17, 1967 and the Black Lions from Company A and the Black Lions from D Company walked into an ambush and almost nobody survived. They lost all the men within the first 30 minutes.

Company A was gone almost wiped out.

So then Company D had the wounded.

The officers were trying to get up there but the fire was so heavy there was no way they could get up there. They tried; a lot of them got killed trying…

And even the Commanding Officer was killed is that correct?

Yes, the First Sergeant, they were all killed.

The Commanding Officer had a father who was a famous officer who served during World War II. He was a great guy, a good guy things just got mixed up that day.

He was a good person who maybe had some personal problems at home whose father had led the Big Red One in World War II.

So now here the son was inside the Big Red One in the Viet Nam conflict.

Exactly I am not sure how long he had been in charge of the 2nd of the 28th but General Shelton said he was a good person and a good guy you know if Shelton says something I believe I would take it to heart.

That is the setting, General Shelton, then a major, listening to the actual battle as it occurred.

Soon you will meet Sgt Gribble, who was a radio man at the time. Major Shelton had pulled him out of the front lines and put him in the communications headquarters?

Right he needed an RTO. He worked on the radio. It is a very big thing, you have to have a good RTO if you don't you are in a lot of trouble. So he needed a new RTO and he looked around. He wanted a squad leader and usually you don't get squad leaders to hold a radio. He found Gribble and he asked him and he didn't want to go but he talked him into it. That was… he knew all the tags and codes… the lingo then Major Shelton thought that would be great for the Black Lions.

Sgt. Gribble's fate kind of changed the Major's life.

He carries a picture around of Ray Neal Gribble for 47, 46 years now and he shows it to everybody he is proud of it. He tried to get Ray to stay in the rear with him but Ray said I need to get back out there with my men and 2 weeks later he was killed.

The Battle of Ong Thanh.

Ong Thanh, see it is even hard to pronounce sometimes just a little place in South Vietnam where so many lives were changed. I tried to find a way to explain this battle to you but I think I am just going to let the people who were at the battle do it so pay attention if you want to hear a good story.

(Translated from Vietnamese (Viet Cong) speaker) B-52's dropped bombs that night so I knew they would attack the next morning. Where I was there was lone tree left standing. On the street a monkey kept climbing up and then half-way down the tree. Soldiers asked for permission to shoot the monkey because they hadn't eaten for 5 days. I thought of the monkey how similar its situation was to ours it just wanted to live like us. I ordered the soldiers not to shoot it.

Meanwhile in the American camp: When we came in for breakfast that morning I would say there is going to be a big fight today got plenty of ammunition? (Oh yes sir yes sir)

Well they told us we were going to a place that was going to be pretty rough and that is all. They didn't tell us what was waiting on us. Not sure they knew. You had no choice you just went.

I do not believe that Colonel Allen had ever moved with a command group on the ground until the 17th. He was new to the company, and the son of a great Big Red commander.

Alpha Company was leading and right behind Alpha Company was Delta Company there was like 130 of us and I thought this is one of the biggest forces we ever sent out. There is no way they are going to mess with us.

From the Viet Cong positions. (Translated from Vietnamese) They seemed ready; they had their own observation posts. We had scouts in the trees they were watching the Americans move up and let them get within 30 or 40 meters.

An American reported. "I happened to see a tree move to my left front, I don't remember who was sitting behind me but I did tap him on the shoulder and I pointed to the tree and I took my M-16 and I put it on automatic and then he looked at it and he said there is nothing there."

Suddenly there was this series of clicking sounds and then the battle started. It sounded like every weapon in the world was being fired at that point from all directions on us.

I saw Breeden fall; I saw Ceresco fall and I saw Gribble fall.

We heard a lot of fire ahead of us which we knew was Alpha Company.

They were firing out of the trees, they were firing out of bunkers all you could shoot at was muzzle flashes.

We had 160 men.

(From Vietnamese) We had more soldiers than they did but we didn't have the same fire power. They were within 10 meters we wanted to stay close so we couldn't be bombed.

A few minutes I guess or whatever a huge Claymore mine went off that hit Farrell and hit Sgt. Johnson who was lying next to me. To this day I see them just lying in their blood. FUTURE PTSD?

Alpha Company disappeared and now the fire was directed against us, against Delta Company.

(From Vietnamese) Then the L collapsed only soldiers attacked on the right flank.

It was the second bunch of firing that started killing my guys. When I came back to see Col. Allen I said, do something! Bring artillery give me the artillery give me the command give me something. I thought about the Mutiny on the Bounty there that ran through my mind that should I take over?

They were coming in right on us. I seen one run up to one of our machine guns and blow a Claymore mine.

Sikorski our machine gunner is dead! Somebody get the gun! Get the gun!

I didn't give him that much time! Too many people were dead. Too many people were wounded. I could not... couldn't even have run away because that would have left Alpha Company's dead and wounded.

Lt. Welch was moving around among the people telling them where to fire I seen him get hit at least 2 times and I seen him fall a couple of times and he would get right back up.

It is just good for the men to see you are up and moving because if you are cowering down it makes them think it is really bad.

I went to Colonel Allen and he was looking at a picture and my words to him were "What the hell are you doing looking at a picture and I am going to fire artillery" and he said "no you can't fire artillery because Alpha is the lead" "Sir, Alpha Company is gone! I am firing" and a bullet came overhead and hit him right in the helmet but it just blew the top part of his head away. When he fell forward he fell like that and I could then see it was a picture of 3 little girls.

Anybody in the shade was safe; anybody that was in the sunshine was getting shot.

I can't remember his last name, but he is looking at me and reaching out saying, "Help Me! Help Me!, and every time he tried to move to get some cover they would shoot him. If I had got over the fear and felt braver I probably could have run out there and saved his life, you know. Be like Superman just run out and grab him... boom... and back. Then all of a sudden they just disappeared it was all over, they were gone.

(From Vietnamese) Those they see have no mission so they attacked and left the field.

I went through I don't know how many different bodies crawling around trying to find somebody that was alive. I mean there was people with no faces, arms and legs missing.

I was there when the firing stopped. I do not know when I became unconscious the final time.

I looked around and everything was just dead silence. It was just such a lonely feeling.

142 Americans went out 64 died as a result of that fight and almost everyone else was wounded.

We were just massacred, just massacred and my men… my men… what can you do… just massacred.

(From Vietnamese) The Viet Cong came back to the battlefield and they were amazed at what they had done. They all shuddered too because they realized that they were small in frame compared to the American soldiers. What he is saying is that they never understood why the Americans came to Vietnam anyway and attacked them.

5 helicopters brought them back from the battle.

If it took 20 helicopters to move us in and out of a night defensive position and this day there were 5 helicopters. This Sergeant was standing there this grizzled Sergeant and the tears were just running down his face and he said "my God sir is that all that is left?"

The next call I got was that of Major Shelton to see if I could go down and identify bodies so I went down and I saw all my buddies and I just felt like how could anything be worse than this?

In some of these body bags there were just parts.

In the search and destroy operations that characterized the war in this part of Vietnam it is usually a case of search and not find. This time practically by accident the Americans and the Viet Cong did find each other.

We were ordered to make ourselves available in front of the Alpha Company area, they had set some chairs up and we were debriefed before we went into the hooch to interview with CBS news that we were NOT to mention that it was an ambush. From my perspective I was pissed because it was an ambush I felt at that time and I still do now that there was a cover up.

I understand why General Hay didn't want to use the word ambush because an ambush means you are incompetent. The problem is what was said about it was a spin which made it sound like this battle was part of something bigger which was very successful.

It was a total fabrication of what really happened. It was like a show, like a victory. The Americans held them off blah blah 103 enemy killed and all this stuff and that haunted me. I am not a cynic but I started to become one of history as it was taught to me, what the hell… who the hell knows what really happened.

Author's note:

You know, several battles in American history have been reported poorly. For some reason someone decides to misrepresent or to flat out not tell the American people the truth!

Listening to the battle with Tom Mercer there was a description of three men that fell and the third one that fell was Ray Gribble.

"Yes," said Tom.

Ray Neal Gribble is the same man that we talked about earlier that General or Major Shelton at the time was attached to because he wanted a radio man to stay back where it was safe.

He didn't want to be where it was safe. He wanted to go back out in the field with his men and they were needing some better leadership than what they had. I guess, but he just wanted to be back out with his people. So he had bonded with his men just like Major Shelton had bonded with all the men. It was OK for him to put himself at risk because he felt better because he knew he could do more good with them than he could do in the tent or back at the headquarters.

I think he felt kind of bad having his men out there and him living the good life in the field. He was in the rear, clean clothes and good meals, but he wanted to be back out in the field. He was offered safety not because he was a coward but because he was good at communicating on the radio and could keep everybody together. He didn't want that, he wanted to be with his men.

Author's note:

Tom wrote a song about Sgt. Gribble.

Tom replied, "I sure did! Ray Neal Gribble's son wanted me to write it for him and he told me all the facts and I put it down and wrote it and this is the way it came out.

It is about one of the men who died on October 17, 1967:

Sgt. Gribble
LYRICS: (Tom Mercer)

October 1967 was a day that went wrong
Friends died in a battle that they called Ong Thanh
They all died heroes fighting in the far away land
And all were good soldiers
And real good men

They were young men who fought hard that day
They had been in battle and fought the right way
Most men in A Company knew how and what to do
And one was Ray Neal Gribble
Was a squad leader too

At the end of September I needed an RTO
And call signs of battalions he would have to know
Being a good squad leader Ray Neal would be right
Good with men and the radio so I gave him the invite

He came with me but was looking back
A man of God carried a bible in his pack
Ray Neal was a leader and his men needed him back

That is a song about a soldier that was closer to his men and his unit than he was to the overall command. And cared more for his brothers than for his safety.

He knew he could have stayed back and been safe but he went into the battle and it cost him his life.

Right after the battle the Viet Cong pulled away real fast. 1) They had another mission to do but 2) they knew if they hung around they were going to get bombarded by American artillery or American B-52's. So they pulled away and that gave the American's time to go in and get the wounded and pull them out. When I looked at the video I saw all those faces of those men that were on the helicopters when they realized that just remnants were coming back and you know they left at 8:00 am and from what I can learn that battle was over by noon… by lunch time.

It didn't take long.

So in 4 hours they walked up the trail and ran into an ambush, an L-shaped ambush. They were in single file. They ran into a line of Viet Cong.

Yes, and that tapping you heard in the tree on the recording… that was a person up there watching. He had a spot marked out. When the first guy got to that spot that one Company, the whole company all the American Soldiers of the Big red One, Black Lions. Company A were in that ambush. That is when the Viet Cong opened fire.

Author's Note:

I wondered, so I asked.

"What would have been standard procedure when the ambushers opened up? If you had a straight line column what would have been the procedure for the soldiers? "Would they have fanned out?"

Tom answered, "Well, no probably not in this situation. It happened so fast. You don't have too much time to think. You need to make good decisions.

Most of them probably jumped to one side and the other side rotates if you can think of doing that. But it hit them so fast they didn't have time most of them were killed before they could hit the ground.

But if you jumped to the right you might have jumped into mines.

If you jumped to the left you would have run into the other wall of the L.

So, all of a sudden you have danger on all three sides and you couldn't back up because you were in a big long line.

Exactly and I don't care what the news team said, that was an ambush. You don't have snipers up in trees just walking through the jungle.

No not by accident! No way!

The author of the book, THE BEAST WAS OUT THERE was a Major when it happened.

He told us the whole story about that battle.

Since he was an S3 and he was in the rear he knew what was going on. He was on the radio on every one of those calls that went in and out he knew what happened.

He was probably 45 or so at that time. So he was a generation away from the kids that were in the fight. He was not part of the baby boom these kids were the first issue of the baby boom coming in and they were his… they were his boys

He loved those young men.

He listened on the radio while they died not one at a time but sometimes 2 or 3 at a time.

Then he heard their names being called out as fallen or KIA or wounded in action.

Author's note: I listened to him tell the story by phone on my radio program. I could hear the tremble in his voice, the sadness in the telling of the story. The love he had for Sgt. Gribble. And the pride he felt by telling the story of his men.

If you carry that hurt and pain for years, it takes its toll. It does not go away. It's why they call it POST Traumatic Stress.

CHAPTER TEN

Dak To

General Giap takes the next phase of the war
from guerillas to proffesional soldiers

General Giap was such a powerful force in the Vietnam War.

He thought into the future, knowing how he wanted the Americans to act
and behave in battle.

He led them by conclusion, and got them in position to kill.

General Giap, remember him? He entered a new phase of his master plan
when he initiated the battle of Dak To. He wanted to lure American

Soldiers and their allies out of the cities in preparation for the upcoming Tet offensive. Those of us who were at home watching TV at dinner time saw the battles as they entered our living rooms. From November 3 to November 27, 1967 the battles raged, Then the People's Army of Vietnam withdrew. Presumably in hindsight to prepare for the Tet Offensive. The intense fighting grew quiet.

The battles on the hill masses south and southeast of Đắk Tô became some of the hardest-fought and bloodiest battles of the Vietnam War. In 1967, under the overall direction of commander of Special Forces in Vietnam, Col. Jonathan Ladd, the camp began to take mortar fire. Ladd flew in, organized reconnaissance and identified the entrenched hill bunker complex as the source of the shelling.

Author's note:

Journalist Neil Sheehan quoted Col Ladd recommending, unsuccessfully, to Major General William R. Peers: "For God's sake, General, don't send our people in there…. That's what the bastards want us to do. They'll butcher our people. If they want to fight us, let them come down here where we can kill them."

Đắk Tô lies on a flat valley floor, surrounded by waves of ridgelines that rise into peaks (some as high as 4,000-foot (1,200 m)) that stretch westward and southwestward towards the tri-border region where South Vietnam, Laos and Cambodia meet.

Other terrain features were double- and triple-canopy rainforests, and the only open areas were filled in by bamboo groves whose stalks sometimes reached 8 inches (200 mm) in diameter.

Landing zones (LZs) large enough for helicopters were few and far between, which meant that most troop movements could only be carried out on foot. Temperatures in the highlands could reach 95° Fahrenheit (35° Celsius) during the day and could drop to as low as 55° Fahrenheit (12.78° Celsius) in the evening.

The first fighting of the new operation erupted on 3 November when companies of the 4th Infantry came across PAVN defensive positions. The next day the same thing occurred to elements of the 173rd. The American and ARVN troops soon applied a methodical approach to combat in the highlands. They combed the hills on foot, ran into fixed PAVN hill-top defensive positions, applied massive firepower, and then launched ground attacks.

In all of these instances, PAVN troops fought stubbornly, inflicted casualties on the Americans, and then withdrew.

Members of Company C, 1st Battalion, and 8th Infantry descend the side of Hill 742, located five miles northwest of Dak To. 14–17 November 1967

To expand the coverage of supporting artillery fires, the 4/503rd Airborne Infantry was ordered to occupy Hill 823 (14.626°N 107.648°E), south of Ben Het,

We already learned what they were doing at Ben Het, with Glenn Palmer.

Since the rest of the battalion's companies were already deployed elsewhere, the 120 men of Company B would combat assault onto the hilltop by helicopter alone.

We already learned about CA, combat assault from Henry Carson.

It was just a Thang!

The following is an excerpt from the battlereports.

After several attempts to denude the hilltop with airstrikes and artillery fire, Company B landed unopposed that afternoon, but the hill was not unoccupied. Fifteen minutes later, contact was made with the PAVN. The battle that ensued raged at close quarters until early the following morning when elements of the 66th Regiment withdrew, leaving behind more than 100 bodies. Nine men of Company B were killed and another 28 were wounded.

The following morning Company B was relieved by Lt. Col. David J. Schumacher's 1/503rd, which (against the admonitions of Colonel Livsey) was divided into two small Task Forces. *Task Force Black* consisted of Company C supported by two platoons of Company D and *Task Force Blue* which was composed of Company A and the remaining platoon of Company D. Task Force Black left Hill 823 to find the PAVN who had attacked Company B, 4/503rd. At 08:28 on 11 November, after leaving their overnight laager and following a PAVN communications wire, the force was ambushed by the 8th and 9th Battalions of the 66th Regiment and had to fight for its life.[3]:163-164 *Task Force Blue* and Company C, 4/503rd was sent to relieve the beleaguered *Task Force Black*. They encountered fire from all sides during the relief attempt, but they made it, reaching the trapped men at 15:37. U.S. losses were 20 killed, 154 wounded, and two missing.

McElwain's recommendation for a decoration for Private First Class John Andrew Barnes, III, who had leapt on a grenade and sacrificed his life to save wounded comrades during the action. Schumacher refused to endorse the recommendation, stating that he did not think medals were for "men who committed suicide."[2]:205-6 Barnes was later awarded the Medal of Honor.

The build-up at Đăk Tô

The PAVN simultaneously attacked the three companies of the 3/8th Infantry on Hill 724 (14.593°N 107.691°E). Beginning at 13:07 and lasting for thirty minutes, a mortar barrage rained onto the battalion's laager site. PAVN troops then charged out of the jungle to the attack. By the time the action ended at 19:03, 18 Americans were dead and another 118 were wounded. The 4th Infantry claimed that 92 PAVN had died in the clash. [2]:207

An Associated Press article from 12 November quoted the PAVN death toll to have risen above 500 with 67 US troops having also died.[13]

On the night of 12 November, the PAVN launched the first of many rocket attacks against the Đăk Tô airfield, firing 44 missiles. By 08:00 on 15 November, three C-130 Hercules transport aircraft were in the turnaround area as a PAVN mortar barrage landed. Two of them were destroyed. The resulting fires and additional incoming mortars set the ammunition dump and fuel storage areas ablaze. Explosions continued all day and into the night. During that night's incoming shelling, a mortar round landed on two steel containers of C-4 plastic explosive. They detonated simultaneously, sending a fireball and mushroom cloud high above the valley and leaving two craters 40-foot (12 m) deep. This was said to be the largest explosion to occur in the Vietnam War, knocking men off their feet over a mile away. The explosion destroyed the entire 15th Light Equipment Company compound next to the ammunition dump although no one was killed. Engineer Lieutenant Fred Dyerson thought "it looked like Charlie had gotten hold of some nuclear weapons." Although more than 1,100 tons of ordnance were destroyed during the explosions and fires, this was as close as the PAVN would get to taking Đắk Tô. The rapid deployment of allied forces had upset the North Vietnamese offensive and had thrown them onto the defensive. Previous actions had battered the 66th and 33rd Regiments, and they began a southwesterly retreat, covered by the 174th Regiment. The Americans and the ARVN then began to run into tenacious rearguard actions.

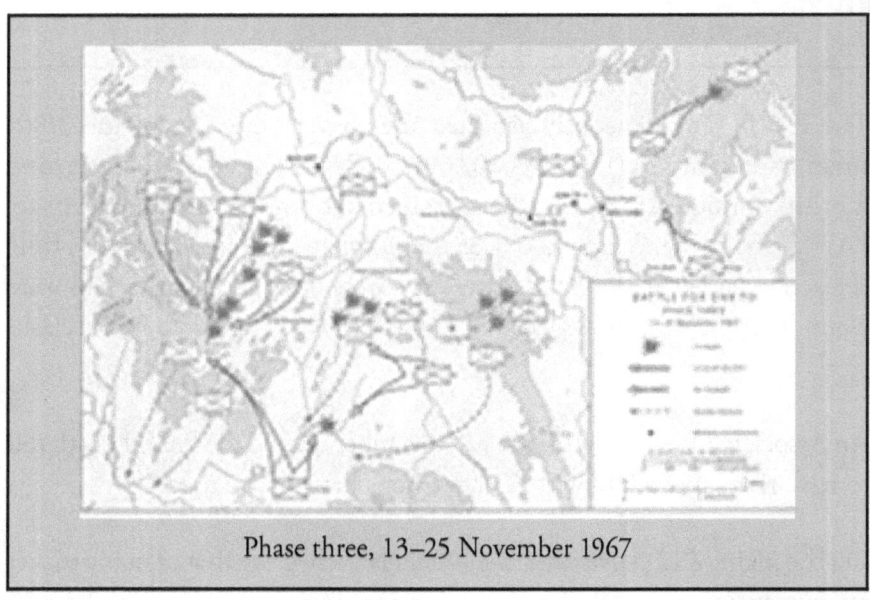

Phase three, 13–25 November 1967

To prevent a repetition of the artillery attack against its base camp, the 3/12th Infantry was ordered to take Hill 1338, which had an excellent overview of Đắk Tô, only six kilometers away. For two days, the Americans fought their way up the steep slope of the hill and into the most elaborate bunker complex yet discovered, all of the fortifications of which were connected by field telephones.

U.S. wounded being moved to an aid station during battle for Hill 882

After scouring the area of the PAVN who attacked *Task Force Black*, the three companies of 1/503rd moved southwest to occupy Hill 882. The force was accompanied by approximately a dozen civilian news correspondents. On the morning of 15 November, the lead company crested the hill and discovered bunkers connected by telephone wire. They were then attacked, and the rest of the Americans rushed to the hilltop to take defensive positions. PAVN troops poured small arms, machine gun, and mortar fire on the Americans and launched several ground attacks. The U.S. commander requested helicopter evacuation for the most seriously wounded, but this request was denied by Col. Schumacher, who demanded that the civilians be evacuated first.[2]:243 When the fighting ceased on 19 November the U.S. battalion had suffered seven killed and 34 wounded. The PAVN 66th Regiment left behind 51 dead.[2]:244

While the action on Hill 882 was underway, Company D, 4/503rd was conducting road clearing operations around Ben Het while being accompanied by a CIDG Mike Force. While calling in an artillery fire mission, an error caused two rounds to fall on the company's position. Six Americans and three CIDG were killed outright and 15 paratroopers and 13 CIDG troops were wounded in the friendly fire incident.[2]:247

ARVN units had also found plenty of action in the Đắk Tô area. On 18 November, on Hill 1416 (14.738°N 107.908°E) northeast of Tan Canh, the ARVN 3/42nd Infantry found the PAVN 24th Regiment in well-fortified defensive positions.[12]:5-241 The elite, all-volunteer ARVN 3rd and 9th Airborne Battalions joined the action, attacking the hill from another direction. The ARVN forces took the hill on 20 November after vicious close-quarters fighting that claimed 66 ARVN dead and another 290 wounded. The PAVN left behind 248 of their own.[2]:295

U.S. intelligence indicated that the fresh 174th PAVN Regiment had slipped westward past Ben Het and had taken up positions on an 875-meter-high hill just six kilometers from the border. The 174th had done so in order to cover the withdrawal of the 66th and 32nd Regiments, which were moving toward their sanctuaries across the Cambodian frontier. On 19 November, BG Schweiter was informed that a Special Forces Mobile Strike Force company had run into heavy resistance while reconnoitering the area. He then ordered his 2nd Battalion to take the hill.

Hill 875

U.S. 105 mm artillery battery in action in the Central Highlands

At 09:43 on 19 November, the three companies (330 men) of 2/503rd moved into jumpoff positions from which to assault Hill 875 (14.579°N 107.595°E).[12]:5-237 Companies C and D moved up the slope followed by two platoons of Company A in the classic "two up one back" formation utilized since World War I. The Weapons Platoon of Company A remained behind at the bottom of the hill to cut out a landing zone. Instead of a frontal assault with massed troops, the unit would have been better served by advancing small teams to envelop possible PAVN positions and then calling in air and artillery support.[2]:254

At 10:30, as the Americans moved to within 300 meters of the crest, PAVN machine gunners opened fire on the advancing paratroopers. Then B-40 rockets and 57mm recoilless rifle fire were unleashed upon them. The paratroopers attempted to continue the advance, but the PAVN, well concealed in interconnected bunkers and trenches, opened fire with small arms and grenades. The American advance was halted and the men went to ground, finding whatever cover they could. At 14:30 PAVN troops hidden at the bottom of the hill launched a massed assault on Company A. Unknown to the Americans, they had walked into a carefully prepared ambush by the 2nd Battalion of the 174th Regiment.

The men of Company A retreated up the slope, lest they be cut off from their comrades and annihilated. They were closely followed by the PAVN. Private First Class Carlos Lozada held the rear guard position for Company A with his M60 machine gun. As the PAVN advanced, Lozada mowed them down and refused to retreat until he was shot dead. For his actions that day, Lozada was awarded a posthumous Medal of Honor. Soon, U.S. air strikes and artillery fire were being called in, but they had little effect on the battle because of the dense foliage on the hillside. Resupply became a necessity because of high ammunition expenditures and lack of water, but it was also an impossibility. Six UH-1 helicopters were shot down or badly damaged that afternoon trying to get to 2/503rd.[2]:269

U.S. troops in combat on Hill 875

At 18:58 one of the worst friendly fire incidents of the Vietnam War occurred when a Marine Corps A-4 Skyhawk fighter-bomber, flown by LTC Richard Taber, the Commanding Officer of a Marine Air Group from Chu Lai Air Base, dropped two 500-pound Mark 81 Snakeye bombs into 2/503rd's perimeter. One of the bombs exploded, a tree burst above the center of the position, where the combined command groups, the wounded, and the medics were all located. It killed 42 men outright and wounded 45 more, including the overall on-scene commander, Captain Harold Kaufman. 1Lt. Bartholomew O'Leary, Company D Commander, was seriously wounded. (Company A's commander had been killed in the retreat up the slope). Chaplain (Major) Charles J. Watters, was killed in the blast while ministering to the wounded. For his gallantry in repeatedly exposing himself to enemy fire to retrieve the wounded on Hill 875, he was awarded a posthumous Medal of Honor.

Author's Note: Could you imagine the emotions this pilot must have had after dropping the bombs in the wrong place? How do you eliminate that from your memory? It becomes part of who you are, and develops its damage over time.

The next morning, the three companies of 4/503rd were chosen to set out and relieve the men on Hill 875. Because of intense PAVN sniper and mortar fire (and the terrain) it took until nightfall for the relief force to reach the beleaguered battalion. On the afternoon of 21 November, both battalions moved out to take the crest. During fierce, close-quarters fighting, some of the paratroopers made it into the PAVN trench line but were ordered to pull back as darkness fell. At approximately 23:00, the 4th Division's 1/12th Infantry was ordered to withdraw from an offensive operations in the southern Central Highlands and redeploy to Đắk Tô. In a night-time air redeployment, the entire battalion redeployed and took up positions around the main fire support base at Đắk Tô in less than 12 hours.

The following day was spent in launching airstrikes and a heavy artillery bombardment against the hilltop, totally denuding it of cover. On 23 November, the 2nd and 4th Battalions of the 503rd were ordered to renew their assault while the 1/12th Infantry assaulted 875 from the south. This time the Americans gained the crest, but the PAVN had already abandoned their positions, leaving only a few dozen charred bodies and weapons.[2]:320–1

The battle of Hill 875 had cost 2/503rd 87 killed, 130 wounded, and three missing. 4/503rd suffered 28 killed 123 wounded, and four missing.[2]:323 Combined with noncombatant losses, this represented one-fifth of the 173rd Airborne Brigade's total strength.[15] For its combined actions during operations around Đắk Tô, the 173rd Airborne Brigade was awarded the Presidential Unit Citation.

Aftermath

376 U.S. troops had been killed or listed as missing-presumed dead and another 1,441 were wounded, in the fighting around Đắk Tô. The fighting had also taken a toll on the ARVN with 73 soldiers killed. U.S. munitions expenditures attested to the ferocity of the fighting: 151,000 artillery rounds, 2,096 tactical air sorties, 257 B-52 strikes. 2,101 Army helicopter sorties were flown, and 40 helicopters were lost.[The U.S. Army claimed that

1,644 PAVN troops had been killed by body count, but this figure quickly became a source of contention due to allegations of body count inflation.

Another figure of some significant contention was the claim from the Vietnam News Agency quoted in an Associated Press report that 2,800 U.S. soldiers and 700 ARVN had perished in the fighting.[16]

In his memoirs, General William C. Westmoreland, U.S. commander in Vietnam, mentioned 1,400 PAVN casualties, while MG William B. Rosson, the MACV deputy commander, By the end of November, the PAVN withdrew back into their sanctuaries in Cambodia and Laos, failing to wipe out a major American unit, yet forcing the U.S. Army to pay a high price. estimated that the PAVN lost between 1,000 and 1,400 men. Not all American commanders were happy with the friendly to enemy loss ratio. U.S. Marine Corps General John Chaisson questioned "Is it a victory when you lose 362 friendlies in three weeks and by your own spurious body count you only get 1,200?

> There were many exhausted soldiers of the 173rd Airborne after campaigning in the Central Highlands

MACV asserted that three of the four PAVN regiments that participated in the fighting had been so battered that they played no part in the next phase of their winter-spring offensive. Only the 24th Regiment took the field during the Tet Offensive of January 1968. The 173rd Airborne Brigade and two battalions of the 4th Infantry Division were in no better shape. General Westmoreland claimed that "we had soundly defeated the enemy without unduly sacrificing operations in other areas. The enemy's return was nil."[17]:280 But Westmoreland's claim may have missed the point. The border battles fought that fall and winter had indeed cost the PAVN dearly, but they had achieved their objective. By January 1968, one-half of all U.S. maneuver battalions in South Vietnam had been drawn away from the cities and lowlands and into the border areas. Just as General Giap had planned it.

The official, post-war, PAVN history is more sanguine, viewing their results as the infliction of casualties on a brigade, two battalions and six companies of US forces.[10]

Operations in and around the Central Highlands including previous battles at Hill 1338 had rendered the 173rd Airborne combat ineffective, and they were ordered to Tuy Hòa to repair and refit.[19]:90–1[19]:153 153 The 173rd was transferred to Camp Radcliff in An Khê and Bong Son areas during 1968, seeing very little action while the combat ineffective elements of the brigade were rebuilt.

Several members of Westmoreland's staff began to see an eerie resemblance to the Viet Minh campaign of 1953, when seemingly peripheral actions had led up to the climactic Battle of Dien Bien Phu.[20] General Giap even laid claim to such a strategy in an announcement in September, but to the Americans it all seemed a bit too contrived. Yet, no understandable analysis seemed to explain Hanoi's almost suicidal military actions. They could only be explained if a situation akin to Dien Bien Phu came into being. Then, almost overnight, one emerged. In the western corner of Quảng Trị Province, an isolated Marine outpost at Khe Sanh, came under siege by PAVN forces that would eventually number three divisions.

Roger Phillips

Volunteered for duty in Vietnam

Joined the 299th Engineers
Motor Pool Battalion C
2 tours

The U.S. Army 299th Engineer Battalion had arrived in South Vietnam in October 1965, and in the summer of 1966 it relocated from Tuy Hua to Pleiku. The battalion remained there for two years—attached to the 4th Infantry Division but assigned to the 18th Engineer Brigade—before it moved to Dak To.

Qui Nhon, in September of 1969, was a hot and dusty small Vietnamese city located on the blue-green waters of the South China Sea and rimmed by the coastal mountains of the Central Highlands. The older women wore the traditional shiny black pajamas. Their teeth were stained and rotted from years of chewing betel nuts. Many of the young women were beautiful and delicate. The few civilian males were mostly very old. Children were everywhere.

Houses of corrugated tin, concrete and bamboo lined the narrow streets clogged with bicycles and motorized carts that looked like gas-powered golf carts, which taxied people and moved freight. Downtown Qui Nhon had a few more substantial buildings: the Catholic cathedral, a railroad station, seedy hotels and restaurants, and banks and government buildings. Though Qui Nhon had the reputation of being sympathetic to the Vietcong, it was relatively safe for American soldiers. The town was neither important nor imposing,

The danger was around the military bases and the roads outside of town. There was a "tank farm" near by.

"Sappers," soldiers carrying explosive devices, crawled across the rice paddies and assaulted the tank farm. Before the attack began, the soldiers inside the tank farm reported activity all around them. The tank farm was guarded by 40 or so American soldiers scattered along an extensive perimeter. The area in front of the gate was a no-fire zone because of the small houses opposite the gate that stood in the direct line of fire. (In a no-fire zone you did not fire weapons unless attacked.)

On the night of the attack, the battalion command headquarters was three miles away. The men inside the tank farm were in constant contact by radio and contact with central command operations downtown. The activity reported by the men at the tank farm was highly unusual. We needed clearance to fire, especially in the no-fire zone; there might be "friendlies" out there. Near 11 p.m. the battalion commander decided to go to the tank farm with some additional troops

Roger Phillips reported remembering the barber in one village who after cutting hair would pace off the camp for future attacks from forces opposing the American troops.

VC? Charlie? North Vietnamese Troops?

Where were the young males of Qui Nhon?

Dead?

Enlisted in the various armies?

Roger Phillips showed me a photo he had with two of his young Vietnamese friends. They disappeared one morning.

Were they "drafted" by one of the local military groups?

Were they now soldiers of the People's Army of Vietnam? i.e the north?

The Army of the Republic of Vietnam. i.e the south?

Or just local militia? Viet Cong?

If we consider the timing, the usefulness of the Viet Cong had been replaced by General Giap's plan of moving in after the TET offensive with his trained army. The People's Army of Vietnam.

Roger operated a 5 ton truck with a crane on it.

He could pick up large loads similar to loads deposited on large ships going to sea. He could pick up a damaged bridge and replace it with a new one.

He had a 50 caliber mount on his truck if needed, and carried a grenade launching rifle.

He has in his possession many letters of commendation for bravery, these letter described his willingness to do any job his commanders asked of him.

One day while on a mission his truck hit a land mine. He was injured, but not disabled. He got care and returned to his job. According to his wife Grace Phillips, he has a cute scar on his butt.

Years later, Roger had bleeding kidneys from the concussion of the land mine, and there is no record of his injury at the Veterans Administration.

How many soldiers have medical issues today, from injuries they felt were unimportant at the time. He has no Purple Heart to prove he was injured in the land mine incident.

The bloody battle described at Dak To in 1967, did not mean the area was secure.

It meant American troops were committed to an area for years after the battle,

Who suffered through Monsoons, and explosions, hearing, watching and experiencing their brothers in arms being injured and dying two and three years later. American bunkers exploding, was it hit because of a Barbers pacing? Did the barber lose a customer?

Roger Phillips and his 299th Combat Engineers, even when having their trucks destroyed right under them, continued to serve heroically and loyally.

After serving two tours, Roger Phillips came home, collects antique cars, lives on a farm in East Tennessee with his wife Grace, lives a wonderful life, helping people associated with his church.

Most do not know of his service, the dangers he endured, and the bravery he showed in a war zone 50 years earlier.

Where else would he have gotten the kidney wound, was it associated to the cute little scar on his butt, and the land mine under his truck?

The loyal soldier got patched up and returned to his duty.

A land mine injury can show up later in life, documented or not.

Roger has no children, and owns may war memories, and souvenirs.

Where does a veteran leave his memoirs and albums of friends he made during wartime?

I was honored to be given a Montagnard cross bow from his Vietnam collection.

It is in a gun case in my living room.

Wars ago, if a battle is won, it is cleared of the enemy. In Viet Nam, from 1967 to 1970, it was a score card, no real military ground taken, just constant work and constant danger.

CHAPTER ELEVEN

The day Martin Luther King was killed

Buffalo Soldiers

> I've seen people turn their heads
> And quickly look away
> Like a newborn baby
> It just happens everyday

Lyrics from Paint it Black
Sung by the Rolling Stones

During the American Revolution: around 9,000 African Americans became **Black** Patriots. As between 200,000 and 250,000 **soldiers** and militia served the American cause during the **revolution** in total that would mean **Black soldiers** made up approximately four percent of the Patriots' numbers. Of the 9,000 **Black soldiers**, 5,000 were combat dedicated **troops**.

Black Americans fought on both sides in the War of 1812. Some in order to escape slavery in the South, chose to join the armies of Great Britain. Others to protect the USA from the tyranny of Great Britain joined the American cause.

Negroes were present at the Alamo, some as American Slaves, some as Mexican Soldiers.

The **Mexican-American War marked a turning point** in the debate over **slavery** in the U.S. by unleashing a massive tension between the North and South on what land would be free and what land would be **slave**.

Some sources theorize the **name** originated with the belief of some Native Americans that the **soldiers'** dark, curly, black hair resembled that of a **buffalo**. Whatever the case, the **soldiers** viewed the **nickname** as one of respect, and the 10th Cavalry even used a figure of a **buffalo** in its coat of arms. By the end of the Civil War, roughly 179,000 **black** men (10% of the Union Army) served as **soldiers** in the U.S. Army and another 19,000 served in the Navy. Nearly 40,000 **black soldiers died** over the course of the war—30,000 of infection or disease. Buffalo Soldiers originally were members of the 10th Cavalry Regiment of the United States Army, formed on September 21, 1866, at Fort Leavenworth, Kansas. This nickname was given to the Black Cavalry by Native American tribes who fought in the Indian Wars.

Buffalo Soldiers originally were members of the 10th Cavalry Regiment of the United States Army, formed on September 21, 1866, at Fort Leavenworth, Kansas. This nickname was given to the Black Cavalry by Native American tribes who fought in the Indian Wars.

Their main tasks **were** to help control the Native Americans of the Plains, capture cattle rustlers and thieves and protect settlers, stagecoaches, wagon trains and railroad crews along the Western front.

Eighteen African Americans earned the **Medal of Honor** during the Indian Wars of the **western** United States. Fourteen were "Buffalo **Soldiers**", members of the **Army's** first peacetime **black** regiments.

The American Indians to honor the black cavalry soldiers for their bravery and fierceness in battle, along with the course texture of their hair, and darkness of their faces called them the Buffalo Soldiers.

All black regiments in the US Army at the time, served in the Spanish American War.

They were a strong force in the Battle at San Juan Hill. Many say they saved the day!

While they fought bravely and valiantly, their brothers and sisters across America were being persecuted and separated from society, some being hung and abused in many ways.

Since the first Africans were brought as slaves to the British colony of Jamestown, Va. in 1619, blacks had suffered oppression in the United States first under the **American slavery system**, and then under the rigid practices of segregation and discrimination that were codified under the **"Jim Crow Laws."** With the entry of the United States into the Great War in 1917, African Americans were eager to show their patriotism in hopes of being recognized as full citizens. After the declaration of war, more than 20,000 blacks enlisted in the military, and the numbers increased when the Selective Service Act was enacted in May 1917. It was documented on July 5, 1917 that over 700,000 African Americans had registered for military service. However, they were barred from the Marines and served only in menial roles in the Navy. Blacks were able to serve in all branches of the Army except for the aviation units.

The government made no provision for military training of black officers and soon created segregated training camps for that purpose. Disheartened, blacks protested against this discriminatory practice. Despite the outcry, Fort Des Moines in Iowa became one of the segregated camps and in October 1917 over 600 blacks were commissioned at the camp as captains and lieutenants.

African-American soldiers provided much support overseas to the European Allies. Those in black units who served as laborers, stevedores and in engineer service battalions were the first to arrive in France in 1917, and in early 1918, the 369th United States Infantry, a regiment of African-American combat troops, arrived to help the French Army. Earning the reputation from the Germans as "Hell Fighters," the 369th was nicknamed the **"Harlem Hell Fighters"** because the regiment "never lost a man through capture, lost a trench or a foot of ground to the enemy." The 369th was also the first to reach the Rhine River and provided the longest service of any regiment in a foreign army. They fought in the trenches for 191 days and the entire regiment received the Croix de Guerre medal for their actions at Maison-en-Champagne.

In a previous book, The Veteran Next Door, I told the story of James Julian who was in the US navy before the start of World War II. Like almost all black sailors they were used as servant for officers. As the war progressed, Mr. Julián fought with 20 and 40mm guns against German and Italian Dive bombers near Greenland, and at Anzio, and then later against Kamikazes at Okinawa. He was present at the surrender of Japan.

I also told the story of a black cotton picker from Mississippi who was assigned as a driver in the Red Ball Express. General Patton had decided he did not want the black man in his fighting ranks and assigned almost all blacks in his army to distribution of supplies to his forces. This man came home to Knoxville, Tennessee, and went to school in New York to be a mathematician and eventually served as the Interim president more than once at the Knoxville College. Primarily a black college.

On **July 26, 1948,** President Harry S. Truman signed an executive order establishing the President's Committee on Equality of Treatment and Opportunity in the Armed Services, committing the government to integrating the segregated military.

The **Korean War** was one **of** the first American wars in which **military** units were not segregated according to race. One exception: The African-American 24th Infantry Regiment participated in all major operations across the **Korean** peninsula, from the defense and breakout at the Pusan Perimeter in 1950, to the United Nations counter-offensive that stabilized near the 38th parallel in late 1951. It was the Korean War, argues Early, which helped truly initiate that integration.

"It was a major institution, it was a major sociological force, and by1954 we could look back and say that the integration of the armed services, while not complete and not perfect, went better than most detractors and most critics thought it would,"

Then there was the war in Vietnam: The number of US military personnel in **Vietnam** jumped from 23,300 in 1965 to 465,600 by the end of 1967. Between October 1966 and June 1969, 246,000 **soldiers were** recruited through Project 100,000, of whom 41% **were black**, while **blacks** only made up about 11% of the population of the US.

In my research, it appears that a larger percentage of black soldiers died in the war 14ish percent, and the total black male population in the USA at the time was on or about 11 percent. Of the 7262 black men who died, ninety-six percent were Army or Marine enlisted men. In 1965-66, when blacks made up 11 percent of our forces in Vietnam, they were 20 percent of the casualties, under the leadership of Black politicians who protested this discrepancy, President Johnson ordered the black participation be cut back in combat units, resulting in 11.5 per cent by 1969.

Freddie Owens, the man to whom I dedicated this book was black, and so was Robert Minter. He was serving in Vietnam the day Martin Luther King was assassinated.

According to Robert Minter:

We came off patrol only to learn about Martin Luther King's assassination.

Many white officers wanted to disarm the black soldiers as they came in from patrol.

We discussed it among our fellow soldiers white and black. We decided we were soldiers here in Vietnam, and need to be unified, not separated by events in the states. We all agreed to hold on to our weapons.

CHAPTER TWELVE

Bad Student
Bad Soldier Prison

Purple Haze all in my brain,
lately things don't seem the same,
actin' funny but I don't know why
'scuse me while I kiss the sky.

Lyrics from: Purple Haze
By Jimi Hendrix

Dean Powell: An angry young man returns to a war he thought he had escaped.

This story starts around 1955-56 when a seven year old child loses his father.

It led to a ministry that helps people get through the same hell he went through.

It is called Focus Prison Ministries. Founded 1991.

A young fatherless boy, who's security base was rattled when his mother took a new mate.

Became a poor student in school, graduating unable to read or write.

Lost a brother in a motorcycle accident.

His older brother was a poor role model, had no help with homework. His mom worked long hours to keep the 3 boys fed and clothed.

He liked to fight a lot, went to school to get by,

Taken aside by his high school principle, and told he was going to OBEY! GO TO SUMMER SCHOOL! Or else!

So he went.

The journey began,

It was not going to be pretty.

Graduated and married a woman a little older the he, who had a child. His Mother was frustrated over the decision.

Was he trying to be the father he lost?

It was a bad relationship, and Dean Powell joined the army to escape the marriage.

A poor student in a bad marriage, and lo and behold, the US Army Poster said I want you?

You are in the ARMY NOW, BASIC TRAINING, and age 19.

Sent to a foreign country in which he could not spell,

A country where he had known his friends in school who had gone before him and had been killed,

Trained as a LRRP> Long Range Recon Patrol

Trained for booby traps, explosives, repelling out of helicopters.

I Corps, northern South Vietnam. 1968

The I **Corps** Tactical Zone (Vietnamese: Vùng 1 Chiến thuật) was a **corps** of the Army of the Republic of **Vietnam** (ARVN), the army of the nation state of South **Vietnam** that existed from 1955 to 1975. It was one of four **corps** of the ARVN. This was the northernmost region of South **Vietnam**, bordering North **Vietnam**. These five provinces are Quảng Trị Province, (Khe Sanh, Đông Hà, Quảng...

As you remember General Giap, wanted to draw American forces out of the cities, and one of those target goals was the battle at Khe Sanh. Activity and concentrations of power in the I Corps vicinity was good for the upcoming Tet Offensive.

A lot of responsibility being a LRRP in Vietnam at age 19.

"To me Vietnam just smelled bad," said Dean Powell.

Smoke, explosives, burning human waste, and having to stir it to make it burn up, fueled with a little jet fuel.

Plus investigating tunnels, crawling in the tunnel hole and scoping it out.

Not quite 20.

Occasional Snatches in local villages to get information.

Author's note:

I learned kidnapping is a crime when one party grabs another to hold for a ransom or for performing the delivery of justice, or for information alone:

A Snatch is the same thing except you are under orders to do it.

The Phoenix Program (Vietnamese: Chiến dịch Phụng Hoàng) was a program designed and coordinated by the United States Central Intelligence Agency (CIA) during the Vietnam War, involving cooperation between American, South Vietnamese and Australian militaries. The program was designed to **identify and destroy the Viet Cong.**

The program was in operation between 1965 and 1972, and similar efforts existed both before and after that period. By 1972, Phoenix operatives had "neutralized" 81,740 suspected VC operatives, informants and supporters, of whom between 26,000 and 41,000 were killed.

Eventually the CIA was forced to cancel the Program.

One day Dean was injured by hot shrapnel, burning his leg, and afraid to touch it, and his fellow soldiers put the heat out with water from their canteens.

He was back in the field a short time later with the burn still healing.

He was close to those 24 or so men in his group.

After six months he got to go home on leave, he had been a good soldier, doing all the right things.

He saw the war protests in California.

Protests like that did not exist in South Carolina.

PROTESTS FROM AN ANGRY NATION.

A NATION WHO COULD NOT SEPARATE THE POLITICS OF THE WAR FROM THOSE WE SENT TO FIGHT IT.

Wounded, a Purple Heart? No more war?

Home for thirty days and gets an order to return to Vietnam!

Promoted from E4 to E5.

Was very angry about having to go back to Vietnam. But off on a jet he went back to his unit.

Where he learned that thirteen of the 24 men in his outfit had been killed.

Yes, this is that same seven year old child, we discussed earlier,

Now angry at his country, had a choice between the alcohol drinkers, the druggies and the straight lacers.

He was already a straight lacer in the past. Look where that got him, so he joined up with the druggies.

He no longer saw himself as a good soldier, turned to marijuana first, and then on to heroin.

He came home from the second trip to Vietnam addicted to HEROIN, An expensive habit for a young man trained right out of high school in the arts of LRRP life in Vietnam,

He reconned local sources of distribution of heroin, placed himself in those positions, and began selling to his friends and customers, enough to pay for his own habit.

His skills learned in the Army of The United States of America, made him a good drug distributor.

He was in cahoots with some public police officers, and his recon skills to find more markets and have more supply got him arrested by the Feds, and off to prison he went.

Now it was THE UNITED STATES OF AMERICA vs Dean Powell.

Not knowing he had not completed his journey to learn what he needed to learn, he had already gotten himself away from the heroin addiction, and gives credit to God, for getting him through it all. With no sweats, or any side effects what so ever. Right with God, but sentenced to prison. The sentence was 8 years, with possible time off for good behavior.

Still unable to read or write.

His first night in prison he cried out to GOD. He wanted to find himself.

He wanted an education, and skills to make it outside of prison.

He began working as a plumber in the prison and began working for four hours and studying for 4 hours.

A man named Donald taught him to write and spell, and read.

He seized an opportunity to go to college, and the GI Bill helped him while in prison.

Remember the Focus Prison Ministries?

The idea came to Dean Powell that he wished there had been support services for him when he came out of the military to help him with the transition back to civilian life. But he was still in prison, and up for parole.

He had been a good inmate.

The result of the parole hearing was the board wanted him to serve a little more time, 1 year and discuss it again at that time.

"I was angry at God, for keeping me in prison. What did he have to do to get out, and God answered him saying, "There are things you need to learn so you will never have to return to this prison.

His second parole was also delayed.

And he knew he was not ready to leave and never come back.

This young man over a 20 year period starting at age seven,

Conflicts and issues all during his life,

No support system or too little,

No tools available to deal with being alone,

Possibly suicidal, feeling the guilt of survivorship, or of morals and ethics,

No one to share stories with, or to turn to when you really need support?

Dean Powell had to go through it before he could help others going through the same traumas.

He believes God kept him where he was so he could do what he does today.

He had so much to learn.

He has helped so many veterans in his ministry after the war.

Author's note: I saw him in action, he learned to help heal his fellow veterans.

This is as it should be.

One wounded veteran helping another with his experience and wisdom.

CHAPTER THIRTEEN

Battle of My Lai aka Pinkville

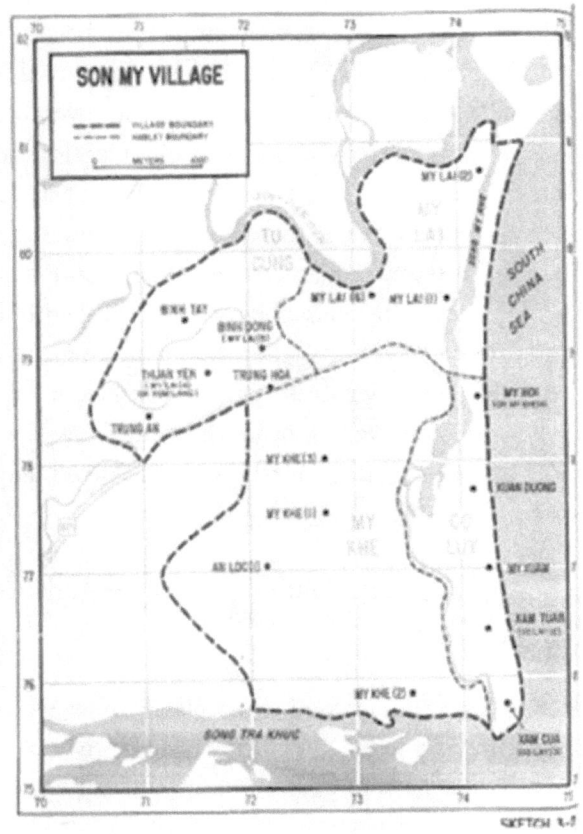

When you are given a direct order by an officer that you know is morally wrong, what do you do?

Oh mother tell your children
Not to do what I have done

Lyrics from:
House of the Rising Sun by THE ANIMALS

I was 13 years old… how old were you? January 5, 1968 Doctor Benjamin Spock was indicted on charges of conspiracy to encourage violations of the draft laws by a grand jury in Boston. Five days later it was announced that the 10,000[th] US airplane is lost over Vietnam. Two weeks after that North Korean patrol boats captured the USS Pueblo. One week later the Tet Offensive began. February 1 a Vietnamese general had his picture taken as he killed a Viet Cong prisoner. No one said what the Viet Cong prisoner had done only that he had been executed without a trial. February 4th Martin Luther King gave one of his famous speeches that turned out to be his eulogy. On February 27th Walter Cronkite reported on his recent trip to Vietnam what he said was after listing Tet and several other current military options as draws and chastising American leaders for their optimism Walter Cronkite advised negotiation not as victors but as an honorable people who lived up to their pledge to defend democracy and did the best they could. Today's story we are going to be talking about a question that military professionals and enlisted men have had to deal with for hundreds of years. The question always runs true when you are given an order do you follow it? Let's see how they dealt with it back in the Civil War. The question was when you are given an order that you know is wrong or you think is wrong or is against your own ethics or your own honor code what are you supposed to do?

A Civil War script of a Confederate officer's trial of the Andersonville POW Camp, after the Civil War

> Let it be clearly understood most clearly now we have a question for the judge advocate which he may or may not answer since he is not of course not on trial here. The question is: What is it an honest man fights for when he picks up arms for his country? Is it the state? Or the moral principles inherit in that state? If the state and the principle are not one is he bound not to fight for that state and indeed to fight against it? Now the judge advocate needn't answer we will make the question more particular. If at the outbreak of the war the government of the so called confederacy had stood on the moral principle of freedom for the black man and the government of the United States had stood for

slavery would a man have been bound on moral grounds to follow the dictates of conscience even if it had led him up to the point of taking up arms against the government of the United States?

BUT, that is not the question.

Author's note: And why is that not the question?

Would he be bound to follow the dictates of his own conscience?

Even to the point of taking up arms against the government of the United States?

Back to the trial:

Mr. Woods we have said that a man does make an inner judgment as to the orders he obeys. Which implies that if those orders offend his humanity deeply enough he may disobey them. General Winders authority over you was not absolute, the question is: "Why did you obey?

The Confederate officer Answered:

I did not think of my assignment at Andersonville in that way. I do not understand what happened here. I thought only in the normal way to obey since he was my military superior.

Not your moral superior sir, no man has authority over the soul of another as we are men we own our own souls and as we own them we are equal as men sir the General the Private, the flag carrier, we are equal as men sir and every man alive being a man knows that as you in your heart knew that and as this situation had become an immoral, grossly immoral situation and as General Winder was not your moral superior you did not have to obey him. The question therefore remains why did you obey him?

Mr. Woods the court would like to hear your answer.

And this is what the Confederate said to the question.

> I would most certainly have been court martialed and if my superiors wish considering that was a time of war and that war had come to a desperate bitter stage at which the word "traitor" could be sounded in a moment. I might have been executed.

> So what does that have to do with decisions made in Pinkville?

> When is it good to disobey an order?

> When does an officer take command of troops who are out of control?

The town in Vietnam on a map, a military map, was known as Pinkville. The situation was: Pinkville had to be cleaned out. The enemy was there and they were sending in American forces that had been beaten up by that same enemy and they were given the chance to get their revenge. Only the United States of America would not cover up what happened. Only the United States of America would prosecute this crime if it indeed was a crime to follow the order at the cost of losing the war and only the United States would use it so forcefully to prevent future incidents.

We are in Vietnam today in 1968. The topic that you may have figured out by now Pinkville on a map of Vietnam is also known as My Lai. There are four My Lai villages and on the map it was referred to as My Lai 1, My Lai 2, My Lai 3, and My Lai 4. There was a massacre at My Lai in 1968 and it remained relatively quiet for some time. There was a trial a few years later to find out who was actually guilty. During that trial it was discovered that the President of the United States didn't order the killing of prisoners of war or civilians. Neither did the Secretary of Defense or the General in Vietnam or even the commanding officer in charge of the Americal Division. So it got on down the rank to the captain, Captain Medina. Captain Medina took a lie detector test and it was proven during the lie detector test that he was telling the truth when he denied ordering or intentionally inferring to his company during his briefing on March 15th that non-combatants be killed. Yet he was not truthful when he denied knowing that his company had killed numerous non-combatants at My Lai and that he was aware that his company was killing numerous non-combatants at My Lai. Since the killing occurred prior to 10:30 in the morning he possessed knowledge during a critical period. The prosecution thus learned that the polygraph examination that Captain Medina had not intentionally ordered this massacre but that he had known about it. He had the ability to stop at least a portion of it and had done nothing to stop it. In more theoretical criminal law terms this information moved the key participant from direct to indirect criminal responsibility since he did not order or participate in the killings yet knew about the killings and had both the duty and the ability to prevent them. CPT Medina was a pivotal figure between personal responsibility and command responsibility. Between ground action and cover up.

Author's note: You might want to reread this above paragraph to get clear on what happened to the chain of command.

Someone had to pay for what happened, and someone had to be identified as the key breakdown of authority occurred on the battlefield, and was never an intended tactic or strategy of the war. Was it?

Our soldier is Roger Taylor. He has asked us to call him Doc Taylor, he was a medic in one of the units that was at My Lai. He was not one of the participants who murdered civilians but he was close enough to hear what was going on and played a small role in part of that action.

This is Doc Taylor's story

Before being inducted in the army, I worked at a place called Magnavox.

Fresh out of high school 18 years old.

I got out of high school and worked at Magnavox then joined the army.

I was assigned the role of medic.

When I joined the army I wanted to get into the combat engineers. I went to basic training and during the last week or so they told us all about what everyone was going to be doing. So the drill sergeant started calling out names of people going to infantry, going to artillery, armored or whatever. The drill instructor said, "Taylor, Roger H, and Fort Sam Houston, Texas. I said what? He said "Combat Medic". I said, "No sir I want to get into engineers." He said, "Private, the army wants you as a Combat Medic and you, are going to be a Combat Medic."

I said, "Yes Drill Sergeant."

"I had no medical knowledge. Not a bit. They said they were going to train me.

I don't know why they picked me to be a medic. Unless it was my test grades when you first go in you have to take a battery of tests. I don't know if they said hmmm this guy here he is maybe a little sharp or a little dense I don't know. They had my test grades.

When we were growing up you know, we all saw the war movies. You saw a lot of infantry and everything but you saw very little of medics, very little. So I didn't know till I got to Fort Sam.

I mean Fort Sam Houston down in San Antonio… well they started the indoctrination there. I probably shouldn't say that. They started to give classes and then at that time Vietnam wasn't a very hot subject. You heard about it once in a while. Then by '65, '67, '68 it really heated up at home here.

I was 19 when I became a medic. I had been in the army for a couple of years before they sent me to Vietnam? It was my last year in the service. I had two years of training as a medic?

I went through school, went to Fort Leonard Wood, MO and I was there for a few months. Worked in the hospital so there were about 20 of us they decided they were going to send out to the line units.

To the line units, the infantry... infantry companies.

Not breaking up our unit, we belonged to the army. but taking about 20 or 25 of us out of this unit you know. The rest were going to stay there. They sent us down to the line units which was the best move they could have made for me. I didn't know it at that time. So we just sat there waiting for orders. We were getting all the dirty details. Finally, we got our orders assigned to the infantry battalions. I was sent first to 4th and 21st that was a new battalion brigade. I was there about 3 days, maybe less than that, all of a sudden they said pack your stuff you are at the wrong place. So they sent me down to 4th and 3rd The Old Guard. Well HHC, Headquarters and Headquarters Company which makes all the decisions. I was there about 2 months and I think about the 7th of December something like that, maybe the 8th we pushed down to Pearl Harbor got on a troop ship and we left. The first day at sea you know being naïve, I started thinking maybe this was just a practice thing we are going to go and fool around for a few days then we will go back and go back to school for a while.

Then I said to myself, "Fool you are going to a war!"

When you were there most up until the Tet Offensive the soldiers were used to fighting in the jungle. Hey weren't used to the city fighting or the street fighting. We were primarily in the jungle.

We were in the foothills. There was a lot of villages around we had to go through villages. Had a lot of real triple canopy. But mostly, a lot of trees and a lot of woods stuff like that.

Kind of like East Tennessee.

OK a lot like East Tennessee but the cows looked different?

Yes the cows there were buffaloes. American cattle wouldn't last five minutes over there they would put them on a spit somewhere.

I was with an infantry platoon I was a fighting medic.

I carried an M-16. And it was working well!

Author's note: Thanks to men like Glenn Palmer who worked on the M-16 so his buddies would not die.

"I never had any problems with my M-16."

We were given cleaning kits.

There were about 33 or 34 maybe 35 to a platoon.

We searched and destroyed. Patrolled and reported?

Whatever we were told to do, search and destroy, patrol, ambush, we would go out an ambush at night. My experience in Vietnam wasn't a war that was fought with battalions or companies or like that it was more of a squad war. A squad consisted of maybe 15 men at the most or a fire team may be 8 or 9 people. But when you go out in a battalion or company, you go out on a patrol or go from one fire base to another fire base it is usually the whole company that goes out. Each platoon will be assigned an area to patrol. It was like a clover leaf the company goes out just so far. Then there would be platoons who would go out from the company and do their patrol and maybe ambush at night. Come back the next morning and the company would go somewhere else. So my war was fought by small units.

I asked Doc Taylor, "What is going on in the mind of a 21 year old man at war in the jungles of Vietnam? You weren't world traveled you were just kind of East Tennessee, Knoxville.

Right out of high school, factory work and then the military. Knoxville and East Tennessee was my whole world.

Then all of a sudden I was in the army traveling to Texas training to be a medic, and on a ship crossing the Pacific in a storm and arriving in Vietnam and witnessed vehicles that have already been destroyed before I ever get into a fight. I felt total panic?

I felt… I said this is not what I am used to. This is not what I have been seeing on the movies. This is not what is in the papers this is completely out of my world it is out of my comprehension. What is going on!!

January to February we were patrolling and getting into occasional firefights with the Viet Cong.

Occasionally snipers would work off a few rounds at us.

But we didn't run into any real fighting. The Viet Cong in our area of operations was more or less a two or three man sniper… they would snipe at you a few times causing you to worry. Then they would take off and they would hide. But the NVA was a trained army totally different bunch of people. Viet Cong they were locals.

The Tet Offensive had begun, but we were not involved in the street fighting. We were not part of the communications. On our level of infantry platoon we didn't hear that. The battalions on up division, brigade yes they may have heard about it. We didn't not until it was too late.

The city fighting that was going on was entirely different new to the soldiers there we weren't doing any street fighting.

Let's put it this way… out in the bush boys like me being out in the county and hunting and fishing and stuff like that… we were in our element because we were used to being out in the field, country boys. When it came to city fighting like Hue and like that the boys that were born and raised in the city had the advantage over us. Because they knew how to operate in the city, we were used to being out in the fields, out in the woods. But when we started into the city fighting the boys that were born and raised in the city were more or less had the upper hand on us "country boys".

I understand that so by the time the Tet Offensive was over and the Viet Cong had pretty well been defeated...... destroyed we came in contact with a little town called Pinkville or... My Lai.

Now this was I think now Delta Company and I moved to Bravo Company and the VC attacked. I will tell you something about that town first... it had been around a few years. It had been mined by five different countries.

Author's note: Mined?

Doc Taylor had done his research.

"Mined oh boy!

World War II mined by the Japanese, French Indo China War mined by the French you can still see the French earthworks around the top (inaudible). Then it was mined by the ROK Marines. It was mined by the United States and mined by the South Vietnamese and how many more people mined it or what units. Nobody knew with all that.

OK, mined by 5 different countries at 5 different times in recent history dating back to WWII. That's why they call it uptight. The Viet Cong had killed and injured many of the soldiers in this area of operation. The soldiers were ripe and ready for revenge,

We don't call it uptight because the hill was real small it wasn't really uptight and the LZ was actually outside the barb wire fence. We were on top of this little hill. We had a battery of artillery and I think mortar battery or platoon whatever it is and we had a company of infantry around it. The other units of the artillery were on the perimeter so it was like that. But it was really uptight.

Tense may have been a better word.

My company was ordered to perform a blocking force near Pinkville. (My Lai)

It was mid-day mid-morning something like that. We had gotten into position there and were where we were supposed to be and we sat there and kept waiting and waiting didn't see or hear anybody. All of a sudden we heard shooting off to our right front. They said they had caught some Viet Cong in the water trying to get away. The first platoon leader of our company was Lt. Willingham. Some way or another I don't know how he did it but he got involved in it in the shooting. It went on for a while then it stopped. Still we didn't know what was going on so then word come down that the operation was over time to move out. Operation over, move out.

Away from Pinkville, start doing your patrols. Follow orders.

I asked Doc Taylor, "What was it like to be on patrol in Pinkville or what is also known as My Lai?"

You are in the boonies and the villages and paddies of South Vietnam and never saw the enemy maybe they lost 15 or 20% of their company through snipers, land mines etc. They never engaged and over the period of over 10, 11 or 12 weeks between the period they landed around New Year's Day of '68 until March 16th they became increasingly brutal, randomly going through a village and whacking people sometimes an old man they saw a soldier would just hit him with a rifle butt and nobody said anything.

Author's Note: As I said earlier, these American soldiers had been beaten up by a disappearing enemy, they knew the people of Pinkville, knew who the Viet Cong were and where they were hiding. They really wanted revenge,

Doc Taylor explained, "Because what happens inevitably is when you don't see an organized enemy and you lose people, lose your buddies and your mates and you are angry you take it out on the villagers.

Author's note: It appears you take your frustration out on the civilian population.

This seems to be how events went down.

One night the Americans were told, "Tomorrow you are going to meet the enemy." They were told the North Vietnamese the regular North Vietnamese battalion is going to be there and you get a chance to get payback. The soldiers mostly 17-20 years old did then what they did then. The young soldiers toked it up and the senior enlisted men and the officers drank it up. It helped break the uptight feeling. They all got up at 3:00 or 4:00 in the morning and jumped on choppers and went to kill and be killed. You have to give them their due. They got into the village and there are no soldiers there. The intelligence was bad as it always is and they gathered people up. There were no Viet Cong to identify and destroy. Just old women and men and children making their breakfasts… heating up water for their morning rice. They gathered them into three large ditches and began to execute them. Paying the Viet Cong families back for the hurt they felt. The officers had lost control. Calley became infamous but there were five or six, first and second lieutenants that were also organizing it. As I later wrote and learned about it I spent a couple of years sort of obsessing with it I wrote a couple of books about it. One was about the cover up almost during the day every senior officer including the major general in charge of the Americal Division. This group was assigned to the Americal Division, and officers were flying over the area. Pretty much everybody knew pretty much what was going on. There you are and I learned there was one of the young soldiers that did a lot of shooting. From a little small hamlet called New Goshen, Indiana and talk about a repressed memory. Many soldiers knew what was going on in some visceral way and reporters knew there was something there. Eventually locating soldiers who were present on the day of the MyLai massacre. The Stories began to build. The major presses were unsure if they should run the stories.

One repressed memory, a reporter identified the young man from Indiana. He had just kept firing clip after clip.

He was one of those who just shot and shot into the ditch. They put people as I said into 3 large ditches. After the shooting was over the soldiers went over eating their lunch really literally next to the ditch next to the bodies. That is how disconnected you get you obviously have to dehumanize the enemy as we have already learned earlier.

They were Gooks, Charlie, VC, not sons, fathers, and family men.

In any case. one mother had tucked a two or three year old child under her stomach and somehow he survived all the bullets and they heard a noise and this little boy climbed his way up through the ditch full of other people's blood, got to the top and began to run away.

Lieutenant Calley turned to the boy from Indiana, his most dependable shooter, others had stopped at a certain point or shot high, and said," Plug him. The boy from Indiana could not do it. And reportedly and Calley then with a very saucy like look, grabbed his carbide, officers had a smaller rifle called a carbide, ran behind him and shot him.

Everybody remembered that because the next morning the boy from Indiana was walking on patrol with the other soldiers. They moved on a few clicks away a mile or so away and began to patrol again as they always did. Just another day's work. I guess I don't know. The boy from Indiana stepped on a land mine. Japanese, French, American Korean, Viet Cong? Who knows?

He stepped on a land mine and blew his right leg off at the knee. When the medevac was coming they called in a chopper to take him away he began to issue an oath, "God has punished me Lt. Calley and God will punish you! God has punished me!" The soldiers were telling about this a year and a half later. All remembering how angry they were "get him out of here, get him out of here" they didn't want to hear this.

Doc Taylor added, "Like I said we didn't know what was going on I didn't see no dead bodies."

We were told operation over, Move out!

We did and began doing our normal stuff.

We started doing our usual thing you know, ducking bullets and dodging booby traps and fighting back to the LZ Sue.

Did Doc Taylor think that a massacre occurred?

189

"If it had, we didn't hear about it. We did not hear about it I didn't hear about it till 1972 when it first hit the fan."

As I said, "Back then if a platoon is more or less isolated from everything, we only knew what we knew. I didn't hear about a massacre myself, 1972.

And I know it is given the name massacre

It was... what else would you call it?

When you shoot kids and women unarmed women and kids what would you call it?

Author's note: Let me ask you this. "I am not a veteran I have never been in that spot. Were those young soldiers ordered to shoot?

Doc Taylor responded, "We were told what the 1st and 20th was told...

1st and 20th being Lieutenant Calley's group.

I know what we was told.

We were told that there was no innocent VN in My Lai 4. There was 3 or 4 different areas but My Lai 4. We were told there was no innocent civilians in My Lai 4 they had all gone to market. The people that was there were Viet Cong and Viet Cong suspects.

Author's note:

These are the same people that every time you all had gone in there they had beaten you up and shot you up?

Doc Taylor replied, "Yes!"

Author's note:

I asked this question in two different ways and you don't have to answer either one of them OK. Had you been ordered to fire would you have fired your gun?

That is difficult to answer now 52 years later. Back then I was a medic. It was my job to save lives and I guess rules that I live by are the medic's rules. If the Viet Cong was injured I tried to save him because that was my job. Now infantry lives by a whole different code than what I was living by. I probably wouldn't have pulled my trigger.

Author's note:

Now let's do this I am going to ask you the same question again. If you met one of those soldiers who had fired their guns and it was just another young man like you at the time and he had told you I was ordered to fire my gun how would you have felt about him?

Well, back then we was told to follow instructions, orders no matter what. If I was to tell you to do something you did it. Later on if something happens you just say that was my orders. If he was ordered to fire his gun he fired it he was doing what he was ordered to do. If he was ordered to do it he was following instructions... followed his orders. Everybody in Task Force Barker in the My Lai area knew we had taken beating after beating We wanted revenge. The opportunity to get revenge was offered to us and we took it. I don't think anybody planned for that to happen it happened. I don't think anybody planned in advance to put people down in the ditch and shoot them.

It was a total breakdown in command, control and communication.

Is the excuse I was only following orders acceptable? Some say yes in a combat situation. The men are young most are between the ages of 19 and 26 leading fire teams and squads in a war against the enemy. Now they are on their own and they have to make a split decision. When you aim your weapon and at the end is a threat then you need to eliminate the threat. If during the exchange of fire a civilian walks in between that is just war. If you aim your weapon and at the end of the barrel is a civilian and you pull the trigger you are wrong plain and simple. If it is a lawful order you are given by a superior you must follow that order. Sometimes it is difficult to determine what is lawful but you cannot have soldiers picking and choosing the orders they are going to follow. If in doubt follow the order. Soldiers are trained to follow orders however soldiers are people just like you and I. If you needed to disobey an order so that your conscience could be clear and you knew it was an unlawful order knowing the difference between a lawful and unlawful order can be difficult so it falls to your conscience. It is possible that you could refuse an order only to be court martialed and convicted if that happened would it have been better to follow your conscience and not commit what you thought was a crime or commit the crime and be walking a free man or woman. Did anything I just said make sense? Well, I was talking about things you ought to do and ought not do in a quick situation you are 19 years old, 20 years old most of the people who pulled the trigger on their guns at the My Lai incident said they were ordered to. Those who didn't pull the triggers on their guns didn't claim that at all they either shot in the air or refused to follow orders. Roger Taylor was a medic he operated under different rules as a soldier he was there to save lives. He said he would not have pulled the trigger then he was ordered to leave the area and walk over the hill and never mention it again.

Four years later he became aware he was nearby that massacre, and has lived with that ever since.

Do you follow an order, even if you know it to be morally wrong?

That Confederate officer was following orders, and felt he could have been executed if he had not starved the union Soldiers in Andersonville. At the German War crime trials many Nazi sympathizers said they were just following orders.

Do our American Boys 17-20 years old get a pass when an officer orders them to do an immoral act?

And when they follow orders, what is the bill that comes in when they have to be treated for POST TRAUMATIC STRESS?

How about being a soldier in the field of battle when you heard this from Walter Cronkite: Soundbite of TV program, "CBS Evening News")

Mr. CRONKITE: (Reading) tonight, back in more familiar surroundings in New York, we'd like to sum up our findings in Vietnam, an analysis that must be speculative, personal, and subjective. Who won and who lost in the great Tet Offensive against the cities? I'm not sure. The Vietcong did not win by a knockout but neither did we.

Then, with as much restraint as I could, I turned to our own leaders whose idea of negotiation seemed frozen in memories of General McArthur's encounter with the Japanese aboard the Battleship Missouri.

We've been too often disappointed by the optimism of the American leaders...

(Soundbite of TV program, "CBS Evening News")

(Reading) Both in Vietnam and Washington to have faith any longer in the silver linings they find in the darkest clouds. For it seems now more certain than ever, that the bloody experience of Vietnam is to end in a stalemate. To say that we are closer to victory today is to believe in the face of the evidence, the optimists who have been wrong in the past.

To say that we are mired in stalemate seems the only realistic, if unsatisfactory conclusion. On the off chance that military and political analysts are right, in the next few months we must test the enemy's intentions, in case this is indeed his last big gasp before negotiations.

But it is increasingly clear to this reporter that the only rational way out then will be to negotiate, not as victors, but as an honorable people who lived up to their pledge to defend democracy, and did the best they could.

This is Walter Cronkite. Good night.

Was this the start of our participation Trophies in Sports?

CHAPTER FOURTEEN

Vietnam - The Montagnards

I once watched an old video on the internet of the Jimmy Dean Show. He was interviewing **Sgt. Barry Sadler who wrote the Green Beret Ballad. He described the Montagnards of Vietnam as Vietnamese Hillbillies.**

They were primitive fighters. Roger Phillips who you met earlier gave me a crossbow used by the Montagnards. The arrow are made of wood, the bow string of a vine.

Who were the Montagnards? And how did the American soldiers, who became involved with them deal with these people who may not have considered themselves Vietnamese?

Earlier we mentioned the role of the Green Berets expanding to include the establishment of civilian irregular defense groups made up of fierce mountain men known as the Montagnard. Montagnard is not their real name. Montagnard is a French word, and the French had called all the mountain people in the central highlands of Vietnam the Montagnard. They were really Degar and H'mong, and lots of other minority ethnic groups. Before the Vietnam War, the population of the central highlands, estimated at between 3 and 3-1/2 million, was almost exclusively Degar. Today, the population is approximately 4 million, of whom about 1 million are Degar. The 30 or so Degar tribes in the central highlands comprise more than 6 different ethnic groups who speak languages drawn primarily from the Malayo- Polynesian, Thai, and Mon-Khmer language families. The main tribes, in order of population, are the Jarai, Rhade, Bahnar, Co Ho, H'mong, and Stieng.

Originally inhabitants of the coastal areas of the region, these "Montagnards were driven to the uninhabited mountainous areas by invading Vietnamese and Cambodians beginning prior to the 9th century. Well, how are our soldiers supposed to know that? We trained our soldiers to shoot the guns and to operate their equipment and to fight a war. We did not train them to understand the social cultures of Vietnam, or did we? French Roman Catholic missionaries converted some Degar in the 19th century but, American missionaries made more of an impact in the 1930's before World War II, and many Degar are now Protestant. Of the approximately 1 million Degar, close to half are Protestant, while around 200,000 are Roman Catholic. This made Vietnam's Communist Party suspicious of the Degar, particularly during the Vietnam War since it was thought that they would be more inclined to help the American forces. So the inhabitants of the central highlands in Vietnam didn't think of themselves as true Vietnamese. They were thought of by the French as the Montagnard.

In the mid 1950's, the once isolated Degar began experiencing more contact with outsiders after the Vietnamese government launched efforts to gain better control of the central highlands, and following the 1954 Geneva Accord, new ethnic minorities from North Vietnam moved into the area. These were the same ethnic minorities that had suffered all the starvation in 1945 right after World War II. The Degar communities felt a need to strengthen some of their own social structures and to develop a more formal, shared identity, so in a way, they became natural enemies of the true Vietnamese, especially the North Vietnamese. When the French withdrew from Vietnam and recognized the Vietnamese government, Degar political independence was drastically diminished.

The Degar have a long history of tensions with the Vietnamese majority. While the Vietnamese are themselves heterogeneous, they generally share a common language and culture and have developed and maintained the dominant social institutions of Vietnam. The Degar do not share that heritage. There have been conflicts between the 2 groups over many issues, including land ownership, language, and cultural preservation, access to education resources, and political representation.

The U.S. Mission to Saigon sponsored the training of the Degar in unconventional warfare by American Special Forces. These newly-trained Degar were seen as a potential ally in the central highlands area to stop Viet Cong activity in the region and a means of preventing further spreading of Viet Cong sympathy. The U.S. military, particularly the U.S. Army Special Forces, developed base camps in the area and recruited the Degar, roughly 40,000 of whom fought alongside American soldiers and became a major part of the U.S. military effort in the highlands.

This information may make it easier to understand the brutality between the Viet Cong and their southern neighbors.

The first time you the reader probably ever became aware of the Montagnard might have been in the John Wayne movie, *The Green Berets*, and if you saw the movie, you'll remember when they went to capture the North

Vietnamese general, the commandos took with them a few half-naked Vietnamese warriors who carried crossbows, and those were the Montagnard.

So the Montagnard never got along with the Vietnamese flat landers, around the beaches, around the rivers, and they most certainly didn't get along with the North Vietnamese, who kept sending people down to take their land and do land reform, so they were prime allies of the American military.

The story I'm about to tell you comes from a newspaper called the *Trident*, the Jungle Warriors. It's an Americal Division newspaper from the 11th Infantry Brigade. It was published in Duc Pho, Vietnam, Volume 2, Number 12, September 20, 1968, and the headline is, "A 105-mm Howitzer is now back in the allied arsenal."

The story went like this!

Two Montagnard informants earned 25,000 piastres each last week by leading infantrymen from the 11th Brigade's 4th Battalion, 3rd Infantry, to a 105-mm Howitzer buried 8 miles west of Quang Ngai City. The artillery piece, captured by the enemy when the Tra Bong Special Forces camp was overrun 3 years ago—this is in 1965—had been reassembled and cleaned and is being used by the 11th Brigade in Operation Champagne Grove. Six months ago, the VC used the cannon during the Tet attack on Quang Ngai City. Our helicopter Crew Chief in an earlier chapter had already been a prisoner of war for three years. The 18-year-old tribesmen, their wives, and one sister turned themselves over to elements of the brigade's Task Force Garcia last month west of Quang Ngai. They claimed the VC used them 6 times as forced laborers and were planning to use them as guerillas before they decided to seek Allied protection. The Viet Cong didn't like the Montagnard. The Montagnard didn't like the Viet Cong.

"Laborers don't usually have valuable information", said the American officer of the Brigade's 52nd military intelligence detachment. "The VC infrastructure is pretty careful about letting forced laborers know too much." That's because the VC knew that the Montagnards were friendly to the Allies. The officer and his Montagnard interpreter asked the 2 boys the routine questions. Did they have any weapons? Did they know the location of any small arms, explosives, grenades, caches? They shook their heads. "Do you know the location of any weapon?" the officer asked. "Yes, one big one," they answered. "How big?" asked the officer. "It took 60 men to carry it," said the boys. "I don't know of any weapon that requires 60 men to haul around," said the officer. I asked them the smallest number of men they had seen carry it, and they replied, "30." But we know 30 Vietnamese can move a mighty large piece of equipment. The history videos of men carrying large field guns up mountains to fight the French at Diem Bien Phu was enough evidence for anyone. The young laborers had no idea what type of weapons they had carried into the hills. One VC referred to the cannon as a "dai bac," which means an 82-mm recoilless gun. "They look somewhat like a 105," said the officer, "but the 82 has metal wheels." The informants said the 2 wheels were rubber, just like our jeep tires. They also said the barrel was 8 feet long, and these 2 things indicated an artillery piece. All of this left one important question unanswered: Where had the VC buried the cannon? The 2 boys had helped to bury the weapon in 4 well-camouflaged holes shortly after Tet in early February. During the Tet attacked on Quant Ngai, the Viet Cong recruited them as laborers, and they had seen the weapon with empty shell casings beside it. The cannon was pointed towards Quang Ngai. After Tet, they were again forced to work for the VC and help drag the 4800-pound cannon to a streambed. Later, they returned to the spot where they dug holes to bury the weapon. NVA soldiers had dismantled and prepared the gun for burial. A few days before turning themselves in, they passed the streambed and noted the camouflage had not been disrupted. They didn't have any idea where they had buried the gun. They couldn't find the place on a map or even tell the difference between east and west, and there's a lot of little streams out there. It took the interrogation team over 6 hours to narrow the spot down to a grid square. "The hamlets they knew weren't on our maps," said the officer. "We used their word pictures and crude maps they drew to locate the spot. After hours of map-tracking, I felt pretty sure we had the right square. The boys had been honest with us all along, but I told them I thought their story was crazy, and I didn't believe it. They said they would lead us to the weapon to prove they weren't lying." This was before any monetary incentive had been offered.

A few days later, the 2 boys joined Bravo Company, 4th Battalion, and 3rd Infantry on a hilltop west of the province capital. "We had a hell of a time getting down that hill," said the officer of B Company. We were all slipping around, and they seemed to be leading us in circles, but when we got to the bottom, they became surer of themselves. I was walking up front, firing my M-79 into the trees behind the stream. The interpreter was afraid there'd be an ambush near the weapon. Then he pointed into the underbrush and said, "They say VC artillery there." We pushed through the tall grass and dug into the sand. We got about 6 inches down when I hit something. It took the old guard soldiers 2 hours to dig the cannon out of the four holes. "Every thing's there accept the panoramic telescope," said the officer. "It's pretty rusted, but the VC put the small, movable parts in plastic bags. I imagine it could be cleaned up and fired without too much trouble." The infantryman lugged the barrel, shields, cradle, and wheels across a small rice paddy where a chinook lifted the weapon back to Landing Zone Bronco to be reassembled. It took 11 men just to move the barrel a few meters. They had heard about the 30 or 40 Vietnamese who had dragged the 2-1/2-ton cannon through the hills. "Where were those 30 men when we needed 'em?"

This story was brought to me by Doc Taylor. You met him in the My Lai story. He was a medic for the Americal Division in Vietnam. He was on a hillside following orders to block the mountain escape at a little village called My Lai. He knew it as Pinkville. He told me his version and viewpoint concerning a captured 105-mm cannon in Vietnam, and I asked Doc, "How was a Green Beret involved in this search?

This is what he said:

"You had a captain in charge of the Green Beret attachment.

The A team.

You would have a captain from the South Vietnamese Army up there, too, and his company, or whatever he has, and this was a counterpart. You have one American and one South Vietnamese.

They were training but, they didn't need that much training, 'cause the South Vietnamese and all Vietnamese soldiers from both sides had been fighting for decades.

So, they just needed to be trained in the updated equipment—

But, a lot of times their primitive, obsolete—whatever you want to call it—weapons that they used on us, did better than what our sophisticated weapons did on them. They can go underground and hide, and—and bombs wouldn't touch 'em. Then when they came out ready to fight, they were ready to fight.

And they had been doing that for years. They had been doing that since World War II, or beforehand.

A lot of those tunnels had already been dug.

We still don't know where they're all at. It's been 40 years, and (LAUGHTER) we still don't know where they're all at.

Doc Taylor told me about the 105 that was buried.

"Well, this was a very, very good weapon. It saved our bacon more times than I care to remember. We'd get in a bind, we'd call back to a fire base, LZ Uptight, LZ Sue, or Dotty, or nearest fire base, and give 'em coordinates. They would fire what was called a smoke round, which was a "Willie Pete," white phosphorous. It was a marker round.

So they would shoot the marker round over, and you'd say, "Yeah," that's the spot you want?

Or move it so many meters this way or that way. Then it would fire for effect. Then you adjust the next round from there. You say "fire-for-effect or put a cap on it," and all 4 of 'em would open up.

When you say "put a cap on it," that means the explosive shell?

That means—put a cap on it—that means "hit it!"

This Howitzer that we're talking about was sent to Vietnam in 1965?

Well, maybe even before.

It all depends on when that fire base was built.

And right now we're talking about the Tri Bong fire base, and that was Special Forces? It wasn't Marine or Army, it was Green Berets?

It was Army, but Special Forces.

I told Doc Taylor that in 1965, there was a battle at Tra Bong. He did not know anything about that battle?

That there was an American 105 captured when the camp was overrun, and that the Viet Cong had reassembled and cleaned and used it during the Tet Offensive. So the North Vietnamese Army was using American equipment.

During the Tet Offensive, they were using some of our guns they had captured and in some cases, instead of actually towing it behind equipment, when the American soldier would go in with a 105 Howitzer either being pulled by a truck or landed by a helicopter or pulled by a jeep, the North Vietnamese soldier would have 30 or 40 men carry it. Just like in '54, Diem Bien Phu?

This is Doc Taylor's version:

"OK, so we've got this Howitzer, then, in the possession of the North Vietnamese, and they used it in the Tet Offensive in February '68—

Um-hmm, and probably even before then.

Then one day a couple of Montagnard informants who were not slave labor—or I guess they *were* slave labor, weren't they?

Well, it was—like this. The Montagnard did not like the low-lander Vietnamese or the Viet Cong…

And the flat-landers, North or South didn't like the Montagnard.

And, you know, they hated each other with a purple passion.

And—if they wanted to use slave labor from the Montagnard, you know, they'd use 'em! The Montagnard didn't like that, and didn't trust the flat-landers, and the flat-landers didn't like and didn't trust the Montagnard.

But the Montagnard were fierce fighters, and mostly pro-American.

They were mostly pro-American because, Green Berets went in there and set fire bases and showed 'em a little bit of respect, had medical people there taking care of 'em, paid 'em.

Doc Taylor wanted to talk about one of the platoons in his Company. The article that he brought to me said that the Montagnard informants came up and told them they knew where the gun was, but they didn't know how to read a map, the Montagnard didn't, so they had to try and show the American military where the guns were.

"Normally", said Doc Taylor, "and usually, my impression of American soldiers coming across a cache of weapons was— they were just patrolling an area, and they would find a suspicious spot and go in, or they would be looking for a cache because they knew about it. In this case,

It was a—going looking for 'em, having an informant, just by happenstance, find it.

But more or less, when we go into a village, we search the village, turn over—underneath the fire pit, they'd dig a hole underneath the fire pit where they cooked and hide stuff down there, and, you know, put a cover over it, build a fire, and usually they have ammunition, grenades, whatever they have underneath there. And you'd go by there, and you'd have to search the village. And you may find an AK, or a carbine, or something like this, or grenades, or some ammunition, something like this, but finding a real big cache—very few and far between."

I asked Doc Taylor, "How would a patrol like that be handled?"

"Well," he said, "we would try to have an interpreter there, to begin with. We'd send back to Division, try to get an interpreter to interpret what these guys were saying, because we're, you know, we're dummies. We can't speak that language. (LAUGHTER) We would go out in a—it's a platoon. We'd put them guys out in front with a man right behind 'em, with orders. If they run, don't let 'em run.

If they look like they're going to take off on you, you know, run away, don't let 'em.

You can read whatever you want to into that.

OK, because if they're running—we're in an ambush. They're trying to save their own bacons.

All right. We take our time, let them lead, and follow and hope we don't get hit. (LAUGHTER)

In 1965, the Montagnard had been resisting invaders taking away their land, lifestyle, and freedom for over 20 years. That's not counting the 1050 years they had lived up on the central plateau region of Vietnam. The North Vietnamese Army and the Viet Cong treated them as slave labor and sometimes as expendable soldiers. How would an American soldier know that in advance? How would they know that the 2 men were Montagnard and not Vietnamese or Viet Cong or disguised North Vietnamese Army soldiers? And then, being a young American soldier from East Tennessee, how are you supposed to know all that? And on top of that, sometimes when an American soldier was going on search-and-destroy, he carried a weapon, but he also had a Red Cross patch on his shoulder or on his helmet, and all the guys in the squad knew that he was the Doc. Docs were held in much esteem and when they were needed, and they always knew when they were needed, all a soldier had to do was cry out, and the Doc would be there. The Doc on many of those search-and-destroy mission was Doc Taylor.

The combat medical badge was conceived March 1, 1945 by the War Department. The combat medical badge could specifically be awarded to officers and enlisted personnel of the medical department who were assigned to or attached to a medical detachment of the infantry. The combat medical badge was to recognize medical aid men who shared the same hazards and hardships of ground combat on a daily basis with the infantry soldier. The combat medical badge was never intended to be awarded to all medical personnel. Due to the uniqueness of ground combat in the infantry, it was intended to be awarded only to those medics who served under direct fire with the infantry. To be awarded the combat medical badge, the infantry unit to which the medical personnel were assigned or attached must have engaged the enemy in active ground combat. Medical personnel must have been personally present and under fire in order to be eligible for this award. During the Vietnam War, the requirements were so stringent that recommending officials were required to document the place in 6-digit coordinates: The time, the type of engagement, and also the intensity of fire to which the medical personnel were exposed. The combat medical badge could also be awarded to U.S. Navy and U.S. Air Force medical personnel as long as they met all the requirements of Army medical personnel.

Doc Taylor served his time in Vietnam. He was a very young man and at the time did not know the many things that he knows now about the Vietnam War, and he has spent a lifetime researching the details and understanding the maps and all the information to find out where he was and what he was doing there other than just observing as a young American man. Thank you, Doc Taylor, for all you've done. Thank you for sharing your information with us, and thank you for caring enough about the rest of us to want us to know.

The Montagnard inhabited Central Highlands became open to the Vietnamese only under French rule. The word savage (moi) was used by the Vietnamese against the Montagnard Degars. Who fought both the South Vietnamese and the united Communist Vietnam government for twenty years after the end of the Vietnam War and the scale of Vietnamese attacks on the Montagnards are alleged by one US author as having killed over 200,000 Montagnards after 1975. The Vietnamese were leasing land to Japanese companies to harvest lumber in the area. Munitions, weapons, and 5,000 rifles were given by the Chinese to some Montagnard groups after some Montagnards requested help from China. China has never really gotten along with Vietnam through time.

I have already described the first Tet offensive against Chinese forces earlier in this book. The Americans had refused to help against the Vietnamese. [14] Montagnard courts were abolished by South Vietnam and the Central Highlands became flooded with Vietnamese colonizers under the direction of the Vietnamese government.

Torture and mass arrests by the Vietnamese military were used in the Central Highlands against the Degar/Montagnard during the February 2001 protests against Vietnamese oppression.

The animosity goes back to post World War II issues.

The conflict also is traced to the independent mind set of the Montagnards.

This was the situation in 1963. Heavy Chinese influence from Vietnam, and heavy Indian influence from the Cambodians and Laotians also led to conflict of these mountain folk who wanted their own autonomy.

Colonists flooding into the Central Highlands has significantly altered the demographics of the region. Violent demonstrations with fatalities have broken out due to Montagnard anger at Vietnamese discrimination and seizure of their land since many Vietnamese were settled by the government in the Central Highlands once the Americans were gone.

The demographics of the highlands was drastically transformed with the mass colonization of 6 million settlers from 1976 to the 1990s, which led to ethnic Vietnamese outnumbering the native ethnic groups in the highlands.

A 2002 article in the Washington Times reported that Montagnard women were subjected to forced mass sterilization by the Vietnamese government for the Montagnard's population to be reduced, in addition to stealing lands of the Montagnards, and attacking their religious beliefs, killing and torturing them in a form of "creeping genocide".[38]

Former Green Beret and writer Don Bendell wrote a novel based on Vietnam's policies in the Central Highlands with details in his book such as accusing the Communist Vietnamese government implemented a genocidal and discriminatory policy against the native Montagnards in the Central Highlands, banning Montagnard languages and implementing Vietnamese language, having Vietnamese men marry Montagnard girls and women by force, colonizing the Central Highlands with massive numbers of Vietnamese settlers from the lowlands, inflicting terror and on the Montagnards.

The jailed Montagnards had been subjected to torture by the Vietnamese government which caused the mass protests. There were 30 police officers wounded in Buon Ma Thuot in Daklak and Pleiku. Coffee farming and colonization of ethnic Vietnamese in the Central highlands are supported by the Vietnamese government. The natives were attacked by Vietnamese helicopters and soldiers in Daklak and Gia Lia provinces.

The Ratanakiri and Moldokiri based Montagnards numbered 402 people in December 1992. Another wave of Montagnard refugees in Cambodia happened after the Vietnamese government crackdown on the protests in the Central Highlands in February 2001.

Torture was performed by the Vietnamese upon Montagnards who were detained after the protests. The demonstrators were crushed by Vietnamese troops and police after they asked for the land back in non-violent protests in the Central Highlands in 2001. In their own native lands, the Vietnamese have been removing Montagnards since they don't have official documentation and the Highlands have been flooded with Vietnamese colonists supported by the Vietnamese government. Plantations run by the government were built on the land of the Montagnards which were also settled by lowlanders. Montagnards were made to give up their lands for far less than they were worth to the Vietnamese government [47]

The Vietnamese government stole the land of the Montagnards when the Communists came to power. During protests Montagnards were shot. Thousands Montagnards were alleged to have been killed with rivers being used as dumping grounds for bodies by the Vietnamese government.

Ethnic cleansing at its best!

The Montangards were driven to Cambodia after they were left in destitution when their indigenous lands were seized by the Vietnamese in an "ethnic cleansing" plan implemented by the Communist. The Montagnard demonstrators were accused of being separatists who wanted their own country by the Vietnamese government.

The Vietnamese government implemented a campaign to censor and whitewash the events.[99]

Demonstrators were hunted down with dogs in coffee plantations by the Vietnamese.

Because of his desire to promote trade with Vietnam, John Kerry rejected showing any concern for Montagnard rights and voted against the 2001 Vietnam Human Rights Act in the Senate. Kerry said that "communism" was what the people wanted in Vietnam. The current 750,000 Montagnard have been halved from their original 1975 number of 1,500,000.

Such are the spoils of war.

CHAPTER FIFTEEN

The Tet Offensive

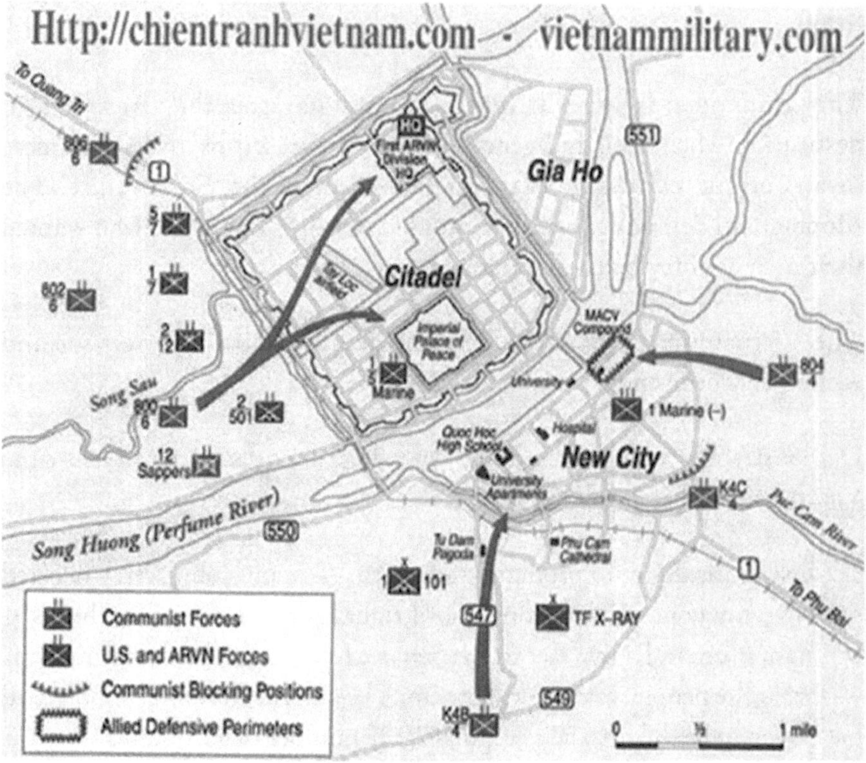

In this dirty old part of the city
Where the sun refuse to shine.

Lyrics from: We Gotta get Out of This Place
Sung by the Animals

The first Tet Offensive most people think was in 1968, but in reality it was in 1789. The United States of America was forming its Constitution. The

Vietnamese were fighting all over their country against the Cambodians, the Laotians, the Thais (they were called Siamese at the time), and the Chinese.

In January of 1789, the Vietnamese army led a revolt against the Chinese army to run them out of the country. They did it in a massive battle with elephants, hundreds of thousands of troops, and on the last day of the Tet New Year celebration, the Chinese retreated after losing several of their officers to having their throats cut and their soldiers surrendering. Although to defeat your enemy was important, the mission was to make it so that the Chinese never wanted to come back.

General Giap. You probably didn't hear his name very much. Most of us think that the leaders of North Vietnam were Ho Chi Minh. General Giap was the general who set the stage for the military strategy to defeat the French at Dien Bien Phu.

We have been mentioning his name many times in this book.

Fourteen years later, he came up with a strategy to defeat the American military during the Tet Offensive in 1968.

The 1968 Tet Offensive proved to be a military disaster for the North Vietnamese, but General Giap was able to achieve some of his political objectives. The offensive showed the North Vietnamese were far from being defeated and significantly contributed to changing American perceptions about the conflict. Following Tet, peace talks began, and the U.S. ultimately withdrew from the War in 1973.

The Tet Offensive in 1968 was conceived by General Giap, commander of the North Vietnamese army and his staff. It started with the Battle of Khe Sanh on January 21, 1968. The mission of Khe Sanh had two objectives besides the obvious objective in defeating the Marines. The first was a diversionary tactic to draw American attention away from the cities of South Vietnam and more towards Khe Sanh up the mountains in the Northwest corner *and* to remind the people of South Vietnam of another battle that took place 14 years earlier at Dien Bien Phu.

The Tet Offensive of 1968 was the first time during the War that actual street-fighting took place in the major cities. This new offensive was immediately brought into the homes of American families through reporting by television and the press. The sensationalization of this reporting brought forth misrepresentation of the actual facts that took place during the Tet Offensive of 1968. Reports led the American people to think that we were losing the War in Vietnam and that the Tet Offensive was a major victory for North Vietnam. This was not the case. The Viet Cong suffered such high casualties that they were no longer considered a fighting force, and their ranks would have to be replaced by North Vietnamese Regulars. The civilian population of South Vietnam was indifferent to both the current regime in South Vietnam and the Viet Cong.

This story is about Captain Alex Wells, Marine Reserves. He left the Marines in 1969, and he was a participant in the Battle of Hué at the Citadel.

I started our interview with a Thank you for his service.

He Replied, "Thank you, Randy, my friend. I'm honored to be on this program, and I appreciate your support of all the active military, wounded warriors, and all those coming back and all of us old veterans.

I grew up in Chattanooga, Tennessee. Up on Lookout Mountain. Right up there on top.

Alex had taken me on a tour. He showed me where his grandfather lived and showed me the country club up there and showed me the land and told me some of the history, but his family goes back a long way in the American military. All the way back to Valley Forge?

Alex told the story, "Well, we had a character whose name was James Wells, and he claimed to be a lieutenant with Washington at Valley Forge. That's about all we know, but he was the first recorded ancestor over from Wales, believe it or not. The Wells from Wales."

I had a great-great grandfather that was in that little event called THE CIVIL WAR.

Actually, I had one on each side. We had a lieutenant colonel in the Union Army at Gettysburg, we know, and then he had a brother who went South, and I believe he joined the Tennessee Volunteers here, the Confederacy, in the battle of Vicksburg.

My Grand Dad Loman, my mom's father, actually went down in the Mexican campaign in 1916 and rode in the last cavalry charge that the U.S. ever made with General Blackjack Pershing against Poncho Villa.

Then there was my father who seems to be the most decorated in the family, in World War II.

Well, he was a PT boat skipper, and the Battle of Guadalcanal, he participated in the sinking of several destroyers coming down the slot there, the Japanese, and the last few days of that battle, which lasted, as you probably know, almost six months with the Marines having a heck of a time and supported by the Navy all the way, February 1, 1943, about 3 weeks before I was born, he had just fired two torpedoes and sunk a destroyer, and as he was coming back on patrol about midnight, he was hit by a Jap night bomber. Probably a 250-pound bomb hit him amidships, cut the PT boat in half, and he spent the next eight hours in the ocean fighting the sharks and trying to tow what was left of his crew, and he got a couple of guys back, and he won the Silver Star for that engagement.

Silver Star—but that is not his only claim to fame. He had a little bit of contact with one of our famous generals. He was a squadron commander in the Battle of Leyte Gulf, and October 24, 1944 he actually took General Douglas MacArthur back on his PT boat, #525, to make his famous return. Actually, they just pulled up on an old rickety dock there off the Gulf, and the Marines were still fighting the snipers on the beach, but the General jumped out on the dock and said, "I have returned. Let's get the hell out of here!" he laughed, "OK, they don't tell the whole story in the books, do they?

Author's note:

OK, so now we come up to the son of the man with the Silver Star, Mr. Captain Alex Wells. He attended one of the military schools in Chattanooga?

Well, I did, but before that, let me just say that I've got a little bit of credit to my uncle on my mom's side, my mom's brother. He's really the only living relative that was in the War, and he was an Ace fighter pilot with the Flying Tigers in Southern China, and he was shot down by the Japs near the Northern Vietnamese border with China and rescued by some Vietnam guerillas who were fighting the Japanese and the French during the Second World War and some Chinese guerillas,.

Author's note:

Remember, Ho Chi Minh was working with the Allies rescuing pilots shot down over Indo China, soon to be Vietnam.

Backing up to my childhood in Chattanooga at the McCauley School when it was full military back in the 50's and early 60's, just followed in the footsteps of my dad and my uncle there.

Author's note: I first learned about McCauley when my daughter Lori had a basketball game against them in Chattanooga in the mid 1990's.

Capt. Wells explained, "I was captain of the wrestling team and played a little football and did a little pole-vaulting. I got a wrestling scholarship to Virginia and fortunately was able to play some polo at the same time.

I took my polo pony down there whenever they had a home game and had a great time, dressed up like a Crazy Cavalier with a sword and a plume hat and all that stuff, big cape, rode around in circles with the football team, but we weren't scoring too many points back then so really didn't have a lot to celebrate but had a great time.

I interrupted the sports memories with Captain Wells, "OK, the Virginia online magazine put out a report about all the different students that they had that were in the Vietnam War, and one of the paragraphs in it has a picture of Marine First Lieutenant Alex Wells, and it says, "Early in his tour,

Alex Wells was Bob Dunphy's artillery forward observer and later survived being surrounding by the enemy for 14 days in the Citadel at Hué during the 1968 Tet Offensive. After that, with his partner, Ron Miller,(deceased) he started and runs a private humanitarian Vietnam reconciliation business group and has gone back to Vietnam a time or two on sanctioned U.S. Government reconciliation visits." Is that you?

Well, that's me, but the operation is actually chaired by my wife, Mary T., and she should have been in that article. I think she was in the original article, but she's the one that put everything together and was our inspiration to actually go back to Vietnam 25 years after the Tet Offensive and film a documentary over there.

Captain Alex Wells is talking about at time when he was Lt. Alex Wells. He told me about the first time he realized he was on your way to Vietnam?

"I got the commission, Second Lieutenant, in May of '66, and I figured from the day they pinned on that LT's bar I was on the way, and later, actually that fall, starting in September, we went through 5 months of officer combat training at the basics school at Quantico, Virginia.

I trained with some Vietnamese troops? We had about 20 South Vietnamese officers that were in the ARVN Marines, and yeah, they were training with us. They had several lieutenants and some captains that were there. They wanted to learn what we as officers did. They wanted to, they took part and participated, but they just wanted to see how we operated as Marines working in conjunction with them, you know, in the War, and we had, of course, Marine advisors with their units, so they participated in most of the classroom work. They didn't like the physical part, but yeah, they were observers and participants both.

Then off to artillery school in Fort Sill, Oklahoma, became an artillery officer and learned how to be a forward observer, calling in light and heavy artillery fire. I was qualified to call to someone far away or nearby and tell them where to drop a shell.

Well, I could call Air in when I had to and also naval guns from time to time, but mainly it was 105-mm artillery and then 155s.

Alex and I had bonded and began celebrating his birthday in an unusual way. This particular conversation occurred on the 43rd anniversary of the Tet Offensive? It was also, the 43rd anniversary of his 25th birthday, which was during the Tet Offensive, surrounded by the enemy.

Forty-third anniversary of your 25th birthday.

"That makes me an old guy right now, Randy.

I responded," you're lucky to be here. Tell me about that beer you had with the colonel. You were telling me about going into a bar and a colonel bought you a beer, or a pitcher of beer, or something.

Here is the story:

I'm telling you that was the most expensive beer that I've ever had in my life, and I was afraid that it might be my last, but I was just minding my own business, had got off duty from target information officer the night of the 9th of February, '68, and the Tet Offensive had been going for 10 days by that time, and I got off about noon, I guess, on the 10th and went over to the old club hooch there and was having a cold beer, in fact a whole pitcher of cold beer, and the colonel came in. Colonel Barr was the artillery commander at Phu Bai, and that's 10 miles south of Hué and the Citadel and the Perfume Rive. He joined me, and we were sipping cold Budweiser, and he said, "Alex," he called me by the first name, as he usually did, and said, "I need you to go into the Citadel for a 24-hour mission to mop up small pockets of enemy resistance for General Truong up there at the first ARVN Division. He just called in this morning and requested a combat-experienced forward observer to help him call in some big guns, which he doesn't have, and I said, "Well, that sounds real good, Colonel, but you know I'm short, and I've been an FO for six months before I got here and by the grace of God lived through that with only one scratch, and so I'm not volunteering for anything, but I'll help you find somebody, and he quickly said, "Lieutenant, get on the chopper at 1630 hours and bring your radio operator with you." He wasn't looking for a volunteer. He had already volunteered me, I guess.

He was not telling me the whole truth. The Citadel had already fallen at that time.

I don't really believe he knew it, and if he did, I need to find him today and have a little chat with him, but the intelligence was so pitiful because the South Vietnamese would never really give us the straight scoop when they had been overrun by Viet Cong or NVA, and by that time, good Lord, there were 5,000 NVA and main force Viet Cong inside the Citadel, and they'd taken over about 80% of it, so, in effect, they'd captured the Citadel and had General Truong and his headquarters group with a few straggling Rangers and Marines and Black Panther commandos surrounded up in the Northeast corner of the Citadel, and the American intelligence did not know that.

So I got orders after the Citadel had fallen to go in by helicopter with my sergeant and to go into someplace called The Alamo. We actually landed, in fact, trying to fly over the Perfume River, we almost got shot out of the sky with green tracers, which, of course, meant that the enemy was firing at us since we only had red tracers, and all of a sudden, the whole Southern wall of the Citadel, and I mean these were high, thick walls, 30 feet high, 30 feet thick, the Southern wall along the Perfume River opened up on us as we were crossing the Perfume River, We just about got blown out of the sky but had a great pilot, and he flipped the chopper on the side and zoomed out over the South China Sea—in fact, we came over part of the Task Force out there, the Navy Task Force—and we came over the East wall, and finally we set down at the Ta Loc airstrip, but he didn't touch the ground, the hovered about 5 feet off, so the two of us had to jump out, and we were still getting sniper fire at the time.

It wasn't as peaceful and it wasn't quite a mop-up operation as I was led to believe. I think the intelligence was so bad that it was just the opposite of what they told me.

We finally met up with a Black Panther commando sergeant, ARVN and South Vietnamese, and he got us through the enemy lines to General Truong's headquarters. We were briefed there by the General and his Chief of Staff, and they told us they wanted us to go out to a forward outpost near the emperor's Palace of Perfect Peace and set up an operation to call in fire on the West gate of the Western wall, and I told him that would be great, as soon as the American Marines got in, I'd be glad to join them and do that, and he said, "No, they can't get across the river, and we need you there now. This is an emergency." And my orders were actually in support of him, so he was my commanding officer, and I'm telling you, which 24 hours turned into 14 days, and I never saw the American Marines until it was all over.

Well, we ate everything that moved and ended up having a big roasted sewer rat for my birthday on the 19th of February. Twenty-fifth birthday, matter of fact.

I thought it was going to be my last for sure, but a birthday meal never tasted so good in my life. I was just trying to stay out of the way of the NVA guns and stay alive and at the same time carry out my mission of calling artillery on the West gate and the Western wall. We couldn't fire inside the Citadel. Its 3 square miles of residential buildings inside the fortress walls, and it was a no-fire zone, so— no artillery fire. No heavy guns at all.

I had to fire on the Western wall, which really was the ingress and egress for the NVA to resupply and reinforce themselves through the West gate, and then I called in 155-mm artillery from Phu Bai, 10 miles South of the Perfume River, onto the West gate and the moat bridge that crossed the 100-foot-wide moat there from the outside. That's where the enemy was coming across, and then they were going under the moat through the sewer system, and it was pretty bad because we could not stop 'em. But we could see them coming!

Hunkered down like I was, I couldn't see too much, but I could certainly hear 'em, and on the radio we had an enemy radio intercept, so I could hear their voices in Vietnamese, and I was, of course, had a translator right with me, and yeah, I could hear 'em, and I could hear the guns coming closer and closer, and then on the night of the 16th of February, they staged a battalion-size attack from the outside of the West gate and were coming across the moat bridge there, about 1,000 NVA probably, and, fortunately, I called the Artillery, and after about 10 minutes had a round hit the bridge and stop that attack and saved all of our lives, the South Vietnamese and American Marines that were probably a couple of football fields to my East, so that was the last major attack against our position.

I had bombed them into submission. I had also triggered my own location. We were probably 3 minutes away from being overrun, and so if that had happened, we were just going to take as many of them with us as we could, and I kept telling the Battery at my command only if I called it in.

I lost 25 pounds in 14 days? I was a skinny guy after that.

Emotionally, I was shell-shocked and probably still am.

Yes Alex, you have qualified for full disability for PTSD. Thank you for your service.

Lt. Alex Wells had fought inside the Citadel at the Battle of Hué in the Tet Offensive in 1968. He spent 14 days, not trapped, but located in the front of the battle, calling in artillery positions to stop the enemy from advancing on the cornered South Vietnamese troops and the American Marines.

Alex continued his story:

"I want to go back and build a reconciliation center.

Well, Randy, we've really been going back for the last almost 20 years now several times and taking American veterans back to meet the former enemy that we fought against, and it all started with our very first trip. I went back with my wife and some friends, and our Vietnamese partner, Dr. Tran Van, who has been going back over the past few years and doing business in Vietnam. Our tour guide just happened to be a Viet Cong commander that I'd fought against face-to-face inside the Citadel, and he was part of the attack on the 16th and was wounded by my Artillery on the West gate moat bridge but survived. There he was 25 years later, welcoming us with all these beautiful, smiling people at the airport in Hanoi, and then we went down on the train to Huế, and he ended up being the battlefield tour guide and taking us—after the Citadel, down to Da Nang and China Beach and Marble Mountain where I'd been for the first six months as an FO. (Field Observation officer). That's when we realized, my wife and myself. We realized that that was our mission in life, and thank the Lord for our great friend and partner, Ron Miller. He joined us, and we had several other vets in the Atlanta area that helped us get started, and then we just started going back and making friends with former enemies and really going through a tremendous healing process of redemption and forgiveness and really becoming human beings with each other again. It was just the most exhilarating experience that any of us have ever had.

We were just soldiers following orders. We really weren't setting policy, we weren't setting tactics or strategy, we were just following orders and getting done what we had to get done.

Author's note:

Again, General Giap was setting the strategies and tactics and the Americans we reacting to it.

We were just doing our duty as we saw it and fighting for our cause, such as it was, and we had no hatred or animosity on a personal basis. It was strictly a military job, and now I think we can make a big difference in a lot of lives of veterans who've been hurting' ever since the War, and we have found that my taking combat veterans back to meet the men that they fought against face-to-face in certain battles wherever they were at a specific time and date, there is a tremendous healing catharsis that takes place in our hearts and souls and spirits and minds, and it's just a miraculous situation.

Lots of our soldiers come home, and they're wounded emotionally and spiritually and physically and never get the chance to go back and heal, but you have taken this opportunity to go back to Vietnam and take a chance of sharing your experience with the enemy, which—they're not the enemy anymore, are they?

No, it's always the former enemy, and now they're becoming friends and allies government-to-government. At first it was just veteran-to-veteran when we started 20 years ago, but now our governments are working closely together and doing a lot of rehabilitation and reconstruction over there, and it's just an amazing process, but by the grace of God, it is the way that I guess all conflicts should end up. They don't all the time, but it would certainly be an idyllic world if they could end up the way that we're doing with the Vietnamese, and North and South now. We're getting more and more South Vietnamese military both in Vietnam and in this country to join us in sort of a three-way reconciliation.

Alex wrapped up the conversation. "thank you, Randy, I really appreciate this opportunity, and I would just say to all of my fellow American Vietnam veterans, whether you were actually in-country or not, whether you were combat or not, think about going back to a beautiful country with incredibly wonderful people who actually love Americans and realize that Vietnam is a fantastic country. It's not a war anymore, and I believe that it will do your heart and soul a lot of good if you go back with friends and family and spend time there with those people.

The military defeat of North Vietnam after the Tet Offensive in 1968 became a political victory for North Vietnam because of anti-War demonstrations and the sensationalism of the news media. The North Vietnamese interpreted the U.S. reaction to these events as the weakening of America's resolve to win the War. The North Vietnamese believed that victory could be theirs if they stayed their course. From 1969 until the end of the War, over 20,000 American soldiers lost their lives in a War that the United States did not have the resolve to win. The North Vietnamese did not defeat our military. We won every major battle. When I see what is going on in Vietnam today, the commercialism, the desire for trade and tourism, the fact that they want you to come there and spend your vacation, tells me that we may not have lost the War at all. All we had to really do was let them see the life we live and the way to make it happen.

Viet Cong soldier portrayed at The Big Red One Museum.

CHAPTER SIXTEEN

Anonymous Soldier

Author's note:

When I was younger, there was an old black and white movie that came on it was a World War II movie and at the end... it was about the Battle of the Bulge... at the end there were about 10 or 12 ragtag American soldiers that marched off and when they saw some new soldiers coming it they snapped to attention and did their best march as they went by them. They had been fighting for days during the Battle of the Bulge. When the movie was over I thought hey that was a great war movie! I never thought about the fact that those 10 soldiers were, although they could walk off the battlefield, they may have been wounded in many ways and how that affected their lives or what went on. Then it made me think about when I was younger when I would play with my army men I would go in and set them all up and then I would knock some down and I would never think about what was really going on in that life or how that affected that family. Sometimes I would stand them back up or I would say if I had my favorite army man I wouldn't let him get hurt. It never crossed my mind about when I was playing that there were real families or things like that involved and that those folks needed to go home. That is sort of what we are going to be talking about today our guest is Mr. Howard Jenkins.

My cup runneth over...

A particular battle in a place called Phu Nhon.

Phu Nhon or LZ Miller

LZ Miller: That battle and what happened and then we will hear from one of the soldiers that came out of that battle and what happened.

This is a report on the battle.

On the evening of 15 March at 2355 Hours, A North Vietnamese force of regimental size, initiated a sustained attack against Phu Nhon District HQ (Compound Diagram).

FSB MILLER, Attached Regional Forces, co-located U.S. Artillery forces 2nd Platoon, Battery C 1st 92nd Artillery and supporting Dusters of 2nd Platoon section from Battery B, 4th Battalion, 60th Artillery. During the course of the initial evening attack, The North Vietnamese forces attempted to overrun the position by utilizing sapper attacks, assaults by fire with 62 mm mortars, 120 mm mortars, B-40 rockets and ground assaults. The initial attack came from the Southeast against the US. Artillery sector of the perimeter held by the dusters from 4th BN. 60th Artillery and C Battery 1st BN. 92nd Artillery. The enemy was unable to penetrate this area due to the heavy volume of fire and the aggressiveness of the U.S. Soldiers in defense of the artillery sector. The Main attack then moved to the East side, in the vicinity of the ARVN Artillery. The enemy penetrated the wire inflicting damage to the facilities and causing causalities to the

South Vietnamese defenders. The 1st Bn. 92nd Liaison Officer directed all gun ships and other aircraft during the first night and morning of the attack. Very little artillery from surrounding Firebases could be called in because the aircraft and the enemy were too close to the position. The U.S. Artillery and Duster personnel proved their ability by the fact that they had killed 21 sappers within 10 meters of their compound. (The numbers of sappers killed would rise to over fifty before the battle would end.) These sappers were heavily armed with satchel charges, B-40 rockets, Bangalore torpedoes and M16 rifles. But not one enemy gained access to the compound and were unable to inflict any major damage to the compound or wound any artillery men. One Duster personnel was seriously wounded by a .51 cal. round after 16 hours of fighting. Confidence in their leadership and training, and a great deal of individual initiative were displayed by the Artillerymen throughout the 5-day Battle. Despite lack of sleep, C Battery was able to perform their mission of firing and securing their position in an outstanding manor.

The ground attack, which was directed against the eastern and northeastern sides of the perimeter, ran into very little resistance from the ARVN's. Their men on the perimeter were never reinforced as those on guard duty remained inside their bunkers with their families. No reaction force was formed until daylight. When the MACV compound was over run, the ARVN soldiers brought their families to the American bunkers. The ARVN artillery fired no more than 40 rounds and did not fire direct fire. Sappers were running freely thru their compound with little resistance. They occupied several key bunkers and one building while holding dependents as hostages. Finally at 1600 hours 16 March, GS gas grenades were deployed to clear the enemy from the bunkers.

C Btry, 1/92nd, Rebuilding Defenses, Phu Nhon 1971
Photo: Craig Stevens

The enemy was able to cut off the road north and south of Phu Nhon, surrounding the defending forces and cutting off normal land re-supply during the period 16-20 March. Villages held by the enemy were AR865027, Plei Tao-AR863045, Phu Quang-AR870050, and Phu Nhon-AQ862997. 2nd BN. 47th REG. (ARVN) was tasked to move South to clear QL-14, at 1635 hours, on 16 March they encountered a platoon-sized Element of NVA. They exchanged small arms fire, and were pinned down. Gun ships were called in and the NVA broke off the engagement. On 18 March the 1st and 3rd Company 2/47 REG. ran into heavy resistance North of Phu Nhon. A U.S. convoy escort attempting to re-supply our troops arrived on the scene; the Commander of the convoy offered his assistance to the ARVN unit. The convoy had 4 Dusters and one APC. The ARVN troops started another attack. The dusters and APC moved faster than the ARVN, at one point being more than 100 yards in front. The Dusters came under heavy fire, one being destroyed. The other Dusters leveled the village. The NVA moved back North to their former position. Vehicle re-supply was impossible because of the enemy strength. Throughout this period, the Artillerymen were under constant attack. The enemy showered them with 82mm mortars, 120mm mortars, and small arms fire. U.S. Helicopters, (including 1/92 Aviation) provided re-supply by air but were under devastating ground to air machine gun fire. The 1st BN 45 REG. proceeded towards LZ Lonely and linked up with the 3rd Cavalry troops. With the 3rd Cavalry leading the advance, were ambushed but continued their advance towards Phu Nhon. The 45 REG. linked up with the 3rd Cavalry and advanced. They came under intense enemy fire. The 3rd Cavalry received heavy causalities and became ineffective and moved to the rear. The 1st BN. 92nd Artillery Forward Observer with this Task Force was SP-4 Richard Parrish, he did an outstanding job during these assaults. On 20 March an extensive artillery preparation was fired on the enemy position and after it was completed the 1/45th, 4/45th, and the 2/3rd Cavalry conducted an assault on the objective and overcame enemy resistance. The forces split, moving North and South meeting at Phu Nhon District HQ. The enemy encirclement had been broken.

The U.S. Artillerymen distinguished themselves throughout the siege by repeated acts of Individual heroism. The other platoons from C Battery at FSB Weigt Davis and LZ Lonely were instrumental in ending the attack.

Six Day Totals:

1. Attack Totals:
   - 13 Assaults
   - 6 Significant Contacts
   - 5 Road Ambushes
   - 6 Incidents of Ground to Air Fire

2. Re-supply Routes for 94.3 Tons of Supply:
   - SVC Btry 1/92nd Artillery Convoyed to Weigt Davis
   - CH-47 Hook sorties to Weigt Davis and Lonely
   - UH-1 sorties to Phu Nhon from Weigt Davis

3. U.S. Artillery Expenditures (1401 Rounds):
   - 155mm: 1280 Rounds
   - 175mm: 99 Rounds
   - 8 Inch: 22 Rounds

4. Enemy Losses (Personnel & Equipment):
   - 387 KIA's (178 KBA)
   - 48 Small Arms
   - 23 Crew Served
   - 2 Radios (Communist Chinese)
   - 40/B-40(RPG-2) Rounds
   - 12/82mm Mortar Rounds

5. Friendly Losses (Personnel & Equipment):

	1/92nd	Other U.S.	ARVN	RF/PF
KIA	0	1	45	25
WIA	5	16	101	36
MIA	0	0	0	10

Army Commendation Medal with "V" Device for Valor Awarded to:

SFC Roy Ward, SSG. Raymond S. Powers, SP6 Preston E. Travers, SGT. Michael T. Barrett, SP5 Howard C. Jenkins, SP4 Frank Ansaldua, SP4 Paul S. Austin, SP4 Henry A. Bortnowski, SP4 Bennie Decker, SP4 Robert D. Duper, SP4 Michael E. Ford, SP4 Richard O. Gallagher, SP4 Steven Gill, SP4 Thomas Jennings, SP4 Thomas Joyce, SP4 Patrick J. Maloney, SP4 Robert J. Mentz, SP4 Michael Reynolds, SP4 Timothy Shipman, SP4 William E. Stevens, SP4 Michael D. Yates, PFC Barry D. Baird, PFC John Hayes, PFC Michael Hunter, PFC Johnny K. Miller, PFC Raymond Reynaga

The story of SP5 Howard C. Jenkins

I was going to school. I had been to Trevecca Nazarene College for 2 years and then I transferred to Belmont University across town in Nashville. I was 25 years old, and I basically thought the draft was going to pass me by. I was 6 years older than the average draftee.

In fact on some of the fire bases I was on, I was older than the officers.

There was a guy they called Pop but he was only 28 I was 25.

I had been through several physicals and had several deferments. I figured this war was going to pass me by. I had seen it on the news but hadn't paid much attention to it. I was living in a mobile home park where they have all these mail boxes. I went down there and I knew this notice was going to come in one of those yellow or manila envelopes. Before I opened the box I just said to myself I said this is the big one and when I pulled that letter out I sat down and I didn't open it. I just sat down and I thought about it and I said for some reason this is the big one. It was, it was my basic and my draft notice. I don't remember if they told me in there that I had an opportunity to go volunteer or not but my dad was an Air Force recruiter and had been for 5 or 6 years in fact right here in Knoxville. I knew I had that option so that is what I did I went down and got on a 90 day delayed enlistment so I could graduate from college.

You did not go into the Air Force.

No, it was a stronger possibility of becoming an officer in the Army at that time. The Air Force wanted me to enlist and then wait. I didn't want to wait. I knew some guys that had waited for 5 or 6 years and finally got out and never got their commission.

So you went in June of 1969 that was the year after the Democratic Presidential Nominating Convention. The Vietnam War had already changed American society.

That is right, there was a lot of protesting going on and...

That had changed me. My Dad, having been in the service for 24 years in the Air Force and retired I felt like it was the right thing to do. I bought into the Domino Theory you know if Southeast Asia fell then Asia would fall... if Asia fell the Europe would fall. I felt like it was my duty to serve.

I had gotten a degree in Business Administration with minors in psychology and economics. I wanted to get into aviation maintenance management, but the Army had different ideas.

They wanted me to shoot the big gun. The 155 Howitzer is the towed unit like they used in World War II. We had about a 13 mile range and I think everything we shot was strictly within Vietnam itself.

Our primary function was to follow the engineers as they moved south and fire support for them. We had a sister platoon we would move two of us would move at a time... or one of us would move at a time we would leap frog going south. One would jump over the other within our range probably 10 – 12 miles just far enough so we could shoot what they called Delta Tango's or **D**efensive **T**argets. They were standard targets we might just shoot them in the middle of the night for no reason just thinking the enemy might be there. Like playing Battleship.

I was enlisted '69 but I didn't make it to Vietnam until '70.

The Siege was in March of 1971.

I was trained in various things; my secondary MOS was survey which relates to artillery. You might have to survey what they call a registration point, in other words a known point then you would... like a rifle... you would site it in with a Howitzer you would zero in on that target so that you know that the data and the corrections. Some of those Howitzers didn't always fire exactly where you want them to, they are very close but this is a fine tuning of the Howitzer registration point so that is why your secondary MOS might very well be surveying.

When you go into the Army or at least when you went in at that time you chose a combat arm you either went into the infantry, artillery or armor. My philosophy was I don't want to get that close to the enemy in the infantry and I don't want to be in that metal box so I picked the middle ground I took the artillery. That is one of the advantages of volunteering too you get a little more option as to what you can do.

I was in fire direction control, not maintenance. I computed the data for the Howitzers to fire. We would pick a point on the map. A map man would give us an elevation which would mean a correction for the gun based on the height of the mountain or a valley which you have to make a correction for. We would have a radio man that would get the data from the forward observer and I have done all those jobs plus at that time of the attack I was the chief computer or lead NCO in the fire direction control unit. I would actually compute the data, make all the corrections, give them to the radio man and he would send them to the Howitzer and that is what they would put on the Howitzer then they would shoot. All this was done very rapidly.

I felt pretty safe that I had a defensive perimeter around me and was well protected or defended?

I did in that respect. My fear was when I got there and I think this was part of the problem that I had to deal with was you would go for days at a time, weeks at a time, months at a time and never even get a mortar round inside your compound or even get shot at. The guys were so complacent they were much younger than I was I think I had been through more than they had been through. I was 6 years older than most of them and my fear was that well let me put it this way, I heard stories where the guys became so complacent that on one fire base the VC just walked in.

The fact that I was in what they call the TOC the Tactical Operations Center. I have the radios to communicate with the rear areas if they ever got inside the wire. That is what they want to destroy first. They destroy the electricity, they destroy the communications, they destroy the data to the Howitzers we can't fire for the unit down the road and that unit was being hit at the same time we were being hit.

We had several layers of this constantina wire that you see surround a lot of prisons, barbed wire, mostly constantina wire. That is much harder to get through than the barbed wire. At our fire base probably 4 rows of it plus they had trip wires out there. I seen these guys work, I seen them work in the day time. These sappers that would come in. I stood there and watched them in the daytime and if you are not looking right at them I mean you don't know what they are doing or who they are… you don't know they are there. They were that good these are just small guys that take little sticks and they push that constantina wire out and they know just what place to put it in and they just slip through there like a snake almost.

Snipers? I guess there were but I never experienced any of them on a fire base. Maybe once in a while we might get a shot from something but nothing to really… you wouldn't really call them snipers so to speak they were just I think just shooting at us in general.

I do not remember the dates of the siege?

No and I should because I just came back from a reunion but that is one of the things that PTSD does to you. There is a tendency to forget dates and things like that.

I felt like the men that I was serving with had more of a false sense of safety they had become complacent. I don't think it was their fault I think it was just the way things were done and that was Vietnam I realize that now. Like I said my biggest fear was that I had heard stories about guys becoming so complacent that the VC would actually just march into the fire base. Now I don't know if these stories were real or if it was things they were telling us to keep us alert but it worked on my mind. It was on my mind all the time. When I got out on the fire base I thought to myself if they come in on the north am I going to be able to get out on the south if it comes to that.

Earlier when we were talking about the show a little bit you talked about a song that you heard a lotof In-A-Gadda-Da-Vida

Well of course I was from Knoxville and my dad was from Knoxville and I grew up here I guess more with country music. The guys over there they were into that I guess you would call it the heavy metal era so to speak.

Maybe Rock and roll?

Well I was an Elvis fan and they were like Iron Butterfly I can't think of some of the other groups then that were real popular, The Who I guess was another one and they were more into that and I think they played the In-A-Gadda-Da-Vida for my benefit because they knew I didn't particularly care for it.

So, it is daytime and you have just been doing your job and then you get down to a point where the sun is starting to set you are thinking that tomorrow is going to be another day and then you had just gone to bed.

It was about midnight as I recall and the small arms fire woke me. We had heard small arms fire before we had a few mortars dropped on us from different fire bases. I had been at Wake Davis and played coup and things like that happened but somehow I knew it was like the letter from the draft board. I knew something was going on, something was different. I could... I could hear hollering and screaming... not screaming necessarily but I could hear the guys hollering. Go here go there I could hear my officers giving directions I could hear mortars and I knew we were in a serious situation. I got up me and fellow by the name of Michael Ford from Kingsport, Tennessee. We went in our shorts and t-shirts.

When you say went in?

Into the fire direction control which we lived right behind it, we lived in a hooch about 40 foot long we had about 15 foot of it was fire direction control and the rest was living quarters and that was part of the problem.

Wait just a minute now a hooch is a shed? Underground it has got about 2 foot of circulation just above ground... it is so high you can't see out of it but somebody outside could see in it.

Then fire direction control is that another bunker?

That was our office that was like the TOC or Tactical Operations Center and Fire Direction Control all in one.

Was it underground?

It is part of the hooch.

Oh it is part of the hooch.

It is like a 15 foot piece of it then you have got about 25 or 30 feet behind there where the officers bunked and where Fire Direction Control bunk. The fellows on the guns they had their own hooch they bunked together.

Was that a 24 hour living quarters?

Yes (inaudible)

OK so other people weren't sleeping in there while you were working in the hooch it was just your personal...

We had 2 shifts we worked 12 hour shifts. I had just worked from say... I guess I worked from 12 noon to 12 midnight I kind of give the guys the choice of what shift they wanted most of them wanted to work the night shift. So I would take 12 noon to midnight and they would get midnight till 12 noon. I had just gone to bed... just pulled a day shift me and Michael Ford we had just pulled a day shift and we had just gone to bed when this started.

What is it you would be doing during the day?

Probably things like they call just basically administrative work, paperwork they had what they called a MEP which allowed the artillery rounds or allowed an artillery piece to adjust for the atmospheric conditions that would come in a couple of times a day and you would make those adjustments. You had a form you had to fill out which allowed for a correction to be put on the guns. Some of the guys would go out and work on the wire doing things in the perimeter. The guys on the guns had various jobs that they performed every day.

So at 12:30 or whenever the fight started there was already somebody doing your job is that correct?

That is right.

So what did you do?

As soon as we got up we went in and took their job. We didn't even bother to dress we took their job and they went outside to do guard duty or whatever needed to be done out there. We had a sandbag bunker on top of the FDC one of them would man that and one of them would go out on the perimeter.

Did you outrank them?

I was a Spec 5 at that time I was the chief computer I forgot what my other... Fire Direction Control I was the head NCO in FDC. I had just recently gotten that position. So you have gone in and taken this new position what was going on in your mind then... what were you expecting or what did you think?

Well, it was probably the scariest time of my life if I could hear all this small arms fire, I could hear mortars I could hear the guys hollering out there I could hear various things going and I had no idea what was going on. I am sitting there with Michael Ford and my knees are shaking, my teeth are chattering like it was cold and the sweat is running off of me and I looked at Michael I said it is cold tonight isn't it? He said yeah. I said Michael it is not cold we are scared to death aren't we? He looked at me and he said yeah. That was one of the things that really bothered me I am sitting there thinking I have got 25 feet of darkness behind me in this Fire Direction Control bunker. My biggest fear was a satchel charge that they would drop in there now if it came in the Fire Direction Control where it was lit I am wondering what will I do? Will I pick it up, will I throw it out will I freeze will I tell Michael let's get out of here? The worst part was if they threw it back there where it was dark I couldn't see it I kept listening. We are sitting there firing Delta Tango's or firing support for the fire base our sister fire base and I am thinking what am I going to do if they put that in the back? Well the next day I found out that is what they were trying to do. One of the South Vietnamese soldiers shot the guy that was headed for the Fire Direction Control.

Where you were?

Where I was, I go outside and they had a... that next day when we had daylight... they had what looked like maybe a culvert that had been cut about 3 foot high and about 3 foot in diameter and that is where they threw all the unexploded ordinance. I look in there and there is that satchel charge then I hear one of the officers say they were headed for the Fire Direction Control and that was one of my worst fears. That was my first shock right there... actually my second shock. The first one was all that going on outside when I was inside the Fire Direction Control and the second one was seeing that satchel charge that I had feared.

Well now you weren't doing paperwork… you said you do paperwork on your job so you were on the radio… did you have to stay where you were could you go out and fight?

Well, part of our job would be to call the rear area and tell them we are under attack. There was some serious firing going on and they would say something like are you sure? I would take that mic and key it and say listen to that and I would hold it open and let them hear that firing then I would get back and they said yes, we have choppers on the way and they did. We probably wouldn't have made it if they hadn't sent those choppers out there. They sent Cobra's out there and they were firing so close to the compound that the metal links that were holding the rounds together were falling inside the compound. This compound is probably only 40 foot wide and maybe 80 feet long. Those links were falling inside… I could hear them hitting the roof the top of the FDC and I didn't know what they were at the time.

So the choppers were right overhead?

Oh, yeah!

Were they Viet Cong or North Vietnamese army?

Well, we found out later that there were 300 of them or more out there now we are only 28 guys on a fire base. They were also hitting the fire base down… our sister fire base down the road about 10 clicks. Most of them were North Vietnamese regulars we learned. I never actually saw one of them.

So there were 300 attacking 2 bases?

2 bases at the same time that is what they usually do and that is why they would put us that close together so we could fire for each other.

So again not being a veteran when I read the books of Sun Tzu they say if you are going to attack, attack with 3 times the force of the defenders so you think there were maybe 150 or 300 coming after you all?

Oh yes they told us there were 300 I have no idea how many were actually out there. I know we probably killed about 10 on the wire that night.

How do you maintain personal discipline when that is going on when you are scared?

Well that is one thing I can say about military training, they train you for this. That when you get into something like that your primary function is to do your job! Everybody had a job if everybody does their job things are going to come out better. If somebody panics or doesn't do their job then somebody had to fill that hole. We did… everybody in my outfit everybody there did their job in fact I talked to the Lieutenant that was there that night and his comment was… well my comment was first "you saved our lives that night". We had 3 officers there but we might as well only had 2 they might as well stayed at home. His comment was, "everybody did their job" that is why we came home. That doesn't mean that the guys that didn't come home didn't do their job but it means if you do your job you are more likely to come home. We did everything we were supposed to do we did it like we were trained and we had one good leader there that night.

Let me hear you talk about Michael Ford and I hear so many veterans from Vietnam talk about old friends did you all have nicknames for each other or did ya'll call each other by your names or by your ranks?

I would say Michael was probably 18 or 19 but I think maybe we had a closer relationship because he was from Tennessee, he was from Kingsport. All of us shared things when we would get a care package but it was especially significant to me when I would get something or he would get something and there was always something in there from my wife or from his family he wasn't married that would remind us of home so I think we had a camaraderie that him being a country boy and me too basically.

You didn't go home at the same time did you?

No, I think Michael was still there. See, a lot of guys would stay a few extra months so that when they come back they didn't have any time left in service. I had a wife and I wanted to get out of there. I had a year left in service when I come back. I would have had to stay another whole year and I wasn't going to do that.

Did you stay in service for that year?

I had a year to go but, I got a 6 month early out they were pushing guys out.

Were you feeling the effects of that battle six months later?

No it didn't hit me till about '75 when I divorced my wife.

4 years?

Yes.

You divorced her or she divorced you?

I divorced her. She had put me through college. I had helped her go. She was going to University of Hawaii. That is where I was when I got divorced and I just got to the point that I felt like I wasn't really the man that she needed. I couldn't give her what she wanted. In fact, I just came back from Florida a couple of months ago and the first time I was able to tell her that. It wasn't that I didn't love her it was just that I loved her so much that… I couldn't give her what I thought she needed. She was a good woman.

I am not going to ask you why but do you think it was because of that battle experience?

Oh it was definitely Vietnam it was post-traumatic stress disorder. I would fly into fits and rages and for no reason at all I can remember some of them like they were yesterday. Nothing she did it was all me.

Now was this a creeping disorder or disease?

I think it got worse for a period of time I think it was building up till probably '75 that was probably the high point of my depression. After that it kind of alternated between rage and depression and I was subjecting her to this. We tried to get back together once and I wasn't over the trauma yet.

Was it thoughts or memories that would trigger it or was it just a general overall reaction to civilian life?

Well, I was having nightmares I was waking up I wasn't sleeping well. Most of the time for no apparent reason something that somebody would say or she would say would just set me off. I kept trying to tell myself that this was righteous indignation and it wasn't it was PTSD, I know that now. When did you get diagnosed?

Didn't get diagnosed till 2005, I was in denial for 30 something years.

So you did not seek help?

Well, I divorced my second wife and I didn't have any insurance so I went to the VA at Mountain Home Johnson City and I got to talking to one of the nurses and she asked me some questions. She said have you ever been tested for PTSD? I said no and she said you need to be because you have answered all these questions in a positive manner for PTSD. I was at the point then where I had been through 2 divorces, I was going through a lot of depression and I was willing to try anything. I said ok let's give this a shot you know, it has cost me enough of my life, let's give this a try.

Mr. Jenkins it affected your first marriage, you said you had a second marriage that you were telling me a few minutes ago about your children... it affected your children can you tell us a little bit about how PTSD would affect children?

Well, after my first wife and I divorced in Hawaii in '75. I went for ten years just by myself. PTSD is a series of mountain peaks and valleys. I got on a mountain peak. I met this lady. We hit it off. We got married. She told me she couldn't have any children and I said, "well, you have never been married to a Jenkins before either have you?' She said, "No" So we had a daughter. She said, I bet you cannot do that again." I said, "I bet I can!" Thirteen months later we had a son but, my experience with my second marriage and my children was some good parts and some bad parts. My children experienced or lived with this PTSD through me in different ways. My daughter withdrew but, withdrew into her books. Did good in school. Went to Middle Tennessee State and graduated but, after she left home she wouldn't speak to me for 6 years. My son went the other way. He withdrew, got into drugs. He is doing good now. I finally explained to my daughter one day, I said, "You need to ask yourself, "Do you feel like that I was deliberately doing what I was doing and we lost our relationship. I want you to remember this one thing… we are both victims of Vietnam. We are getting back together now we have had dinner together and lunch a couple of times I have been over there taking some stuff to her she lives in Nashville. Like I said my son got into drugs had a problem with them. He is doing good now. One thing I wanted to share with you that I think was very important to me was I asked him one day I said… this was back in the period of time when they were showing this commercial on TV with these 2 boys in the seat of a car and his dad sticks his head in the window and he looks like a monster. I was thinking about that when I asked my son, I said, "What did you think of me when you were growing up? I said, "I need an honest answer," and he gave me an honest answer when he said, "Dad you were a monster". I needed to hear that. I suspected as much, but that has helped me more towards my recovery because I asked him a couple of months ago, I said, "how am I doing?" He said, "Dad, you are doing better" That meant more to me than any military award or anything I can think of or any part of my recovery.

What do you think the cause of you doing better was?

Well, after so many years, the VA finally decided they were going to give us some help with this PTSD. I started seeing a Dr. Gannon over at the VA hospital or VA clinic here in Knoxville. She helped me a lot. She helped me to realize that ineede to get this out. I needed to talk about it. She asked me one day if I would be interested in going into a group therapy. I said, "oh yeah, I need that. I want that. So I got into a group with Dr. Richardson. You get into this group and it is good. I have never been in to

AA or NA, but it was not like that. You get in there with a group of guys that have been through what you have been through and they tell stories about what happened to them and you think, "Oh, I have been there, I have done that. I know what you are saying, and you are telling my story!" Then, when I told my story, I could tell they were reacting the same way. "I have been there and one that, that is my story, too. You are in the group about six months or a year you see guys that came in crying, or who could hardly talk about their experiences, and you see those same veterans patting people on the back, and asking how they are doing. We all know in our minds and hearts where they have been, what they have come through. That is part of the healing process.

Mr. Jenkins where are you going with this now we have... where are you taking this cure?

Well, as a group we got out of the VA and got into VET to VET. A national organization formed by a fellow by the name of Bo Armstrong. He had PTSD and was told he was alright by the VA to go home, and not to worry about it. He did not feel they were right, So we decided we were going to help ourselves. We formed a group called Legacy Peer Support Group. It is group therapy only there is no clinician. It is Vet to Vet and as Ed junod said, "Each one, Reach one, Teach one".

This is the message I want to get to all veterans. If you think you have PTSD, and if you are coping with its effects, and it could be ruining your life, it does not matter what war you fought in, there is help available!

Who would they call who can they get in touch with?

Well they can go online at www.tmvhc.org.

For the public out there: it is not that you have post-traumatic stress disorder but it is in your family.

That is true...

OK then briefly tell me about what this outreach program has done for you?

Oh I have made marvelous success with this program I have got to the point where we have actually divided the group into two sections. One of them is a strength based outreach the other is a crisis based outreach… I am a facilitator. That is a little different from being a leader we just kind of make sure that the program is going along we may start it let people talk give everybody an opportunity to say what they need to say maybe ask a person you know, "how do you feel about this?" It has just helped me enormously it actually got me back to thinking that if this group of guys could help me I need to get back into the church because the church is going to help me because they understand where I have been in a Christian sense.

Howard Jenkins who started out as a 25 year old man, went into the military and experienced the difficulties of a battle that stayed with him all his life. It made him… would you call it sick?

PTSD is a mental illness it doesn't mean that you are crazy but it means you have problems coping with particular situations.

But you can use it to strengthen your missions and use it as a guide to help others.

That is right if you use it properly and realize what you problem is you can reach out to other people and help them. That is what helps us is helping other people.

CHAPTER SEVENTEEN

Taking the story of the fallen home and the aftermath on the messengers

Mother, mother
There's too many of you crying
Brother, brother, brother
There's far too many of you dying.

> Lyrics from:
> What's Going On
> As sung by Marvin Gaye.

Death arrives at your doorstep during wartime.

It comes by daylight, while you are having morning coffee. Or it waits at the curb until you come home from work.

It comes as a respectful officer, in full dress uniform.

It's a tradition as old as war.

During World War II, soldiers' families received the news at any hour with a knock on their door and a Western Union messenger delivering a telegram.

During Vietnam, the military decided that a more humane way to deliver the blow was to have military personnel notify the family in person.

Since then, the military has further refined the task, with each branch of service following the same basic procedures.

The next of kin will be notified by specially trained Casualty Assistance Call Officers, called CACOs, within 24 hours. At least two military officials will deliver the message in person. The Air Force sends a nurse or medical assistant with a chaplain and officer.

Vietnam veterans are impressed with how the military's notification system has improved since they were soldiers more than 20 years ago.

"Death is one of the unfortunate realities of war, but the military has done a great deal to cushion the blow," he says.

A soldier, who has had to deliver the news to the families of four Marines in the past, says compassion for the family is the key.

"It's more than just a mechanical notification," said the soldier. "They've given the biggest sacrifice any family could give the corps.

"Provide as much information as possible, but don't go into any gory details," he says of his mission. Usually, the message is simple: "Your son was killed in combat."

The CACOs are advised to use first names rather than military ranks and to deliver the news indoors and away from the media.

"We'll stay with the family as long as we think its doing the family good," he says. "If the person was alone, we'll wait until someone gets there—a relative or neighbor."

Western Union does follow up the official military notification with a telegram within 24 hours, according to Western Union and military officials. Later, the CACO revisits the family to help with funeral arrangements and military benefits.

Besides insisting that all notifications of Persian Gulf casualties be done in person, military posts also have assembled teams of psychologists and clergy to ease families through the anguish.

More than 300 volunteers have registered with the South Florida Veterans Multipurpose Center in Fort Lauderdale, offering everything from child care to travel arrangements for families whose relatives are wounded or killed. Many civilians in Fort Lauderdale, Florida are involved with the center.

While the military has made some efforts to soften the blow to the families, the Pentagon recently decided to scrub the traditional public honors ceremonies for returning war dead, angering some relatives of the thousands of U.S. troops facing the prospect of a bloody ground battle.

The honor guard and military band that have in the past attended the arrival of casualties will not be present.

Except for the honors ceremonies, the procedure for dealing with the dead will be basically the same as during the Vietnam War.

American casualties from the Persian Gulf will return home in body bags—7- foot 10-inch sacks made of rubberized fabric with metal rings. The Pentagon, which calls the bags "human remains pouches," buys them from several private manufacturers.

The bags will be loaded on "killed in action carriers" and flown to the military mortuary in Dover, Del.

A soldier, who served as a funeral escort for six months during Vietnam, remembers the incredible assembly line in the hangar-like buildings at the military mortuary in Oakland, Calif.

There the bodies were clothed in full-dress uniforms, with medals pinned to lifeless chests, and placed in gun-metal silver caskets.

His job was to accompany the body from the mortuary to the gravesite in the soldier's hometown.

Sometimes he also had to persuade families not to open the coffin if the Army had classified the remains as non-viewable.

"Legally, they have the right, but you do everything you can to talk them out of it, They would deny it was their son. It was incredibly difficult, trying to explain to a mother: 'Yes, this is your son in here.'"

Can you imagine having to tag the bodies as we described earlier in the Ia Drang opening battle?

At the gravesite, a flag will be presented that had draped the coffin to the next of kin and recite this speech: "Dear _____: On behalf of the President of the United States and a grateful nation, please accept this flag as a token of appreciation of the extraordinary sacrifices made by your (loved one)."

One mother threw the flag back at him, Kaufman says. Another tried to crawl into her son's casket.

"People have no concept of what is going to happen, until that concept hits home,"

And one soldier noted:

"Some people will cheer the end of the war and for some people it won't matter—it ended when their son died."

WHAT YOU ARE ABOUT TO READ IS A REPRINT FROM THE EXPERIENCE OF a LT.COL.

Para Phrased to protect indentities:

Vietnam Casualty Notification Officer USMC (Ret)

In my 76th year, the events of my life appear to me, from time to time, as a series of vignettes. Some were significant; most were trivial.

War is the seminal event in the life of everyone that has endured it. Though I fought in Korea and the Dominican Republic and was wounded there, Vietnam was my war.

Now 42 years have passed and, thankfully, I rarely think of those days in Cambodia, Laos, and the panhandle of North Vietnam where small teams of Americans and Montangards fought much larger elements of the North Vietnamese Army. Instead I see vignettes: some exotic, some mundane:

- The smell of Nuc Mam.
- The heat, dust, and humidity.
- The blue exhaust of cycles clogging the streets.
- Elephants moving silently through the tall grass.
- Hard eyes behind the servile smiles of the villagers.
- Standing on a mountain in Laos and hearing a tiger roar.
- A young girl squeezing my hand as my medic delivered her baby.
- The flowing Ao Dais of the young women biking down Tran Hung Dao.
- My two years as Casualty Notification Officer in North Carolina, Virginia and Maryland.

It was late 1967. I had just returned after 18 months in Vietnam. Casualties were increasing. I moved my family from Indianapolis to Norfolk, rented a house, enrolled my children in their fifth or sixth new school, and bought a second car.

A week later, I put on my uniform and drove 10 miles to Little Creek, Virginia. I hesitated before entering my new office. Appearance is important to career Marines. I was no longer, if ever, a poster Marine. I had returned from my third tour in Vietnam only 30 days before. At 5'9", I now weighed 128 pounds – 37 pounds below my normal weight. My uniforms fit ludicrously, my skin was yellow from malaria medication, and I think I had a twitch or two.

I straightened my shoulders, walked into the office, looked at the nameplate on a Staff Sergeant's desk and said, "Sergeant _____, I'm Lieutenant Colonel _____. Here are my orders and my Qualification Jacket."

Sergeant _____ stood, looked carefully at me, took my orders, stuck out his hand; we shook and he asked, "How long were you there, Colonel?"

I replied "18 months this time." The Sgt. breathed, "You must be a slow learner Colonel." I smiled.

"Colonel, I'll show you to your office and bring in the Sergeant Major. I said, "No, let's just go straight to his office. Nodding and hesitating, he lowered his voice, "Colonel, the Sergeant Major. He's been in this job two years. He's packed pretty tight. I'm worried about him." I nodded.

The LT.Col. was escorted into the Sergeant Major's office. "Sergeant Major, this is Colonel _____ the new Commanding Office. The Sergeant Major stood, extended his hand and said, "Good to see you again, Colonel." I responded, "Hello, how are you?" The escorting Sgt. looked at me, raised an eyebrow, walked out, and closed the door.

I sat down with the Sergeant Major. We had the obligatory cup of coffee and talked about mutual acquaintances. His stress was palpable. Finally, I said, "Son, what's the hell's wrong?" He turned his chair, looked out the window and said, "Sir, you're going to wish you were back in Nam before you leave here. I've been in the Marine Corps since 1939. I was in the Pacific 36 months, Korea for 14 months, and Vietnam for 12 months. Now I come here to bury these kids. I'm putting my letter in. I can't take it anymore." I said, "OK If that's what you want, I'll endorse your request for retirement and do what I can to push it through Headquarters Marine Corps."

The Sergeant Major retired 12 weeks later. He had been a good Marine for 28 years, but he had seen too much death and too much suffering. He was used up.

Over the next 16 months, I made 28 death notifications, conducted 28 military funerals, and made 30 notifications to the families of Marines that were severely wounded or missing in action. Most of the details of those casualty notifications have now, thankfully, faded from memory. Four, however, remain.

MY FIRST NOTIFICATION

My third or fourth day in Norfolk, I was notified of the death of a 19 year old Marine. This notification came by telephone from Headquarters Marine Corps. The information detailed:

- Name, rank, and serial number.
- Name, address, and phone number of next of kin.
- Date of and limited details about the Marine's death.
- Approximate date the body would arrive at the Norfolk Naval Air Station.
- A strong recommendation on whether the casket should be opened or closed.

The boy's family lived over the border in North Carolina, about 60 miles away. I drove there in a Marine Corps staff car. Crossing the state line into North Carolina, I stopped at a small country store / service station / Post Office. I went in to ask directions.

Three people were in the store… A man and woman approached the small Post Office window. The man held a package. The Storeowner walked up and addressed them by name, "Hello John. Good morning Mrs. Cooper."

I was stunned. My casualty's next-of-kin's name was Cooper!

I hesitated, then stepped forward and said, "I beg your pardon. Are you Mr. and Mrs. Cooper of (address?)

The father looked at me – I was in uniform – and then, shaking, bent at the waist, he vomited. His wife looked horrified at him and then at me. Understanding came into her eyes and she collapsed in slow motion. I think I caught her before she hit the floor.

The owner took a bottle of whiskey out of a drawer and handed it to Mr. Cooper who drank. I answered their questions for a few minutes. Then I drove them home in my staff car. The storeowner locked the store and followed in their truck. We stayed an hour or so until the family began arriving.

I returned the storeowner to his business. He thanked me and said, "Mister, I wouldn't have your job for a million dollars." I shook his hand and said; "Neither would I."

I vaguely remember the drive back to Norfolk. Violating about five Marine Corps regulations, I drove the staff car straight to my house. I sat with my family while they ate dinner, went into the den, closed the door, and sat there all night, alone.

My Marines steered clear of me for days. I had made my first death notification.

THE FUNERALS

Weeks passed with more notifications and more funerals. I borrowed Marines from the local Marine Corps Reserve and taught them to conduct a military funeral: how to carry a casket, how to fire the volleys and how to fold the flag.

When I presented the flag to the mother, wife, or father, I always said, "All Marines share in your grief." I had been instructed to say, "On behalf of a grateful nation…." I didn't think the nation was grateful, so I didn't say that.

Sometimes, my emotions got the best of me and I couldn't speak. When that happened, I just handed them the flag and touched a shoulder. They would look at me and nod. Once a mother said to me, "I'm so sorry you have this terrible job." My eyes filled with tears and I leaned over and kissed her.

ANOTHER NOTIFICATION

Six weeks after my first notification, I had another. This was a young PFC. I drove to his mother's house. As always, I was in uniform and driving a Marine Corps staff car. I parked in front of the house, took a deep breath, and walked towards the house. Suddenly the door flew open, a middle-aged woman rushed out. She looked at me and ran across the yard, screaming "NO! NO! NO! NO!"

I hesitated. Neighbors came out. I ran to her, grabbed her, and whispered stupid things to reassure her she collapsed. I picked her up and carried her into the house. Eight or nine neighbors followed. Ten or fifteen later, the father came in followed by ambulance personnel. I have no recollection of leaving.

The funeral took place about two weeks later. We went through the drill. The mother never looked at me. The father looked at me once and shook his head sadly.

ANOTHER NOTIFICATION

One morning, as I walked in the office, the phone was ringing. The Sergeant held the phone up and said, "You've got another one, Colonel." I nodded, walked into my office, picked up the phone, took notes, thanked the officer making the call, I have no idea why, and hung up. Jolly, who had listened, came in with a special Telephone Directory that translates telephone numbers into the person's address and place of employment.

The father of this casualty was a Longshoreman. He lived a mile from my office. I called the Longshoreman's Union Office and asked for the Business Manager. He answered the phone, I told him who I was, and asked for the father's schedule.

The Business Manager asked, "Is it his son?" I said nothing. After a moment, he said, in a low voice, "Tom is at home today." I said, "Don't call him. I'll take care of that." The Business Manager said, "Aye, Aye Sir," and then explained, "Tom and I were Marines in WWII."

I got in my staff car and drove to the house. I was in uniform. I knocked and a woman in her early forties answered the door. I saw instantly that she was clueless. I asked, "Is Mr. _____ home?" She smiled pleasantly and responded, "Yes, but he's eating breakfast now. Can you come back later?" I said, "I'm sorry. It's important. I need to see him now."

She nodded, stepped back into the beach house and said, "Tom, it's for you."

A moment later, a ruddy man in his late forties, appeared at the door. He looked at me, turned absolutely pale, steadied himself, and said, "Jesus Christ man, he's only been there three weeks!"

Months passed. More notifications and more funerals. Then one day while I was running, Sergeant Jolly stepped outside the building and gave a loud whistle, two fingers in his mouth... I never could do that... and held an imaginary phone to his ear.

Another call from Headquarters Marine Corps. I took notes, said, "Got it." and hung up. I had stopped saying "Thank You" long ago.

The Sgt asked, "Where?"

Me, "Eastern Shore of Maryland. The father is a retired Chief Petty Officer. His brother will accompany the body back from Vietnam."

The Sgt shook his head slowly, straightened, and then said, "This time of day, it'll take three hours to get there and back. I'll call the Naval Air Station and borrow a helicopter. And I'll have the Captain get one of his men to meet you and drive you to the Chief's home."

He did, and 40 minutes later, I was knocking on the father's door. He opened the door, looked at me, then looked at the Marine standing at parade rest beside the car, and asked, "Which one of my boys was it, Colonel?"

I stayed a couple of hours, gave him all the information, my office and home phone number and told him to call me, anytime.

He called me that evening about 2300 (11:00PM). "I've gone through my boy's papers and found his will. He asked to be buried at sea. Can you make that happen?" I said, "Yes I can, Chief. I can and I will."

My wife who had been listening said, "Can you do that?" I told her, "I have no idea. But I'm going to break my ass trying."

I called Lieutenant General _____, Commanding General, Fleet Marine Force Atlantic, at home about 2330, explained the situation, and asked, "General, can you get me a quick appointment with the Admiral at Atlantic Fleet Headquarters?" The General said," you be there tomorrow at 0900. He will see you.

I was and the Admiral did. He said coldly, "How can the Navy help the Marine Corps, Colonel." I told him the story. He turned to his Chief of Staff and said, "Which is the sharpest destroyer in port?" The Chief of Staff responded with a name.

The Admiral called the ship, "Captain, you're going to do a burial at sea. You'll report to a Marine Lieutenant Colonel until this mission is completed."

He hung up, looked at me, and said, "The next time you need a ship, Colonel, call me. You don't have to sic THE GENERAL on my ass." I responded, "Aye Aye, Sir" and got the hell out of his office.

I went to the ship and met with the Captain, Executive Officer, and the Senior Chief. We trained the ship's crew for four days Then Jolly raised a question none of us had thought of. He said, "These government caskets are air tight. How do we keep it from floating?"

All the high priced help including me sat there looking dumb. Then the Senior Chief stood and said, "Come on Jolly I know a bar where the retired guys from World War II hang out."

They returned a couple of hours later, slightly the worst for wear, and said, "It's simple; we cut four 12" holes in the outer shell of the casket on each side and insert 300 lbs. of lead in the foot end of the casket. We can handle that, no sweat."

The day arrived. The ship and the sailors looked razor sharp. The General, the Admiral, a US Senator, and a Navy Band were on board. The sealed casket was brought aboard and taken below for modification. The ship got underway to the 12-fathom depth.

The sun was hot. The ocean flat. The casket was brought aft and placed on a catafalque. The Chaplin spoke. The volleys were fired. The flag was removed, folded, and I gave it to the father. The band played "Eternal Father Strong to Save." The casket was raised slightly at the head and it slid into the sea.

The heavy casket plunged straight down about six feet. The incoming water collided with the air pockets in the outer shell. The casket stopped abruptly, rose straight out of the water about three feet, stopped, and slowly slipped back into the sea. The air bubbles rising from the sinking casket sparkled in the sunlight as the casket disappeared from sight forever.

The next morning I called a personal friend, at Headquarters Marine Corps and said, "General, get me out of here. I can't take this anymore." I was transferred two weeks later.

I was a good Marine but, after 17 years, I had seen too much death and too much suffering. I was used up.

Vacating the house, my family and I drove to the office in a two-car convoy. I said my goodbyes. My Sergeant walked out with me. He waved at my family, looked at me with tears in his eyes, came to attention, saluted, and said, "Well Done, Colonel. Well Done."

I felt as if I had received the Medal of Honor.

Author's note:

PTSD is not always on the battlefield, or maybe better said the battlefield extends all the way to completion of the funerals.

The words to this song helped me cope with the chapter you just completed.

Riding With Private Malone

As sung by:
David Ball
Written by: Thom Shepard

I was just out of the service thumbing through the classifieds
When an ad that said old Chevy somehow caught my eye
The lady didn't know the year or even if it ran
But I had that thousand dollars in my hand
It was way back in the corner of this old ramshackle barn
With 30 years of dust and dirt on that green Army tarp
And when I pulled the cover off, it took away my breath
What she called a Chevy was a 66 Corvette
I felt a little guilty as I counted out the bills
What a thrill I got when I sat behind the wheel
I opened up the glove box and that's when I found the note
The date was 1966 and this is what he wrote
He said, my name is Private Andrew Malone
And if you're reading this, then I didn't make it home
But for every dream that's shattered, another one comes true
This car was once a dream of mine, now it belongs to you
And though you may take her and make her your own
You'll always be riding with Private Malone
Well, it didn't take me long at all, I had her running good
I loved to hear those horses thunder underneath her hood
I had her shining like a diamond and I'd put the ragtop down
All the pretty girls would stop and stare as I drove her through town
The buttons on the radio didn't seem to work quite right
But it picked up that oldie show, especially late at night
I'd get the feeling sometimes, if I turned real quick I'd see
A soldier ridin' shotgun in the seat right next to me
It was a young man named Private Andrew Malone
Who fought for his country and never made it home
But for every dream that's shattered, another one comes true
This car was once a dream of his, back when it was new

And he told me to take her and make her my own
And I was proud to be riding with Private Malone
Well, one night it was raining hard, I took the curve too fast
And I still don't remember much about that fiery crash
Someone said they thought they saw a soldier pull me out
They didn't get his name, but I know without a doubt
It was a young man named Private Andrew Malone
Who fought for his country and never made it home
But for every dream that's shattered, another one comes true
This car was once a dream of his, back when it was new
And I know I wouldn't be here if he hadn't tagged along
Yeah, that night, I was riding with Private Malone
Oh, thank God, I was riding with Private Malone
Private Malone

Songwriters: Thom Shepherd

CHAPTER EIGHTEEN

Vietnamization

Vietnamization was a policy of the Nixon Administration to end U.S. involvement in the Vietnam War. Through a program to "expand, equip, and train South Vietnam forces. and assign to them an ever-increasing combat role, at the same time steadily reducing the number of U.S. combat troops." Brought on by the Tet offensive, the policy referred to U.S. combat troops specifically in the ground combat role, but did not reject combat by the U.S. Air Force, as well as the support to South Vietnam. U.S. citizens' mistrust of their government that had begun after the offensive worsened with the release of news about U.S. soldiers massacring civilians at My Lai. The invasion of Cambodia and the release of the Pentagon Papers.

The name "Vietnamization" came about accidentally. At a January 28, 1969, meeting of the National Security Council stated that the Army of the Republic of Vietnam had been steadily improving, and the point at which the war could be "de-Americanized" was close. "What we needed was a term like 'Vietnamizing' to put the emphasis on the right issues." Nixon immediately liked Laird's word.[2]

Nixon said Vietnamization had two components. The first was "strengthening the armed force of the South Vietnamese in numbers, equipment, leadership and combat skills", while the second was "the extension of the pacification program [i.e. military aid to civilians] in South Vietnam." To achieve the first goal, U.S. helicopters would fly in support; however, helicopter operations were too much part of ground operations to involve U.S. personell. Thus, ARVN candidates were enrolled in U.S. helicopter schools to take over the operations., To qualify an ARVN candidate for U.S. helicopter school, he first needed to learn English; this, in addition to the months-long training and practice in the field, made adding new capabilities to the ARVN take at least two years.[4] Palmer did not disagree that the first component, given time and resources, was achievable. However: "Pacification, the second component, presented the real challenge… it was benevolent government action in areas where the government should always have been benevolently active… doing both was necessary if Vietnamization were to work."

The policy of Vietnamization, despite its successful execution, was ultimately a failure as the improved ARVN forces and the reduced American and allied component were unable to prevent the falloff Saigon, and the subsequent merger of the north and south, to form the Socialist Republic of Vietnam.

How many of the young people you have learned about understood the politics of the Vietnam War when it began? If you ask me, not many.

And when they began to realize that the friends they lost in Vietnam, and the time they lost with their families and the Dear John letters, the sicknesses caused by Agent Orange and debilitating injuries were for a lost cause. That they were not celebrated like soldiers in the past with parades and accolades. That their country had gotten into an unpopular war, and could not separate it from those our country sent to fight it? That someone had to be blamed and that it would take decades for us as a nation to see how wrong we were to treat them in this way? How do we undo the wrongs we as a nation committed against these brave soldiers who did what they were told to do. How do we replace the children of our Gold Star Moms and Dads? Since most of the parents of these soldiers are long gone, can we not honor their sacrifice by being more diligent in our foreign entanglements? Can we not listen to their fears and anquish, and do what we can to honor their service to our country.

As Mr. Jenkins remarked, PTSD is not always just an individual illness, it is in the family.

After the Vietnam War, we had a series of minor squabbles in the south, and then came the Middle East confrontations. Many of which were led by Generals who were JR. and medium level officers in Vietnam.

We lost few military battles in Vietnam, but we lost so many lives over the presidencies of TRUMAN, EISENHAUER, KENNEDY, JOHNSON, NIXON and possibly even FORD. We were divided by the amnesty offered Americans by Jimmie Carter, who had fled the country to avoid the Vietnam draft calls.

In all, seven Presidencies were involved. And millions of American put at risk and suffered so much pain.

Today we buy many products from Vietnam. Could we not have just spent the money developing trade relations at the time?

When Freddie Owens of Knoxville, Tn set foot down at Ia Drang, and experienced the loss of so many of his friends, and pain and suffering of Agent Orange exposure and still came home a Patriot, and full of care and desire to make the lives of his fellow soldiers better than our country wanted to provide.

When William Robinson spent over seven years as a prisoner of war, and came home to be sure all Air Force sergeants knew that the day after graduation they could become prisoners of war, and they needed to know how to act, and what was expected of them.

When Tom Mercer a.k.a. Pointman who had a needed to see his former fellow warriors so bad he organized reunions of the Big Red One.

When JLTucker decided to distribute bicycles to veterans with no transportation. He learned that by helping others with PTSD he could relieve his own pain.

When Henry Carson would tell his scared battle mates that the upcoming battle was "just a thang" and carried the shrapnel of many battles still in his body, and can honorably wear the Soldiers Medal on his chest awarded to only 109 Vietnam veterans including Colin Powell.

When Glen Palmer would modify and correct issues with the M-16 and volunteer to go to a hell hole called Bin Het.

When General James Shelton carried the pain of listening to his former command get destroyed in an ambush and carry the photo of his fallen radio man, in his wallet for decades.

When Roger Phillips can make a gift of a war souvenir, and Robert Minton refuse to hold his white fellow soldiers responsible for the death of Martin Luther King.

When Dean Powell can overcome the drug addictions and prison terms associated with his Vietnam experiences and lead a ministry to help other veterans suffering from the same issues.

When country boy Doc Taylor can become an amateur historian in order to tell the story of My Lai and the Montagnards.

For the Montagnards to ally with America only to suffer ethnic cleansing after the war.

When many anonymous soldiers serve the families of fallen soldiers becoming victims of PTSD for doing that horrible job.

When Alex Wells after being forced to kill hundreds of enemy soldiers, and having to eat a rat for his birthday dinner, and for being trapped in rubble for a long time, surrounded by enemy soldiers and then wanting our two countries to heal from the war, and work together in peace.

When Howard Jenkins can choose to help Veterans from all wars by sharing his story and raising money to help their causes.

And last but not least an unknown warrior named Ed Junod, who was a friend of Freddie Owens and a fellow Vietnam veteran who has done so much to ramrod the solutions for so many veterans in their battles and disagreements with the Veterans Administration.

How can we as a nation of civilians not have so much gratitude for their service to us and their fellow veterans.

CHAPTER NINETEEN

What is PTSD?

A wide variety of symptoms may be signs that you are experiencing post traumatic stress disorder. The following are some of the most common symptoms of PTSD that you or those around you may have noticed:

- Feeling upset by things that remind you of what happened
- Having nightmares, vivid memories, or flashbacks of the event that make you feel like it's happening all over again
- Feeling emotionally cut off from others
- Feeling numb or losing interest in things you used to care about
- Feeling constantly on guard
- Feeling irritated or having angry outbursts
- Having difficulty sleeping
- Having trouble concentrating

Being jumpy or easily startled is not just the symptoms of post traumatic stress disorder but also how you may react to them that can disrupt your life. You may:

- Frequently avoid places or things that remind you of what happened
- Consistently drink or use drugs to numb your feelings
- Consider harming yourself or others
- Start working all the time to occupy your mind

Pull away from other people and become isolated.

If you show signs of PTSD, you don't just have to live with it. In recent years, researchers have dramatically increased our understanding of what causes PTSD and how to treat it. Hundreds of thousands of Veterans who served in the Army, Marine Corps, Navy, Air Force, and Coast Guard have gotten treatment for PTSD and found significant relief from their symptoms.

Two types of treatment have been shown to be effective for treating PTSD: counseling and medication. Professional therapy or counseling can help you understand your thoughts and reactions and help you learn techniques to cope with challenging situations. Research has shown several specific types of counseling to be very effective for treating PTSD. Medications can also be used to help reduce tension or irritability or to improve sleep. The class of medications most commonly used for PTSD is called "selective serotonin reuptake inhibitors," but a doctor can work with you to figure out which medication works best for you.

- In therapy I learned how to respond differently to the thoughts that used to get stuck in my head."
- In just a few months, these treatments can produce positive and meaningful changes in your symptoms and quality of life. They can help you understand and change how you think about your trauma and how you react to stressful memories.
- You may need to work with your doctor or counselor and try different types of treatment before finding the one that's best for dealing with your PTSD symptoms.

The earliest time in historic literature in my opinion of a man with POST TRAUMATIC STRESS is in the story of Achilles.

A man of many wounds that could have killed him, but he survived. He fought fearlessly as if no battle wound could kill him. It began to affect his behavior, and his leadership skills. I am sure PTSD was a diagnosable event in any war story.

During the Civil War, when a soldier came home not quiet himself as he was before he left, he was considered to have Soldier's Heart.

After World War I and II it was called Shell Shock.

During and after the Vietnam War it began to be called Post Traumatic Stress Disorder.

In addition to getting treatment, you can adjust your lifestyle to help relieve PTSD symptoms. For example, talking with other Veterans who have experienced trauma can help you connect with and trust others; exercising can help reduce physical tension; and volunteering can help you reconnect with your community. You also can let your friends and family know when certain places or activities make you uncomfortable.

> "I wanted to keep the war away from my family, but I
> brought the war with me every time I opened the door.
> It helps to talk with them about how I feel."

Your close friends and family may be the first to notice that you're having a tough time. Turn to them when you are ready to talk. It can be helpful to share what you're experiencing, and they may be able to provide support and help you find the right treatment for you. Every day, Veterans from all military service branches and eras connect with proven resources and effective treatments for PTSD. Here's how to take the next step: the one that's right for you.

Corona Virus can also cause PTSD. Read VA's latest coronavirus information. If you have flu-like symptoms such as fever, cough, and shortness of breath, please call before you visit your local medical center or clinic. If you have an appointment, consider making it a telehealth appointment.

New to VA? Apply for health care benefits.

- Getting started is simple. Create a free account online to help ease your enrollment process. To prepare to apply for VA health care in person, by telephone, or by mail, explore VA's "How to Apply" page.
- Not sure whether you are eligible for VA health care benefits? Read about eligibility for VA health care.

- Unsure of what kind of help you need? Call 1-877-222-VETS (1-877-222-8387) to find the right resources to meet your needs, Monday through Friday, 8 a.m. to 8 p.m. ET. If you have hearing loss, call TTY: 1-800-877-8339.
- Veterans' family members and caregivers can see whether they qualify for VA medical benefits as a spouse, surviving spouse, dependent child, or caregiver. Explore family and caregiver health benefits.

Already enrolled in VA and interested in mental health support? Schedule a mental health appointment.

- **If you're already enrolled and using VA health care,** the fastest way to schedule VA appointments is to call the VA facility where you want to receive care.
- **With VA Appointments tools**, you can schedule some VA health care appointments online, view details about upcoming appointments, and organize your health care calendar.
- **If you're not using VA medical services,** contact your nearest VA medical center or Vet Center to talk about your needs.

What about other options at VA? VA offers a variety of tools and resources.

- **The Veteran Training online self-help portal** for overcoming everyday challenges includes modules on managing anger, developing parenting and problem-solving skills, and more.
- **Mental health apps for Veterans** cover a variety of topics, ranging from PTSD to anger management to quitting smoking.
- **VA TeleMental Health** connects you with a VA mental health provider through a computer or mobile device in your home or at your nearest VA health facility. You can learn more about this option from your local VA medical center.
- **Vet Centers** provide support, counseling, and readjustment services for Veterans and active duty service members (including members of the National Guard and Reserve) who have served

on active military duty in any combat theater or area of hostility or have experienced a military sexual trauma. Find a Vet Center near you or call 1-877-WAR-VETS (1-877-927-8387) to talk with a fellow combat Veteran about your experiences, 24 hours a day, 7 days a week, 365 days a year.

What about support beyond VA?

There's a whole community of support ready to help with whatever you're going through. Use this tool to find resources near you.

A reprint:

Dr. Matthew Friedman

Exec. Dir., VA National Center for Post-Traumatic Stress Disorder

The term "Soldier's Heart" was first coined in the post-Civil War era when people were looking at these veterans returning from Civil War combat and trying to understand why they had been changed, because there was general recognition that they had been changed, and that many of those changes were not for the good. [And back then] there were two different models trying to explain this. One was a psychological model, and the other model was a physiological model.

Soldier's Heart comes from the physiological model, the observations that people's cardiovascular system in terms of their heart dynamics, their blood pressure, a pulse rate, seemed to be altered. We can now incorporate that under the PTSD construct, but starting with Soldier's Heart, Irritable Heart... it was [Jacob Mendez] Da Costa, who I believe was a 19th-century cardiologist, who made these observations.

Then, in World War I, another physical explanation was shell shock, the notion being that being close to the big guns pounding out the artillery on both sides of the barbed wire in the trench warfare was somehow disrupting neuronal connections, so nerves were actually affected. Combat exhaustion, combat fatigue—all of these are physical types of manifestations. Following the Gulf War, some people felt that the unexplained medical symptoms [were] on a continuum going back to Soldier's Heart, as you've asked.

The parallel trajectory is about the psychological models. And in the Civil War, it was very interesting; the psychological model was nostalgia. The notion was that a Vermonter who found himself with Sherman marching through Georgia who exhibited psychological symptoms was doing so because he was nostalgic for being back in Vermont. Being in this alien Georgia terrain was somehow psychologically so disconcerting that he was having these kinds of symptoms. So this was another model under the influence of the Freudian psychoanalytic school. This got transformed into notions of traumatic neurosis and on and on.

And what's really interesting about PTSD is that it incorporates both the physical manifestations—and certainly our research has shown that people with PTSD have alterations in their physiology and even are at risk for medical problems as well as psychological problems—and it incorporates, of course, the psychological symptoms. The first person who really discovered this was an American psychoanalyst [Abraham Kardiner] working with World War I veterans.… And what he observed, in addition to the psychological distress that they were manifesting and that he was diagnosing as traumatic neurosis—which was the term that was used for these symptoms in those days—he also noticed that they were physiologically altered. Particularly he noticed that they were very jumpy, that unexpected loud noises would produce in them a startled reaction…

Tell me about the breakthrough concerning understanding how the mind and body connect.

Well, you know, this mind-body dualism that has infected medical thinking for centuries, since Descartes, if you will, is the notion that what happens in the mind doesn't affect the body. And hopefully everybody now recognizes that we're talking about the brain, and the brain is a part of the body. And it also is the part of the body that produces the phenomenology that we also talk about as mind.

And I'd say in the last 10, maybe 15 years, there has been extraordinary progress. And I'm proud to say that the National Center for PTSD has been at the forefront of this progress, showing that people with PTSD have alterations in certain structures of the brain. And they have alterations in how the brain processes information, particularly how it processes information perceived to be dangerous or information that might be reminiscent of a tour in Iraq or of other traumatic situations. So this really is becoming much clearer now in terms of why both the body and the brain are affected in people with PTSD and other post-traumatic problems.

Andrew Pomerantz

Chief of mental health services for the VA in Vermont

: Read the
Full Interview

...Did World War II vets talk about PTSD?

...The classic story for a World War II veteran is, [he] came home from the war, drank a little bit too much, maybe partied a little too much, got in some fights here and there, had a hard time settling down. Eventually, with a lot of support and perhaps [a] push from the family, he said, "OK, I'm done doing this," and then worked two jobs for the next 30, 40 years, sometimes having an occasional nightmare but basically having the whole experience shut off from the rest of [his] life—"I put it behind me"—not talking very much about it with family members or with others, many not associating with other veterans' groups or anything that might bring back some of the remembrance of what they went through.

And then many of those folks, as they reached retirement, as they developed illness, as they went through family stresses or they lost loved ones, suddenly would wake up one night in the middle of a nightmare saying, "Where'd this come from?" And I've seen many of those people from that moment on be plagued by symptoms....

It was a different world, it was a different culture that they came back to. It was a culture of a post-Depression era—"We won the war; we're really great."... When I ask them one of my standard questions—"Have you ever talked with your family about what happened?"—the answer is almost invariably no. Almost to a person, it's always "No, I haven't." "Well, why not?" Well, it's "They don't want to hear it; they wouldn't believe it; I don't want them feeling sorry for me; they haven't asked about it." When you ask their families if it ever gets that far, they say, "Well, we always [knew we] should never ask Dad that question; there were some things we just had to stay away from." ...

Society didn't want to hear it, you know. You don't want to hear that your hero who has just come back from winning the war is troubled by what he did over there and the people he bombed, the people he shot. People didn't want to hear that kind of thing. All anybody wanted to hear at the time was: "Isn't it wonderful? We won. We've saved the world. Thank you."...

There's a fellow from the other side of the state that I see from time to time, who worked lots of jobs, had positions of authority, was very effective in his work. Within a week after he retired, he was just flooded with symptoms. "Where'd this come from? I have no idea what this is about. I remember these events, I remember how awfully it felt at the time, but I thought I put those behind me years ago. Why are they here now? Why are they back?"

It's a very common response from people who are just now reexperiencing stuff that they thought was long gone, long buried. The mind is a wonderful thing, what it can do. It can protect us from things that are too upsetting. And sometimes we get away with it; sometimes we don't. Sometimes it comes back years later....

Sometimes people come back to these experiences at the end of their lives.

I think the best piece of work I ever did in treating anybody with PTSD was a Korean War veteran who had been a POW who had helped his fellow POWs escape. Part of the process of that was coming up behind somebody and putting a piece of cord around his neck and strangling him.

This man lived with that image for his whole life. It would come to him occasionally while he was working, but not in a big way. When he was dying, I think the best thing that I was able to do for him was help him find a way to talk to his pastor about it. [A] pastor came from the local church and listened to the story and provided the kind of forgiveness that for this man only a pastor could do. Psychiatrists can't do that; we don't have that kind of power.

These people, their spirituality is deeply affected by what they've done. And I've seen many people when they are dying—and I've done a lot of work with that population—they start talking about things that happened 50 years ago. Many are looking for forgiveness. Some have given up looking for forgiveness. They just feel this is something that does not fit with how they've lived their lives. Part of the work of dying... is putting your whole life in context, looking at how it all fits together, and for people like this, this doesn't fit. This is not how they lived. This is not how they were raised as children; it's not how they have functioned as adults. It's an interlude that lasted a year or two, and it does not fit anywhere. And it's very hard work....

How do the services available now compare with what Vietnam, World War II, or Korean War vets got?

I think that the person returning from Iraq is going to see a mental health service that is more sophisticated in its knowledge about what to do to be of help to them.... They won't necessarily find more resources, but hopefully they will find more effective resources than they did 30 years ago.... People came home from Vietnam and [were told,] "Well, you're just crazy." They got put into this psych thing; they got treated with major tranquilizers. There were not a lot of specialized programs. So now at least we have specialized programs that not only are specialized but actually have some expertise....

One thing we know is that [today's] veteran, more than any other, has a much higher likelihood of actually being in combat. This war is everywhere, in the streets; there's no safe place. In Vietnam there were at least some safe places, relatively safe places that you could be. In Iraq there's no safe place. So people who are coming home will have been on peak alert for 365 days or more, will have had all of their senses tuned to the slightest disturbance, the slightest sound of trouble, so I think it's going to be a very sensitized population. It will have a much higher prevalence of people who have had bad things happen, who have seen combat, who have been in combat, who have lost people close to them, who have had the guy standing next to them blown up, the person in the Humvee sitting next to them blown up. We will see a lot more of that....

Even the World War II veterans who won't say anything to their families, have never spoken to their friends, when they get going in a group of them who are all flooded with memories, they have a lot of stories to tell. They won't tell anybody else. And they will say: "It's because Joe understands. Nobody else would understand, and most people wouldn't believe it."

We're beginning to see some of that same trajectory with some of the Vietnam veterans who have been very productive citizens [and] who are now getting into their 50s and 60s. We're seeing more and more and hearing more and more of them coming into treatment saying:

"I don't understand what's happening, you know? I've been doing fine all these years, and all of a sudden I'm having trouble. I don't understand." So I expect we will be seeing Vietnam-era people for the next 30 years....

Thomas Burke

Director of Mental Health Policy, U.S. Dept. of Defense

: Read the
Full Interview

...Historically, what has been the percentage of veterans suffering from PTSD?

The historical experience, for example with PTSD, of people who have been POWs [is] about 50 percent. Vietnam veterans, 25 to 30 percent had PTSD. Of Gulf War I veterans, 10 to 15 percent had PTSD. There was a study done that was published in the *New England Journal of Medicine* [**Editor's Note:** See the "Readings" section of this Web site for the study]... that showed that about 15, 16, 17 percent of soldiers coming back from deployments to Iraq and Afghanistan reported symptoms consistent with anxiety depression or PTSD.

This was really a very unique study because it was done on soldiers almost immediately after they got off the plane. This wasn't a study done 10 years later. This was a study done immediately, or almost immediately, after exposure to the situation that you would expect to be the risk factor for PTSD. So comparing that 15, 16 percent to the 10 to 15 percent that we saw in Gulf War I, it wasn't surprising that there were soldiers coming back who were reporting these kinds of symptoms. We are concerned about those soldiers and want to provide the best possible care for those soldiers.

The other thing that the study showed is that some of the soldiers were reluctant to seek out that care. That's something that we need to work on: making sure that all of the soldiers who need care, because of what they have seen and been exposed to during their deployment to Iraq and Afghanistan, get the care that they need....

What has driven this progress in our understanding of PTSD?

I think it's fair to say that the Vietnam veterans and the fact that they were so socially active, and that the Vietnam veterans' advocacy groups were so politically active, were very important in getting PTSD defined, getting research resources allocated for the research into PTSD, and getting it on the map politically. It was pressure from the Vietnam veterans' advocacy groups that really pushed the mental health community into defining PTSD and putting it into the *DSM IV*.

So you do think our treatment and understanding of PTSD has improved?

Certainly I think that that's true. I think that because the mental health community, because mental health as a science and as a medical art, has come such a long distance, we have more to offer. I think that there's also been awareness through the military physicians who have been around since Vietnam,... and they have really worked to develop the doctrine and the organizational structures, the mental health resources to be a part of the combat force that goes into war.

For Gulf War I, [the Army] was using the new units, combat stress control units, that were structured and had a doctrine in training that allowed them to not be clinic-based, where the soldiers had to come away from where their units were deployed and come to a central location for care, but to take that care forward to where the units were, where the soldiers were, where they were being exposed to the things that were causing them problems. [These units] provide more proactive care, more preventive health... and also a particular type of mental health care for soldiers with Acute Stress Disorders, with what we call combat and operational stress reactions.

This is a particular type of disorder, and it's treated far forward, near the soldier's unit. They pull them out of the violent situation that they are in to a safe place, but not very far away from their unit. They provide a very simple regimen of sleep, including medication for sleep if they need it; rest, a couple of, three days of rest; hot food; hot showers; clean uniforms. They keep them close to their unit, so that they can maintain that identity with their unit and so that they can also have chain of command.

Their commanders can come and visit them, and they maintain that sense of belonging in that social structure. That's important for making them feel like they're not a patient; they're not sick; they're not in a hospital. They're still part of their unit. They're treated with the expectation that they're going to get better in a couple of days and go back to work.

[But that was not always the case, was it? In the past, what was the procedure for soldiers suffering from PTSD?]

Our experience with that has gone back all the way to the First World War. They evacuated shell shock casualties, and a large proportion of them went [on] to develop chronic mental health disorders. [It was] the same experience [when] we looked at the experience from World War II and Korea and from Vietnam. The first Gulf War was the first time that the Army, the American Army, had tried to use the specific types of units with this specific type of training and doctrine in treating that particular kind of Acute Stress Disorder.

In the 10 years that has gone by, because of the successes in using that unit and that doctrine and the research,... those units have been made a permanent, formal part of the Army's structure. So when the Army goes to war, they take their tent hospital with them, but they also take the combat stress control units with them. And that's a regular part of the way the Army does business.

The Marines are starting to adopt some of those Army structures and organization. [They are] adapting it to their own organization and culture, but they are starting to use the embedded, organic mental health resources and not just depend on the tent hospital system that the Navy provides to them.

CHAPTER TWENTY

Reprints from the VA

Have you ever been in danger and really scared? Overwhelmed with fear, helpless? Fear is not only emotional, but it can trigger physical changes in your body chemistry. Sensing danger, your body prepares to defend against the danger or avoid it if possible. All of us when placed in this situation will make a "Fight or Flight response". Once the danger has subsided it is natural to relax and let the ordeal come to an end. You survived a tight spot and lived to tell about it. You may even have the T-shirt.

If the danger is so intense it leaves a permanent emotional scar that will not go away, and returns periodically when a trigger event occurs, and this occurs continuously, even when you are no longer in danger, it is called Traumatic Stress. The fact It occurs after the terrorizing event has ended, and may take years to come to the surface, the emotional behavior associated with Traumatic Stress is called Post Traumatic Stress Syndrome. i.e. PTSD. This can develop after the ordeal usually involving physical harm, or the acute threat of harm. It can be a situation that threatens the individual or a loved one.

It does not happen just in war time, it could be a mugging, a hostage situation, abuse, rape, car accident, terrorist act, plane crash or even a natural disaster, or any other incident. A PTSD victim will be stressed or frightened even when the danger is over.

The probability of reliving the trauma repeatedly in the form of nightmares, or repeated recollection behaviors during the day is common.

"In therapy you learn how to respond differently to the thoughts that used to get stuck in head."

A PTSD Patient may respond to therapy, or may be treated after diagnosis with drugs, and staying medicated is the primary treatment.

If you are primarily being treated with drugs and for some reason get arrested, and separated from your family, and if the jailers cannot get your drugs to you, you may get worse being held incarcerated, even in a short period of time.

A bad situation can get worse very quickly.

Most people with PTSD repeatedly re-live the trauma in the form of nightmares and disturbing recollections during the day. They may experience sleep problems, depression, feeling detached or numb, or being easily startled. They may lose interest in things they once enjoyed and have trouble feeling affectionate. They may feel irritable, aggressive or even violent. Seeing things that remind them of the traumatic incident may be distressing, which could lead them to avoid certain places or situations that bring back memories. Anniversaries of the event can be difficult.

Alex Wells and I celebrated the 43 anniversary of his 25th birthday. Remember, he spent that day in a collapsed tower called the Alamo at the TET Offensive.

PTSD can occur at any age, including childhood. Having nightmares and intrusive thoughts and in addition developing sleep disorders. Many people are afraid to seek help, or fear stigma of being treated. It could cause problems on the job or in the career. Ideas of suicide just to relieve the pain are not uncommon. In our community of veterans, these suicides happen every few minutes of each day. The emotional scars of losing friends in battle can cause the thoughts repeatedly years after the event occurred. Death can be a welcoming option when the emotional pain of PTSD. It can be very confusing. Lack of focus on current events and no sleep can and will affect, personal relationships, work relationships and even military command. Unknowingly, a PTSD victim may or may not be aware of these behaviors.

Claustrophobia in elevators, crowds and even July 4th fireworks celebrations can make PTSD behavior reappear. Small events or normal situations can cause trauma from being help captive, to seeing horrible sights.

Can you imagine the hidden pain of a Dear John letter while a prisoner of war, of experience20 hours of horrible death an mutilations coming to you for identification and cleaning. Of having to sit inside a death trap and being ordered to stay. Of crawling into a burning helicopter, or having your legs shot up and still performing battlefield surgery, on dying men. Or the memory of eating a rat because of hunger, and learning later the rat was fat from the men you had killed. The experience of heroin addiction and prison soon after your return from war?

The emotional numbness caused by these repeat emotions and the effect it has on your fight or flight reflexes. Will eventually tear away all of the relationships in your life if you don't learn to unlock them [and] get those emotions out.

This is why treatment and counseling must accompany the drug prescriptions and diagnosis.

In many cases treatment is lacking for many reasons.

No close encouragement by friends and loved ones, or even medical doctors just stopping at diagnosis and drug therapy to pursue counseling as an ongoing project.

Reports in the past say, about 15 out of every 100 **Vietnam veterans** were currently diagnosed with **PTSD.** It is also commonly believed that 30% of **Vietnam veterans** have had **PTSD** in their lifetime.

9,087,000 military personnel served on active duty during the official Vietnam era from August 5, 1964 to May 7, 1975. **2,709,918** Americans served in uniform in Vietnam.

Fifteen percent of 2,709,918 is 406487 cases on the low end.

Thirty percent of 2,709,928 is 812074 cases and seemingly would include undiagnosed cases.

Not counting those from our Middle Eastern wars to date.

Since PTSD can take time to establish itself, we as a nation will have much more of this to accept and treat.

How Can I Qualify for VA Benefits for PTSD?

Navigating the VA disability process can be difficult, and you will need to build a compelling case to have the best chance of obtaining the benefits you need. As your veterans disability advocates, we gather substantial evidence on your behalf to build a strong case that supports the maximum amount of benefits to which you are entitled.

Your monthly benefit amount is based on how severe the Department of Veterans Affairs (VA) believes your condition is, which is gauged by the frequency and severity of symptoms. VA acknowledges that these symptoms can impact social factors, such as family relationships, and the ability to maintain gainful employment. To qualify for VA disability benefits for PTSD, you must meet the following requirements:

- You must have been discharged under other than dishonorable conditions;
- You must have a diagnosis of PTSD;
- Your symptoms must be tied to a traumatic event, or "stressor," that occurred during your military service;
- You must have documented medical evidence from a medical professional that the in-service stressor is what caused your PTSD.

Compensation and Pension Examinations for PTSD

As discussed above, veterans must show a link between their PTSD and military service in order to receive disability compensation. When it comes to establishing a medical nexus opinion, VA will likely order a Compensation and Pension examination (C&P exam) in order to have a doctor opine on whether your PTSD is related to your service. During a **C&P exam for PTSD**, the medical examiner will likely complete a **Disability Benefits Questionnaire (DBQ)**.

A DBQ uses check boxes and standardized language so that the disability evaluation can be made quickly and correctly. Specifically, healthcare providers will "check a box" next to a description that most accurately depicts the disability in question – in this case, PTSD. However, it is important to note that a DBQ will not be used if the veteran is undergoing an initial exam for PTSD.

Diagnosing PTSD during a C&P Exam

VA uses criteria from the **Diagnostic and Statistical Manual of Mental Disorders, Fifth Edition (DSM-V)** to evaluate whether there is a valid diagnosis of PTSD. This diagnostic criteria section of the DBQ is broken down into six categories (Criteria A-F). The subsequent section lists additional symptoms related to PTSD. Assuming a veteran meets all of the criteria from the DSM-V necessary for a PTSD diagnosis, the symptoms section of the DBQ will then help determine an appropriate disability evaluation.

Another important section of the DBQ addresses the veteran's level of occupational and social impairment. Here, the level of impairment due to PTSD ranges from no diagnosis to total occupational and social impairment, with various levels in between. Veterans should be honest and forthcoming about how their PTSD affects their everyday life. Doing so will further help the examiner see the full extent of the condition.

How Does VA Rate PTSD?

After the C&P exam is complete, VA adjudicators will review it along with all of the other evidence in the veteran's claims file. Specifically, VA rates PTSD under **38 CFR § 4.130, Diagnostic code 9411**, and assigns a disability rating ranging from 0 to 100 percent with in-between ratings of 10, 30, 50, and 70 percent. The rating assigned is based on the level of social and occupational impairment, and the frequency, duration, and severity of symptoms. **10% PTSD Rating**

A 10 percent PTSD rating is the lowest compensatable rating offered by VA's rating criteria for mental disorders. As such, the rating criteria reflects very minimal and often well-controlled symptomology. When assigning a 10 percent PTSD rating, VA will look for the following:

- "Occupational and social impairment due to mild or transient symptoms which decrease work efficiency and ability to perform occupational tasks only during periods of significant stress, or symptoms controlled by continuous medication."

In this case, a veteran may experience certain PTSD symptoms that are exacerbated during periods of stress, but ultimately do not impair his or her ability to work in most occupations. Furthermore, the increase in severity of PTSD symptoms during periods of stress implies that the symptoms tend to be episodic otherwise. This means that they are not always present and therefore do not significantly interfere with occupational and social functioning. Moreover, when symptoms are present, it is likely that you have the ability to control them with treatment or medication.

30% PTSD Rating

The criterion for a 30 percent PTSD rating under 38 CFR § 4.130, Diagnostic Code 9411, is as follows:

- "Occupational and social impairment with occasional decrease in work efficiency and intermittent periods of inability to perform occupational tasks (although generally functioning satisfactorily, with routine behavior, self-care, and conversation normal), due to such symptoms as: depressed mood, anxiety, suspiciousness, panic attacks (weekly or less often), chronic sleep impairment, mild memory loss (such as forgetting names, directions, recent events)".

The criterion for a 30 percent PTSD rating is meant to represent mild PTSD symptomology. In this case, "occasional decrease in work efficiency and intermittent periods of inability to perform occupational tasks" might mean that you are starting to periodically miss work due to your lack of motivation associated with PTSD.

However, your PTSD does not fully prevent you from performing and succeeding in a work environment. Furthermore, you may experience symptoms such as depressed mood, anxiety, and panic attacks. This may cause you to occasionally isolate yourself. Nonetheless, you are still able to maintain relationships with others. Overall, a 30 percent PTSD rating is assigned when a veteran demonstrates these symptoms presented in a mild manner, intermittently over time. **50% PTSD Rating**

To receive a 50 percent PTSD rating, veterans must demonstrate the following:

- "Occupational and social impairment with reduced reliability and productivity due to such symptoms as: flattened affect, circumstantial, circumlocutory, or stereotyped speech; panic attacks more than once a week; difficulty in understanding complex commands; impairment of short- and long-term memory (e.g. retention of only highly learned material, forgetting to complete tasks); impaired judgment; impaired abstract thinking; disturbances of motivation and mood; difficulty in establishing and maintaining effective work and social relationships".

The 50 percent PTSD rating criterion involves an escalation in the frequency, duration, and severity of PTSD symptoms. Furthermore, there are several additional symptoms included in this criterion that were not included in the lower ratings. If you receive a 50 percent PTSD rating, it is likely that you are beginning to display more noticeable cognitive deficits such as difficulty following instructions or making decisions that depart from past behavior.

Additionally, some of the mood-associated symptomology including depression and anxiety may begin to manifest in physiological ways, such as a flattened affect. In other words, due to feelings of depression, you might speak in a monotonous tone and lack facial expressions. The symptoms mentioned above might then cause a decrease in your ability to efficiently complete work-related tasks.

70% PTSD Rating

To be eligible for a 70 percent PTSD rating, the following criterion must be met:

- "Occupational and social impairment, with deficiencies in most areas, such as work, school, family relations, judgment, thinking, or mood, due to such symptoms as: suicidal ideation; obsessional rituals which interfere with routine activities; speech intermittently illogical, obscure, or irrelevant; near-continuous panic or depression affecting the ability to function independently, appropriately, and effectively; impaired impulse control (such as unprovoked irritability with periods of violence); spatial disorientation; neglect of personal appearance and hygiene; difficulty in adapting to stressful circumstances (including work or a work-like setting); inability to establish and maintain effective relationships."

The **70 percent disability rating criterion for PTSD** is the most inclusive insofar as it represents a wide array of symptoms. Furthermore, it also reflects a progression of the symptoms included in the lower disability ratings. Namely, a veteran who receives a 70 percent PTSD rating suffers from all of the symptoms included in the 50 percent rating, but at a higher frequency, severity, and duration. Here, the veteran is almost always in a state of panic or depression that affects his or her ability to interact with others.

The veteran may also have trouble controlling his or her emotions in a way that leads to violent outbursts or conflicts with others. The level of occupational and social impairment may be evidenced by the veteran's inability to hold down a job or complete classes for school. Additionally, a veteran may engage in obsessional rituals such as checking the locks on his or her doors multiple times throughout the course of a day as a result of being hypervigilant.

100% PTSD Rating

A 100 percent PTSD rating is often difficult to obtain through VA because it requires a veteran's symptoms to be so severe that they are totally impaired and unable to function in everyday life. The criterion for a 100 percent PTSD rating is as follows:

- "Total occupational and social impairment, due to such symptoms as: gross impairment in thought processes or communication; persistent delusions or hallucinations; grossly inappropriate behavior; persistent danger of hurting self or others; intermittent inability to perform activities of daily living (including maintenance of minimal personal hygiene); disorientation to time or place; memory loss for names of close relatives, own occupation, or own name."

The above-mentioned symptoms represent a substantial decline in cognitive and emotional functioning as compared to the rating criteria for lower percentages. Importantly, this decline results in a total impairment when it comes to a veteran's work life and personal life. Specifically, a veteran may experience hearing voices or perceiving things that are not actually present. Self-injurious behaviors and suicide attempts are also consistent with a 100 percent rating.

In addition to this suicidality, a 100 percent PTSD rating also includes homicidal ideation in which a veteran might have thoughts of harming others. An intermittent inability to perform activities of daily living can involve a veteran feeling too depressed to get out of bed, take a shower, or change clothes. All of these symptoms and behaviors are consistent with the highest level of impairment reflected by the rating criterion.

How Much Can I Receive in VA
Disability Benefits for PTSD?
These numbers will change overtime.

The amount you receive in monthly benefits depends on the disability rating assigned for your PTSD. Each disability rating percentage increment on

VA's rating schedule corresponds to a different monthly benefit amount. The higher the disability rating, the more a veteran receives in monthly compensation. As of 2019, single veterans with PTSD can expect to receive the following amounts after a grant of VA benefits:

- **0% – $0.00 per month**
- **10% – $142.29 per month**
- **30% – $435.69 per month**
- **50% – $893.43 per month**
- **70% – $1,426.17 per month**
- **100% – $3,106.04 per month**

Additional Benefits for Dependents

Veterans with conditions rated at least 30% disabling can qualify to receive additional benefits for dependents in their household, such as a spouse, child, or dependent parent. For example, if a veteran has a **100 percent disability rating** with a dependent spouse, they can receive up to $3,279.22 each month (compared to $3,106.04 for a veteran alone).

Ptsd.va.gov

CHAPTER TWENTY ONE

Summation

Legacy of Caring: Partnership between Veterans Friendly Initiative and Community Faith-Based Organizations.

Since 2001, some 2.3 million Americans have served in Iraq and Afghanistan. U.S. Veterans now comprise more than 7 percent of the U.S. population. That number will increase in the next five years to an additional 1 million or more.

U.S. military officials understand that the nation is going to need the Church's help as these Veterans reintegrate into American society. Many churches lack the understanding and support they need to successfully serve those who have faithfully served their country. There are many barriers that Churches must overcome as they reach out to Veterans as the Veteran's Affairs (VA) face their own barriers to service- the increasing number of returning Veterans are overwhelming the system. Where do we go from here?

Every Veteran needs community support. The need for Veterans to belong and have purpose is one of the best ways to satisfy mental, physical, emotional and other needs. Veterans have given up months and years in support of a cause only to find they are no longer needed on the battle front. Members of the military and Veterans are created by God with God-given needs: physical and psychological health, a desire for meaningful and gainful employment, membership in a community and, more than anything, a Creator who knows, forgives and comforts them. The Christian Church has a unique opportunity to present God to Servicemen and women, as well as Veterans through the provision and exposition of his Word, services and community offered by his people.

Cooperative partnership between Veterans Friendly Initiatives and Faith-Based Organizations are a revolutionary concept. Faith-based organizations are trusted entities within many communities. They provide Spiritual refuge and renewal and have served as a powerful vehicle for social, economic and political change.

Increasingly, we are seeing spirituality incorporated into many models of health and wellness promotion. We only have to look to the VA Chaplain statement: **"VETERANS ARE FIVE TIMES MORE LIKELY TO SEEK HELP FROM THEIR CLERGY THAN EVERY VA SERVICE COMBINED"**. That's a very bold statement

Historically, faith-based organizations have also served as an important gateway to services and care-giving for those living in poverty and in social exclusion. They have taken strong leadership roles in communities and provided job training, housing, economic development, educational support, meals and spiritual support to those in need. Faith-based organizations can bring needed resources, expertise and a shared legacy of caring for those most vulnerable members of society and to assist them in achieving their goals.

EPILOGUE

So now you know the history of the Vietnam War in a very abbreviated text.

The young men in this book did not know what you know. They went to fight a war because they were patriot American soldiers, not old enough to vote, or buy alcohol.

They followed orders.

They fought and died with their friends.

They were blamed for the politics of the war.

Many still carry the emotional wounds 50-60 years later.

Many carry the answers other soldiers from other wars need to hear.

It was an honor for me to meet each of these great American soldiers, and to share their stories with you.

When you see a man or woman with a Vietnam Hat on, thank them for their service. They deserve our honor and respect.

We must never again, hold or blame our soldiers for the government policies they are sent to protect.

When they return, we need to honor them, and treat their injuries whether we can see them of not.

And we must also remember, there is a reason we call it POST, Traumatic Stress.

It develops over time, sometimes over many years.

It seldom goes away.

A PTSD Victim has a lot to offer others suffering from the same conditions.

The causes are all different. The reactions are different,

But the internal pain and frustration can be increased by denial, self-medicating, alcohol, emotional triggers and post military life conditions.

The fight or flight decisions many of us make as civilians is to avoid conflict.

A soldier in many cases is conditioned to prepare to fight.

In a bar, in a traffic situation, a conflict with authority at work.

We never know when the reaction will be tied to an experience of war or any kind of trauma.

The best way to help is to let these veterans help others going through the same life events.

Many are treated at the Veterans Administration with chemicals piled on top of more chemicals.

An Arrest can lead to being cut off from those chemicals causing more damage.

It is up to all Americans to have the proper systems to help these veterans.

Protect them economically, medically and legally. Keeping their families from as much suffering as possible, and getting them balanced when needed.

And, oh yeah, put them in positions to share their experiences with other veterans in similar situations.

Salutes to you all, and thank you for your service.

Thanks for reading my book.

Confidential help for
Veterans and their families

"There is no instance of a nation benefitting from prolonged warfare."

"The greatest victory is that which requires no battle."

SUN TZU

www.ingramcontent.com/pod-product-compliance
Lightning Source LLC
Chambersburg PA
CBHW021216130626
46554CB00004B/1246